NANNIE HELEN BURROUGHS

AFRICAN AMERICAN INTELLECTUAL HERITAGE SERIES

Paul Spickard and Patrick Miller
Series Editors

NANNIE HELEN BURROUGHS

A Documentary Portrait of an Early
Civil Rights Pioneer, 1900–1959

Edited and annotated by

KELISHA B. GRAVES

University of Notre Dame Press
Notre Dame, Indiana

Copyright © 2019 Kelisha B. Graves
Published by University of Notre Dame
Notre Dame, Indiana 46556
www.undpress.nd.edu
All Rights Reserved

Published in the United States of America

Paperback edition published in 2022

Library of Congress Cataloging-in-Publication Data

Names: Burroughs, Nannie Helen, 1879–1961, author. |
Graves, Kelisha B., 1990– editor.
Title: Nannie Helen Burroughs : a documentary portrait of an early civil rights pioneer, 1900/1959 / edited and annotated by Kelisha B. Graves.
Description: Notre Dame, Indiana : University of Notre Dame Press, [2019] |
Series: African American intellectual heritage series |
Includes bibliographical references and index. |
Identifiers: LCCN 2019011960 (print) | LCCN 2019012288 (ebook) |
ISBN 9780268105563 (pdf) | ISBN 9780268105556 (epub) |
ISBN 9780268105532 (hbk. : alk. paper) | ISBN 9780268105549 (pbk. : alk. paper)
Subjects: LCSH: Burroughs, Nannie Helen, 1879–1961—Political and social views. |
African American women civil rights workers—Biography. |
African Americans--Social conditions—20th century. | African Americans—Education. | Burroughs, Nannie Helen, 1879–1961. | African American Baptists—Biography. | Educators—United States—Biography. | Conduct of life.
Classification: LCC E185.97.B95 (ebook) | LCC E185.97.B95 A25 2019 (print) |
DDC 370.92 [B] —dc23
LC record available at https://lccn.loc.gov/2019011960

*To my Lord and Savior, Jesus Christ,
for showing the way.*

*To Suzanna Shaw Wright, my maternal great-grandmother,
whose shiny hands, soft knees, and adorable ebony face
I will always remember.*

*To my parents, Kelvin and Carletta Graves,
and my two sisters, Tamri and Majeste' Graves,
whose love and support are boundless.*

CONTENTS

Acknowledgments   xi

Introduction. "God Will Give Us Credit for Trying:"   xv
Toward an Intellectual History of Nannie Helen Burroughs

PART ONE.   Things of the Spirit: Religious Thought

Reflections on Baptist Theology, the Bible, and Paganism

    What Baptists Believe   3

    What the Bible Is and What It Does for the Human Race   6

    Woman's Day   8

    Are You a Colored Baptist?   10

The Role of the Church in Society

    Exporting Christianity and Cultivating Race Prejudice   16

    How to Hitch Your Old Time Religion to New Conditions   17

    The Church Began in the Home   19

    Definite Work That Uplifters Should Do   20

    Human Waste and Human Responsibility   21

PART TWO.   The Way Up and Out: Social, Political, and Race-Centered Thought

On Black Womanhood, Suffrage, and the Nobility of Labor

    How the Sisters Are Hindered from Helping   25

    The Colored Woman and Her Relation to the Domestic Problem   27

Not Color but Character	32
Black Women and Reform	35
Miss Burroughs Plans a "New Deal" to Conserve Girlhood of the Race	37
Negro Women Must Make Future Brighter, or Continue an Economic, Social Slave	38
Negro Women and Their Homes	40
The Negro Woman Is a Mighty Big Woman	42

Uplift, Patriotism, Respectability, and Education

Industrial Education—Will It Solve the Negro Problem?	45
The Negro Home	49
With All Thy Getting	52
From a Woman's Point of View	55
Manhood, Patriotism, Religion, Going Out of Style among Negroes	57
Bathing Is a Personal Right; Smelling Is a Public Offense	61
How Does It Feel to Be a Negro?	63
"Must Uplift the Masses"	66
The Only Way to Victory	69
Up from the Depths	70

Group Politics, Leadership, and Race Work

Go Down Town and Meet Him	76
Why Our Dispositions Are "Most Nigh Ruint"	77
Nearly All the Educated Negroes Are Looking for Ready-Made Jobs	80
Get Ready—Winter Is Coming, Says Educator; Leaders Idle	81
Educated Parasites and Satisfied Mendicants	83
Writer Asks How Dems Election Will Affect Negro	85
Unload the Leeches and Parasitic "Toms" and Take the Promised Land	86
Twelve Things the Negro Must Do for Himself	88

Racial Violence, Social Justice, Politics, and Democracy

Miss Burroughs Replies to Mr. Carrington	95
Divide Vote or Go to Socialists	97
What Is Social Equality?	99
Legitimate Ambitions of the Negro	100
Why America Has Gone Lynch Mad	104
Race Attitude	107
The Challenge of the New Day: Commencement Address, May 24, 1934	108
Ballot and Dollar Needed to Make Progress, Not Pity	115
Declaration of 1776 Is Cause of the Harlem Riot	118
This Is the War of the Five Rs: Race, Room, Raw Materials, Rights, Religion	120
Education and Justice	123
Put the Leaven in the Lump	124
Second Class Citizens	126
Slavery Was a Success	128
The Meaning of Cooperation	132
Brotherhood and Democracy	134
The Only Way to World Peace	139
The Path to Real Justice	143
The Hope of the World	148
Equality of Opportunity Is the Eternal Goal	150
We Must Fight Back, but with What and How?	153

Thoughts and Words toward the White World

An Appeal to the Christian White Women of the Southland	156
Some Early Trail Blazers in Interracial Service	158
The Best Way to Resent the White Man's Insults	161
The Dawn of a New Day in Dixie	164
Twelve Things Whites Must Stop Doing	169

PART THREE. The Figure of Nannie Helen Burroughs in Popular Thought

Burroughs in Popular Thought

    Saving an Idea   174
    Lily Hardy Hammond

    Evanston Hears Miss Burroughs: Educator, Club Worker   183
    Discusses What to Do with Life
    Mary E. Depugh

    Pointing the Way to Better Womanhood: That's Nannie Helen   184
    Burroughs's Job and She Does It
    Floyd J. Calvin

    A Message from a Mahogany Blond   188
    Era Bell Thompson

Appendix. Chronology of the Life and Times of
Nannie Helen Burroughs   194

Notes   196

Further Reading   209

Index   211

ACKNOWLEDGMENTS

Writing this book on Nannie Helen Burroughs caused me to ponder what kind of education my great-grandmother, Susanna Shaw Wright, might have received if she had only been afforded the opportunity. She raised ten black children in the Jim Crow South. She picked cotton, occasionally sewed her children clothes from potato sacks, cooked in restaurants, and tended "white folks chirren." Even if she didn't know it, her labor was noble. According to my mother, my great-grandmother wanted to be a teacher. Circumstances prohibited her from fulfilling this dream. In His infinite wisdom, God thought it not robbery that I would inherit this dream to educate. I am committed to preserving the wisdom of my elders and carrying forward the tradition of black educators.

While conducting research for this project, I was moved when I saw that Nannie Helen Burroughs used the word "pa'cel" when recounting a story of her grandmother, who had been enslaved, because my great-grandmother used the same word. I immediately knew that this was black women's layman's term to denote "a lot of" or "many." This was important to me because it represented the ways in which black language traditions make history more familial (and familiar) to us than we could have ever imagined. Indeed, history is familial, not ethereal.

Nannie Helen Burroughs had a big vision for her race and a special responsibility to women and girls. Her life's mission was to create opportunities for black women in spaces where they scantily existed. It goes without saying that our nation would look remarkably different without her contribution. She gave ungrudgingly and our world is better because she lived.

The idea for this book came from the realization that the words and ideas of Nannie Helen Burroughs had slipped from view. In reflecting on her long career, it seemed unfair to me that there was no book that took up the task of understanding how she thought about the issues of her time. The sixty years she dedicated to working on behalf of the race, her zeal for social justice, her hatred for enemies of progress, and her quest to build an institution dedicated to the education and edification of black women around the globe more than justifies this project.

Ferreting through archives and conducting research can either be highly collaborative or highly isolating. This book would not have been possible without a host of friendly faces and helping hands. I am indebted to my family for their love and encouragement throughout this long process. Their confidence that this project would come to fruition never failed to provide a good boost when I needed it. I would also like to thank the exceptional staff of the Charles W. Chesnutt Library at Fayetteville State University for their kind assistance in helping me corral various research materials for this book. Specifically they are: Robert Foster, Francine Dixon (former library technician), Gloria Mills, Patricia Flanigan, and Winette Vann. I am also indebted to several academic mentors and intellectual influences. Dr. Linda Tomlinson has been an unfailing mentor since I was an undergraduate student. Her commitment to African American historical scholarship is invaluable and her support for my work and career has been inexhaustible. Dr. Blanche Radford-Curry has been a steadfast mentor and a guide as I launched into the world of African American philosophy. As a pioneer for black women in philosophy, her sense of responsibility to helping young women discover their way in the academy is priceless. Dr. Tommy J. Curry's impact on my intellectual thought must be noted. It was through Dr. Curry's scholarship that I found a kindred spirit. His dedication to understanding the truth of black intellectual thought is changing the way scholars like myself approach black philosophy and intellectual historical scholarship. His insistence that black thought must be understood on its own cultural-logical terms is opening the way for a new genre of work to be done.

I gratefully acknowledge Rev. Kip Banks, chair of the Nannie Helen Burroughs School Board of Trustees, who granted permission to reprint Burroughs's works produced in conjunction with the National Baptist Convention. I also gratefully acknowledge and give credit to the following libraries and archives: Library of Congress, *Crisis Magazine* Archives, Afro-American Newspapers Archives and Research Center, and

Pittsburgh Courier Archives. I thank the Tuskegee University Archives for their permission to reprint Nannie Helen Burroughs's "The Challenge of the New Day: Commencement Address, May 24, 1934," *Tuskegee Messenger* 10, no. 6 (June 1934), 2, 11.

I must also acknowledge and thank the University of Notre Dame Press and the editors of the African American Intellectual Heritage series for considering this project worthy of publication. I am grateful to renowned scholars and historians Dr. Paul Spickard and Dr. Patrick Miller for accepting and reading the initial book proposal. Furthermore, I must thank the University of Notre Dame Press office: Stephen Wrinn, director, Eli Bortz, editor in chief, Matthew Dowd, managing editor, Wendy McMillen, Kathryn D. Pitts, and Katie Lehman.

Finally, I would like to thank the readers who will sit with this book for any number of hours, days, and months. I pray Nannie's words will leave a lasting impact. Our world needs the preserved wisdom of our elders.

Most importantly, I give thanks to my Lord and Savior Jesus Christ for showing the way. Without Him, nothing is possible.

INTRODUCTION

"God Will Give Us Credit for Trying"

Toward an Intellectual History of Nannie Helen Burroughs

She was lauded as the world's most "scintillating Negro woman leader."[1] While Nannie Helen Burroughs certainly sought to be exemplary in her life's work, she would have traded flattery in exchange for the simple privilege of being recognized as a crusader for Christ and an educational evangelist for the race. She considered any tendency to take personal credit for her achievements as self-aggrandizement and vainglory. In a letter to her friend Carter G. Woodson, Burroughs bemoaned a chapter about her in Sadie Daniel's *Women Builders* (1931) as premature: "I have not done enough to be given a place in any book. I hope to accomplish something that will be enduring and really constructive, but up to now I am woefully disgusted with what I have been able to accomplish for the women and girls of my race."[2] By the time of the letter's writing, Nannie Helen Burroughs had founded the National Training School for Women and Girls, of which she had been principal for over twenty years, had established several successful women's organizations, and was a prominent member of nearly a dozen others. She had also been appointed by President Herbert Hoover to chair a fact-finding committee on Negro housing. Yet she was thoroughly underwhelmed with her accomplishments. Perhaps the world's most "scintillating" Negro woman leader would have been astounded to imagine that a collection of her works would finally be considered worthy of their own volume. It has been nearly ninety years since Burroughs penned that letter to Woodson. This work will either be considered belated or right on time.

Despite the bevy of books chronicling late nineteenth- and early twentieth-century African American primary-source material, there has never been a documentary reader that establishes Nannie Helen Burroughs in her own right as a critical contributor to the canon of early twentieth-century race thought. As a result, there is plenty of room to open up a conversation about what an intellectual history of Burroughs might look like.

A survey of recent books analyzing African American women's intellectual traditions reveals that Burroughs has been altogether ignored. Recent texts in the intellectual historical tradition considered seminal are Mia Bay's *Toward an Intellectual History of Black Women* and Kristin Waters and Carol B. Conway's *Black Women's Intellectual Traditions: Speaking Their Minds*. While Burroughs's name and quotes have been featured in hundreds of books, these references to her person usually amount to a few honorable mentions in some larger tome on other figures in African American history. Some of Burroughs's more well-known peer leaders include W. E. B. Du Bois, Booker T. Washington, Anna Julia Cooper, Ida B. Wells-Barnett, Mary Church Terrell, and Alain Locke. Readers comparable to the present volume include Charles Lemert's *The Voice of Anna Julia Cooper*; David Levering Lewis's *W. E. B. Du Bois: A Reader*; Bay's *The Light of Truth: Writings of an Anti-lynching Crusader* on the works of Ida B. Wells; Audrey McCluskey's and Elaine Smith's *Mary McLeod Bethune: Building a Better World, Essays and Selected Documents*; and Leonard Harris's *The Philosophy of Alain Locke: Harlem Renaissance and Beyond*.

However, credit must be given to scholars who, as early as the 1950s, considered it important to keep Nannie's legacy alive. The works laid out by these scholars informed the research for this project. Rev. Earl L. Harrison wrote the first biography of Burroughs in 1956. In the biographical genre, this book was followed by Opal V. Easter's biography of Burroughs in 1995.[3] The mid-1990s perhaps saw the greatest proliferation of scholarship on Burroughs. In the interim between Harrison's and Easter's biographies, Evelyn Brooks Higginbotham emerged as one of the premier historians on black Baptist women. Higginbotham's "Religion, Politics, and Gender: The Leadership of Nannie Helen Burroughs" featured in *This Far By Faith: Readings in African-American Women's Religious Biography* analyzes Burroughs's religious leadership on its own terms while her book *Righteous Discontent: The Women's Movement in the Black Baptist Church, 1880-1920* looks at Burroughs within the broader context of black women's activism in the Women's Convention, Auxiliary to the National Baptist Convention.[4] Thereto, Bettye Collier-Thomas's magnum opus *Jesus, Jobs, and Justice: African American Women and Religion* highlights Burroughs as a key figure in the national network of black women's religio-political and social activism during one of the greatest periods of American change and growth.[5] In peer-reviewed scholarship, Sharon Harley's "Nannie Helen Burroughs: 'The Black Goddess of Liberty'" and Audrey McCluskey's "We Specialize in the Wholly Impossible: Black Women School Founders and Their Mission" look at Burroughs through a feminist lens, considering her social education work and school-building legacy.[6] Susan Lindley's "Neglected Voices and Praxis in the Social Gospel" moves Burroughs into religious studies discourse proper by arguing for her inclusion as a pivotal contributor to the early social gospel movement.[7] The following dissertations represent the most prodigious works produced about Burroughs in the last twenty years: Karen Johnson's "Uplifting Women and the Race: A Black Feminist Theoretical Critique of the Lives, Works, and Educational Philosophies of Anna Julia Cooper and Nannie Helen Burroughs" (later a book); Traki Taylor's "God's School on the Hill: Nannie Helen Burroughs and the National Training School for Girls, 1909-1961"; Lolita C. Boykin's "Integrating Natural Coping and Survival Strategies of African American Women into Social Work Practice: Lessons Learned from the Works of Nannie Helen Burroughs"; Ann Michele Mason's "Nannie H. Burroughs' Rhetorical Leadership during the Inter-War Period"; and Shantina Jackson's "To Struggle and Battle and Overcome: The Educational Thought of Nannie Helen Burroughs, 1865-1961."[8] Johnson, Taylor, and Jackson discuss Burroughs's educational philosophy, her founding of the National Training School for Women and Girls, her curricular and pedagogical vision, and her social reform agenda. Boykin's and Mason's dissertations treat the topics of Burroughs's rhetorical style and social work praxis, respectively. In recent years, scholars like Sarah Bair, Christine Woyshner, and Alana Murray have offered analyses of Burroughs's crusade for a black-centered curriculum in social studies. Together, such scholarship has saved Burroughs's work from slipping into obscurity.

Nannie Helen Burroughs is an example of the richness of the black intellectual tradition. Her style was an interesting fusion of high learning and practical experience. She was preoccupied with a variety of topics that ranged from classical Greek literature to domestic science. She could recite poetry with fluidity and at the same time make an argument for taking a bath! She was widely read and deeply invested in activities that grew her mind. A quick look at her archive reveals a woman who moved seamlessly between the gospel, education, and politics. She considered her work as a crusader for Christ to be her foremost call to the world. It was through this articulation of the self as a gospel crusader that she established a school to produce self-determined, Christian women. Her National Training School was a microcosm of the colored world, welcoming students from Africa, Central America, and the West Indies, and best exemplifies her worldview and how she molded her politics around the concept of multicultural brotherhood and sisterhood.

Burroughs did not need to attend college in order to be brilliant, although she received an honorary doctoral degree from Shaw University in 1944 when she was in her mid-sixties.[9] She did not need to matriculate through a doctoral program to earn the title "doctor"; her life dignified the title. Perhaps she inherited this natural aptitude from her absentee father who was considered to be "too smart" for ordinary work.[10] Burroughs never considered herself to be too smart for the ordinary. She was smart enough to know that the hand and the mind were interdependent, that one could not rise without the other. Her genius was organic. Life experience and sensitivity to the needs of people were as central to her intellectual development as any of the books she read. She was equal parts eloquent and folksy, bodacious, and brutally honest; her deep ebony skin made her majestic. She was intensely proud and proudly black.

Nannie Helen Burroughs was a force to be reckoned with, both in life and posthumously.

"She Made Us Country Folk Proud": Finding Nannie

Nannie Helen Burroughs was born on May 2, 1879 in Orange County, Virginia, two years after the end of Reconstruction.[11] Implemented by

Congress immediately following the American Civil War, the Reconstruction period (1865–77) was aimed at rebuilding the nation and solving the problem of readmitting the recalcitrant South back into the Union. The idea that four million formerly enslaved African Americans might thrive in America unchecked provoked widespread antiblack violence and antiblack legislation in the form of black codes throughout the South.[12] The postbellum period and the failure of Reconstruction represent what historian Rayford Logan called the nadir.[13] Here ensued the bloody battle between the South's neurotic urgency to persevere white supremacy and the ambitions of black folks to uplift themselves from the dishonor of enslavement.

The late 1870s was a period in which African American thinkers began to consider what their racial destiny might look like and if a racial future in postbellum America was even possible. As Logan writes in his tour de force, *Betrayal of the Negro*, "determining the place that Negroes should occupy in American society was the most difficult of the 'racial' problems that confronted the American government and people after the Civil War."[14] The Thirteenth, Fourteenth, and Fifteenth amendments "ended slavery, offered equality under the law, and granted black males voting rights," but even if universal emancipation, citizenship, and the franchise were guaranteed on parchment, they were only respected in theory.[15] As Johnson notes, "during this era, the federal government moved away from its policy of promoting the civil rights and educational rights of blacks . . . there was an increase in lynching, mob violence, verbal and literary attacks on Black women's morality, legalized segregation brought about by state governments; the extra-legal terror wrought by the Ku Klux Klan, and the economic peonage of the sharecropping system, all worked together to ensure the continued social and political dehumanization, exploitation, and subordination of the African American."[16]

Two main traditions of black intellectual thought during the postwar era reflected the debate over whether blacks should remain in America or pursue a mass exodus. These two traditions are defined here as *emigrationism* and *political assimilationism*. On the one hand, the emigrationist tradition maintained that African Americans would never be able to achieve equality in America. Proponents of this tradition included Bishop Henry McNeal Turner, Alexander Crummell, Martin

Robinson Delany, Henry Highland Garnett, and Henry Adams. These thinkers envisioned a mass black exodus to Liberia as their redemption. Turner was an outspoken critic of the nation's enduring antiblack discrimination. He blasted American democracy as a hypocrisy and expressed antipathy toward the U.S. Constitution: "The U.S. Constitution is a dirty rag, a cheat, a libel, and ought to be spit upon by every negro in the land."[17] In a petition drafted on January 5, 1878 to President Rutherford Hayes and Congress, Adams, who headed the National Colored Colonization Council, lamented that "our only hope and preservation of our race is the exodus of our people to some country where they can make themselves a name and nation."[18] If Turner and Adams reflected the pessimism experienced by African Americans during the Reconstruction period, at the same time there were African Americans who considered it their mission to make America a hospitable home for the race. Proponents of this political or social assimilationist tradition included thinkers like Frederick Douglass, Booker T. Washington, and Roscoe Conkling Bruce. Here the term *assimilationist* represents those African Americans who saw promise in the ability of Africans Americans to make a way in America, to carve out a niche of opportunity. In essence, they believed that American society could be made (through hard, honest work) livable for black folks. Nannie Helen Burroughs was an heiress to and a proponent of the latter tradition. She considered herself to be a real patriot and situated her political rhetoric "within the constitutional principles of democracy, equality, and justice."[19]

As the daughter of formerly enslaved parents, Nannie entered this life without any pedigree except to say that her "mother's people and her father's people belonged to that small and fortunate class of ex-slaves whose energy and ability enabled them to start towards prosperity almost as soon as the war which freed them was over."[20] In contrast to some of her contemporaries like Booker T. Washington, Mary Church Terrell, W. E. B. Du Bois, and Anna Julia Cooper, Burroughs did not have the kind of skin advantage that might afford her entrance into the upper echelons of the colored world. The girl from Orange County was an amber-skinned woman without any genealogical claim to whiteness that she could tell. She did not have the aristocratic pedigree or "blue-vein society" connections of Terrell nor the heroic familial claims of Du Bois.[21]

Nevertheless, Burroughs glorified her blackness. She was what she called a "thoroughbred, legal heir to the throne."[22] However, the fact remains that Burroughs and her contemporaries were born into a world founded upon the exploitation and denigration of African-descended people. The world she inherited was one in which the solution to the "Negro problem" was manifested as violence and terrorism against black life.

As the descendant of enslaved Africans, she inherited a predetermined status at the very bottom of American society. Even if everything in her world conspired to disempower her, Nannie had an early awareness that to remain on the underside of American life was not a foregone conclusion. As a "colored girl" she would be destined to navigate a world where opportunities for her kind were narrow and fleeting. However, as Nannie matured from girlhood to womanhood, the earliest lesson she learned was that the most immediate assets available to a colored girl were a pair of hands ready to serve, a heart pointed toward God, and a mind open to innovation. She recognized that within the bosom of the black community existed a repository of "gifts," a unique culture that could be relied upon to elevate the race.

Like many early twentieth-century black women who were not only the inheritors of Victorian propriety but also the daughters of women whose claim to interiority was snatched away by slavery, Burroughs never willingly volunteered information about her private life or her past. As Burroughs's biographer and friend, Earl L. Harrison, recalled, "like a tree she is better known by her fruit. She is so full of ideas and so imbued with the passion for service that she had no time to talk about Nannie."[23] However, we do know something about her parents.

Both of Nannie's parents were involved formally and informally in the world of learning. Her mother, Jennie Poindexter Burroughs, was a Sunday school teacher while her father, John Burroughs, was an itinerant preacher who received some formal education at Richmond Institute (later Richmond Theological Seminary in 1886, and Virginia Union University in 1899).[24] The institute was an all-male Baptist college founded by the American Baptist Home Mission Society to provide education to formerly enslaved blacks. Although described as "personable," John Burroughs was a haphazard father whose presence in his daughter's life appeared peripheral at best. Whatever the reason for his noted "irresponsible" nature, Nannie recalled that her father's family "seemed to think that he was 'too smart' to do ordinary work and he concurred with their opinion."[25] Burroughs had one sister, Maggie, who died during childhood, and her father either died or deserted the family at some point in the early 1880s.[26]

With her father effectively absent from her life, the most significant influences in Burroughs's early years were female, namely, her mother and grandmother Maria. Burroughs described her mother, who worked in domestic service to make ends meet, as "independent, proud, sweet, industrious, [and] a marvelous cook."[27] She described her grandmother, who had been formerly enslaved, as a "seamstress" and "philosopher."[28] The lessons she gleaned from each woman had a distinct impact on her intellectual and philosophical development. Jennie Burroughs's work in domestic service and her struggle to provide for her family as single woman would give Nannie an intimate awareness of the vulnerabilities faced by working women. Maria Poindexter, who lived by the motto "we ain't no hung-down-head race," instilled in her granddaughter a deep sense of racial pride and an infinite respect for folk wisdom.[29]

Jennie Burroughs was determined that Nannie would not be confined to a life of domestic service. Not unlike most black Americans, she believed that an education would open up a greater field of opportunity for Nannie. Thus, in 1883, when Nannie was five years old, Jennie moved the family to Washington, DC, to secure better schooling for her daughter. Although a bout with typhoid fever kept Nannie out of school for two years, upon returning to her classes, she quickly redeemed lost time. After completion of the primary and grammar grades, Nannie enrolled in the Preparatory High School for Colored Youth. Established in 1870, the Preparatory High School was the first public high school for black students in the nation. By the early 1890s, when Burroughs was a student, the school was known as M Street High School due to its location on M Street near New York and New Jersey avenues in DC.[30]

During Nannie's matriculation at M Street, she crossed paths with and learned from some of the race's most exceptional thinkers and educators. She counted among these exemplars Anna Julia Cooper and Mary Church Terrell. Cooper, who was born into slavery, worked at M Street for over thirty-five years. She placed emphasis on a classical curriculum that emphasized subjects like literature and philosophy. Terrell, who was born free and into a wealthy family of mixed racial heritage, saw the home as the primary source of uplift and believed that it was the responsibility of the educated class to uplift the masses from degeneracy. She taught at M Street before she was required by law to stop teaching once married.[31] Another exemplar was Francis L. Cardozo, the politician-educator-clergyman and principal of M Street who "developed the District's first trade and business curricula."[32]

As the nation's preeminent public institution of black higher learning, M Street boasted a comprehensive curriculum offered through three courses of study: academic, scientific, and business. The academic and scientific tracks required three years while the business track required two years. Although Nannie's major area of study was business and domestic science, she distinguished herself as a brilliant pupil with an affinity for oratory and classical literature. While a student, she organized the Harriet Beecher Stowe Literary Society, a club that provided students an "outlet for both literary and oratorical expression."[33] As the reader will glean from this volume, Burroughs's writings and speeches reveal the breadth of her educational training and her familiarity with a diversity of literatures and genres.

Burroughs graduated from M Street School in 1896. Despite her stellar academic record, a series of broken promises and closed doors forced her to assume the kind of jobs her mother likely wanted her to avoid. Although Burroughs applied for two positions, as an assistant to the domestic science teacher at M Street and as a typist and stenographer at Tuskegee Institute, neither of these opportunities materialized. It was suggested that her dark skin and lack of pedigree had everything to do with it. Terrell in particular, whose husband had also taught and served as principal of M Street School at one point, was known to disfavor women outside her ilk. As Willard Gatewood reveals in *Aristocrats of Color: The Black Elite, 1880–1920*, "opposition . . . developed late in the 1890s against Mary Church Terrell, a school trustee, who was accused of favoring 'society' women for teaching positions over more-deserving applicants outside her own social circle."[34] John Edward Bruce, a forefather of black nationalist thought, routinely expressed his disdain for Washington's "fair-complexioned" aristocracy and their bourgeois politics. According to Bruce, Washington's "upper tens," the so-called "fust families," were little more than the "illegitimate progeny of the vicious white men of the South." He considered it "absurd" that this "illegitimate progeny . . . should attempt to pose 'as representatives of the better class of negroes.'"[35]

Supposedly denied because of her complexion, it was at this point that Burroughs resolved to establish her own school, a school unencumbered by color politics and petty traditions. Burroughs recalled,

> An idea struck out of the suffering of that disappointment that I would some day have a school here in Washington that school politics had nothing to do with, and that would give all sorts of girls a fair chance, without political pull, to help them overcome whatever handicaps they might have. It came to me like a flash of light, and I knew I was to do that thing when the time came.[36]

Still, in the late 1890s, the manifestation of her vision was afar off. Burroughs eventually left Washington, DC, and arrived in Philadelphia, Pennsylvania, to work as an associate editor for the Baptist newspaper the *Christian Banner*. After "scoring high on a civil service exam," she returned to DC where she anticipated taking a job as a clerk.[37] When this opportunity failed to materialize, Burroughs "began working as a janitor in an office building and a bookkeeper for a manufacturer."[38] The four years following her graduation seemed to have been filled with dashed hopes and odd jobs. Nevertheless, she maintained a steadfast desire to one day start an institution where she could provide the kind of opportunities that seemed to consistently elude her.

Around 1900, Burroughs moved to Louisville, Kentucky, where she began to implement aspects of her woman's industrial school curriculum. She rented a house and organized the Woman's Industrial Club through which she taught evening classes on domestic science, millinery, and "everyday things needed in the home."[39] She worked closely with Mary Virginia Cook Parrish, a prominent black Baptist woman and champion of women's initiatives.[40] A local newspaper article heralded Burroughs's efforts to educate young women, praising the "remarkable young colored woman . . . who has added to her natural abilities a very liberal education and who is fired with enthusiasm for the advancement of her race—advancement, too, along the most practical lines."[41]

In Louisville Burroughs began to work out her vision for what would ultimately become the National Training School for Women and Girls. Her career as a public intellectual was officially launched in 1900, when at the age of twenty-one, she delivered a rousing speech at the annual meeting of the National Baptist Convention (NBC) in Richmond, Virginia. Her speech was entitled "How the Sisters Are Hindered from Helping." Harrison reflected: "She was young, dashing, and spellbinding . . . she charmed the old and the young with her logic, wit, and wisdom. She made us country folk proud. We had not seen or heard such gift displayed in a Negro woman."[42] That year she was elected as corresponding secretary of the NBC's Women's Convention. During her first year as secretary, Burroughs is said to have "labored 365 days, traveled 22,125 miles, delivered 215 speeches, organized a dozen societies, wrote 9,235 letters and received 4,820."[43]

Beginning in 1900, Nannie Helen Burroughs's public career as an intellectual would span six decades until her death in 1961. This documentary reader features key writings she produced during that sixty-year period. Over the course of her life, her profile of work would grow and diversify prodigiously as her platform expanded from denominational work proper with the National Baptist Convention to a larger engagement with American politics and social reform initiatives. The organizations to which Burroughs belonged were myriad. Those she founded or helped found include the short-lived National Association of Wage Earners, the International Council of Women of the Darker Races (ICWDR), and the National League of Republican Colored Women. She was a member of the National Association for the Advancement of Colored People (NAACP), the National Association of Colored Women (NACW), and the Association for the Study of Negro Life and History (ASNLH, now the Association for the Study of African American Life and History, or ASALH). Her involvement in clubs and organizations brought with it a large circle of colleagues and co-laborers that included such luminaries as Carter G. Woodson, Mary McLeod Bethune, Charlotte Hawkins Brown, and Margaret Murray Washington.

Burroughs understood herself to be foremost a racial evangelist, a beneficiary and vindicator of a religiously grounded race-centered intellectual tradition handed down by black thinkers like John Jasper, Bishop Henry McNeal Turner, Alexander Crummell, Maria Stewart, Jarena Lee, Harriet Tubman, and Sojourner Truth. Her long life ensured that she would witness the rise of the civil rights movement even while she did not live to see its bloody culmination in the assassinations of its most cherished leaders. She would marvel the ascent of Martin Luther King Jr. as the premier moral voice in the nation and cringe at the rousing self-defense tactics of Robert F. Williams. Although she did not live to see the emergence of the Black Power and Black Arts movements of the late 1960s, she would have appreciated the zeal of young African Americans to claim black as beautiful, while simultaneously abhorring what she would have considered to be militant manners that did not reflect well on the race. Similarly, she would have found it difficult to square her Victorian sensibilities with the Black Panther Party's Marxist-Leninist pro-communist ideology while at the same time endorsing their emphasis on empowering the proletariat.

A comprehensive biographical account of Burroughs's life exceeds the scope of this work. For a fuller biographical account of Burroughs's life, the reader can review the sources listed in the notes and Further Reading list at the back of the book. Instead, my interest is in the portrait that emerges from the sum total of her life and work. Moving toward a more robust intellectual history of Nannie Helen Burroughs demands that we consider the major ideological components of her thought and how she resolved to deal with the realities of limited opportunity and antiblack racism.

A Prophesying Daughter: Theology According to Burroughs

To speak about Nannie Helen Burroughs as a theologian is to raise questions about the ways in which she thought about God, Christian life, society, and the church. In extending the discourse on Burroughs from a social history analysis to an intellectual history analysis, my goal here is to provide a broad overview of Burroughs's religious thought and demonstrate the way in which Christian theology served as the dominant infrastructure through which she articulated every other major idea in her life. Matters concerning Burroughs's leadership role within the Women's Convention and her oftentimes difficult relationship with some of the church's male leadership have been discussed in detail by scholars like Evelyn Brooks Higginbotham, Traki Taylor, and Bettye Collier-Thomas, and thus I do not address them here.[44]

Throughout her life, Burroughs upheld the "'holy grail' of finer womanhood."[45] Her ideal of pious, clean, and godly Christian womanhood reflected the nineteenth century's emphasis on "true womanhood." The cult of true womanhood was the prevailing ideology of the time, tying a woman's virtue to piety, purity, submissiveness, and domesticity.[46] Central to the cult of true womanhood was the ideology of separate spheres for men and women: the sphere of womanhood was the home and the pews, while the sphere of manhood was the public arena, politics, and the pulpit. Susan M. Cruea writes, "In a rapidly changing world where men were charged with the task of creating and expanding an industrialized civilization from a wilderness, a True Woman was expected to serve as the protectress of religion and civilized society."[47] Although, as Linda Perkins notes, "the 'true womanhood' model was designed for the upper and middles class white women," black and white thinkers alike embraced the cult of true womanhood and the ideology of separate spheres.[48] According to Anna Julia Cooper, these separate spheres gave symmetry to society: "There is a feminine as well as a masculine side to truth; that these are related not as inferior and superior, not as better and worse, not as weaker and stronger, but as complements . . . in one necessary and symmetric whole."[49] In the great struggle for what Cooper called symmetry, men were said to possess certain qualities like reason and abstract thought, while women were said to possess certain qualities like extreme sensitivity and emotionality. Kelly Miller, the African American mathematician and sociologist, maintained that although woman "is far superior to man in purely personal and private virtue," she is "inferior in public qualities and character."[50]

Even while nineteenth-century thinkers supported the idea of separate spheres, as Charles Lemert makes clear, black women also engaged in "strategic transformations of the true womanhood doctrine."[51] As early as the antebellum period, black women articulated a doctrine of womanhood that reflected their claim to the public sphere as a domain of racial uplift. As Chanta Haywood notes, early black religious women such as Jarena Lee, Julia Foote, Maria Stewart, and Frances Gaudet legitimated their right to public work (or the male sphere) by taking cues from biblical passages, particularly Joel 2:28–29: "I shall pour out my spirit on all mankind: your sons and your daughters will prophesy . . . I shall pour out my spirit in those days even on slaves and slave-girls."[52] Like her foremothers in the faith, Burroughs interpreted Christianity as empowerment for service. She validated her right to the public sphere by drawing upon the example of biblical men and women. Often she recalled her life as a parable with various biblical correlates. In reflecting on her own work to establish the National Training School, Burroughs likened herself to Abraham: "I felt like I think Abraham must have felt when God told him, 'in thee shall all the people of the earth be blessed.'"[53] In his biography, Harrison also likened her to biblical figures like Caleb, Moses, John the Baptist, Elijah, Deborah, and the Apostle Paul. Nannie knew her voice belonged to God and she considered her ideas to be divinely inspired. With this awareness she burst upon the public scene in 1900 as "prophesying daughter" in the prophetic tradition of John the Baptist. Hers was a female voice "crying out in the wilderness."[54] She was "too often on the floor [with] too much to say." As Harrison recalled, occasionally complaints arose: "Why in the name of heaven don't that gal sit down and shut up? She gives no one else a chance to say anything."[55] Burroughs saw herself as a prophet of uplift, an evangelist to her race, challenging black people to forsake the sacrilege of unbelief in God's plan and to live out righteousness.

As a prophesying daughter she positioned herself as a hearer of women's needs. She cautioned women against paganism and superfluity because they were the shapers of the home and thereby progenitors of civilization itself. She informed her female pupils that their uplift could be found in Jesus Christ. According to Burroughs, Christ had done for women what all the philosophers of Greece and Rome could never do. She said: "Jesus brought [Christianity]. It gave woman a soul, and lighted her face with supernal smiles; warmed her heart with lofty sentiments, turned her caresses into spiritual fervor. . . . It put her feet in the path of service and lifted her head up to show her proud equality with man in mind, heart and spirit."[56]

While scholars have traditionally framed Nannie Helen Burroughs as a "pragmatic thinker" and a "feminist" she would have preferred to be remembered as simply a good Christian.[57] Harrison reflected that Burroughs was "as deep as the sea, as wide as the human family, and as high as man's faith in God."[58] Burroughs considered herself to be a missionary "to the least of these" in the broadest sense and an evangelist for the race in a specific sense. She was most concerned with how her life's work would serve the broader purpose of elevating her people from ignorance to enlightenment through the application of Christian values. Thereto, Burroughs never considered her life's work to be her own. As she saw it, the deeds Christians accomplished on earth did not belong to them but to God. She said: "It's His work. I began it for Him, I take it to Him day by day."[59] Burroughs belief that God's work was a privilege and not property perhaps best explains why she refused to own the school she founded. She decried religious leaders who "love to boss things."[60] The school did not belong to her, she maintained, it was "God's school on the hill."[61] Although she admitted that she was "jealous of this spot of ground," she made it clear that she was merely a custodian of the work God had given her: "Who owns the school? Well, one thing is certain. I don't own it. . . . what would I do with houses and land? I've put my whole life in this hill, but I have done it for God. He has chosen my little life to build something for humanity, a place where the women and girls of my race can come and learn some sense, about how to live to the glory of God."[62]

Burroughs maintained an optimistic philosophy of life that interpreted trials and tribulations as necessary afflictions that fortified believers to keep "pressing forward." Her disposition was always one of perseverance and hope. She stated: "When failure peeped in on me . . . God always slammed the door in his face."[63] When probed with questions concerning her life, Burroughs always responded in ways that suggested that she did not approach life as a haphazard series of events. Rather, she measured the whole of her experiences (whether good or bad) as always working "together for the good to them that love God, to those who are called according to His purpose."⁶⁴ She saw her life as a part of God's divine plan. An address delivered at a meeting of the Women's Convention in Austin, Texas, in 1904 adequately captures Burroughs's Christian philosophy of life:

> Life is not always sweet, the road is not always smooth, yet we thank God because in the bracing atmosphere of high aims, the very roughness of the way has only stimulated us to 'steadier and steadier' step, and the trials have prepared us for the ordeals through which He knew we would have to pass. Under the shadow of earthly trials our Redeemer has been walking by our side. The intricate web of life, woven as it is by unseen hands and made up of materials infinitely varied and even diverse have spread before us and have challenged our souls. Our hands have been heavy laden, our h[e]arts full of care, unwelcome nights have followed unwelcome days, and dreams divine have ended in awakening dull, but it is life, and life is cause for praise.⁶⁵

Burroughs considered Christianity to be the highest form of enlightenment. Enlightenment, she maintained, could only be achieved through salvation and an adherence to the Bible, which she upheld as the greatest articulation of God's plan for humanity. Although she understood her particular audience to be members of her own race (her Jerusalem), Burroughs conceptualized her role within the broader world of Christendom as establishing a righteous example that could speak to all of humanity. Her all-encompassing concern for the salvation of society positions her as a proponent of the social gospel, albeit a "neglected voice." Susan Lindley accurately recognizes that Burroughs has never been acknowledged as a "social gospel figure" and she has never been "included in traditional histories of the movement."⁶⁶ However, she "did attempt to apply the teachings of Jesus and the message of Christian salvation to society and institutions as well as individuals. Her own strong faith demanded activism in this world."⁶⁷

On a deeper level, to speak about Burroughs as a proponent of the social gospel is to raise questions about the way in which she approached the quest for universal brotherhood as an extension of the more involved question of theological anthropology. Theological anthropology is concerned with human beings and their relationship to God. It specifically asks the question: what does it mean to be made in the image of God? For Burroughs, "being made in the image of God" provided the justification for universal equality. As Burroughs saw it, the "prophetic principle of human equality"[68] was predicated on two theological truths: 1) all human beings are equal because we are made in the image of God; 2) all human beings are equal because "we are all sinners before God."[69] Burroughs believed that skin color was a superficial difference. Enlightenment as to the true nature of race and equality, she argued, could only be found through the Bible. In her 1950 essay "What the Bible Is and What It Does For Humanity" she wrote: "[The Bible] shows by human conduct and character, that all mankind is alike in all essentials, regardless of superficial differences. All mankind is born alike, sin alike (sin is sin), suffer alike, crave for creature needs alike, die alike, and receive Heaven's just rewards alike."[70]

Even while Burroughs believed in the universal equality of all human beings, she also thought that black people had a special purpose in God's redemptive plan and that their historical suffering had meaning. In the same way God called prophets throughout history to awaken nations to righteousness, Burroughs believed that God called black folks to awaken America to righteousness. Unlike some of her contemporaries and predecessors who considered a racial future outside of America, Burroughs maintained that blacks could not abandon the nation because God had given them a redemptive purpose to work out. In her 1927 article "With All Thy Getting," Burroughs wrote,

> The Negro must not, therefore, contribute to [America's] doom, but must ransom her. . . . The Negro . . . has gifts of greater value. The most valuable contribution which he can make to American civilization must be made out of his spiritual endowment. He must do it in self-defense, and in defense of America. She needs it. Without it she will never dispense justice and will be consumed by her own folly and wrath. The Negro has helped save America physically several times. He must make a larger contribution to her spiritual salvation. Who knows but that the divine purpose for bringing him into this country was that, in due time, he might make just such a contribution.[71]

The idea that "the Negro" possessed unique gifts, even if primarily spiritual in nature, is not unusual. The dominant racial theory of the nineteenth century maintained that each race had its own particular *geist,* or spirit; this is what W. E. B. Du Bois called "soul." Du Bois believed that each race had a responsibility "to develop for civilization its particular message, its particular ideal, which shall help to guide the world nearer and nearer to that perfection of human life for which we all long . . . this had been the function of race differences up to the present time."[72] Similarly, Anna Julia Cooper believed, "Each race has its badge, its exponent, its message, branded in the forehead by the great Master's hand which is its own peculiar keynote, and its contribution to the harmony of nations."[73] Following this tradition, Burroughs extended what Chike Jeffers calls "the black gift thesis"[74] to her audience: "I believe it is the Negro's sacred duty to spiritualize American life."[75] Burroughs's idea that blacks had a mission to spiritualize American society (and white people) fits with the racial conservationism of the late nineteenth and early twentieth centuries. What readers might consider more controversial is the way in which she used the Christian discourse of divine election as the prism through which the history of slavery—and the African American generations that emerged from that experience—should be understood.

In 1950 Burroughs made the controversial statement: "American slavery was a success. It did not do anything for the Negro, directly, but it did three important things to him. 1) It woke him up. 2) It made him work. 3) It brought him in."[76] She went on to say, "It also happens, again and again, that the by-products turn out to be more valuable than the primary invention. Then, too, through experimentation, by-products are often various, more beautiful and profitable. That was true of Slavery."[77] In Burroughs's mind, slavery uplifted the benighted African from heathen to Christian. She maintained: "The Negro went into slavery a heathen, he came out a Christian. He went in ignorant, with no inner desire to learn, he came out—hungering and thirsting after knowledge. He went in an unskilled hewer of wood and drawer of water, he came out with many skills and delightful manners."[78] Despite however controversial and callous contemporary readers might take this to be, Burroughs achieves an interesting theological and philosophical somersault. Even if she offends our sensibilities with her justification of slavery as having done something positive *to* black people, what is more important is what Burroughs believed she was accomplishing by introducing this particular reading of the black past. At the highest level, she is doing theodicy and taking African Americans through an axiological reformation of their historical suffering.

Theodicy wrestles with the problem of evil and specifically maintains that God's goodness and mercy abounds in spite of evil. The end result of theodicy is the exaltation of God's omniscience. In other words, even if human beings are guaranteed to face suffering in life, God (as the ultimate Knower of the end from the beginning) has a plan for it. Suffering thus becomes redemptive as opposed to destructive. As the theory of value, axiology is specifically concerned with what can be called good. In this way, axiology is an evaluative exercise. For example, an axiological reframing of slavery from Burroughs's theological position would read the experience as ultimately working for the good of the race because there was good that could be perceived in the survivors. Burroughs did not excuse nor endorse slavery. However, she did have a tendency to see the glass as half full as opposed to half empty. In her estimation, slavery was a trial the race survived in order to serve God's greater redemption plan for America. Thus, it was not up to us to always know the historical *whys* of God. Burroughs accepted the fact that "God moves in a mysterious way, His wonders to perform."[79]

Burroughs's framing of African Americans as the "valuable by-products" of slavery reflects not only how she optimistically interpreted the African American experience but also how she 1) conceptualized black suffering as a theodicean saga that sought to make sense of the evil committed against the race; and 2) achieved an axiological renovation of history by reclaiming the corporate negative experience of enslavement and handing it back to black folks as a positive resource from which to draw cultural and spiritual value. She wrote: "That's why Negroes can hold up their heads and 'strut' in rags, that's why their songs begin in trouble and end in hallelujahs. The Negro has a future in America. He feels it in his bones."[80] Burroughs spiritualized the African American historical experience by transforming a history of suffering into an evangelical narrative of hope.

An overview of Burroughs's religious thought reveals a woman who had very clear ideas about the relationship between God and humanity. For her, God and humanity were involved in an intimate partnership that required humans to work out His will on earth. To question God's will was to question His plan. Nannie Helen Burroughs spiritualized every element in her life. Even when she spoke about politics, she did so from an evangelical perspective that sought to proselytize her audience. Her theology reveals a woman who believed that Christianity empowered believers for service and that God would cause America to prosper because of blacks in general and the Church universal in particular.

Determining the Way Up: The Social-Political Thought of Burroughs

Nannie Helen Burroughs believed that blacks had a place in the world and she aimed to help them find it and occupy it. By the early twentieth century, the United States had fully emerged as the world's most potent industrial power. The late nineteenth and early twentieth centuries were periods of incredible industrial growth, technological advances, massive immigration, and urbanization. The late 1870s to early 1900s is what historians refer to as the Gilded Age, a period known for its superfluity, political corruption, and worker exploitation. Throughout her sixty-year career, Burroughs was consumed with establishing programs that would equip black people to compete in a nation where industry dominated. However, the rise in immigration threatened to displace what Burroughs's considered to be the Negro's place. She was adamant that

> unless the Negro is prepared, he will be easily dislodged by foreigners. By skill and skill alone can he press his claim to economic justice. The Negro is in eminent danger of being displaced by aliens from battle scarred, war ravaged Europe. Now is the time for every Negro to make an opportunity to learn a useful trade. . . . America would rather trust her known white enemies than to trust her tried and true Negro citizens.[81]

Burroughs was not anti-immigrant in the xenophobic sense; however, she remained convinced that the influx of foreigners would disrupt the flow of opportunities that might otherwise go to African Americans. As the descendants of slaves, she said, "The Negro has done more to help lay the economic foundation of American and has given more to protect her homes and her flag than all aliens who have come from other lands combined. But these aliens are enjoying full opportunities under the stars and stripes." She also said, "No other race under the sun has or will ever suffer as much in silence and do as much in service for this nation."[82]

If elevating people from darkness to light speaks to the theological predicate upon which Burroughs founded all of her work, then industrial education was the educational model she considered most appropriate to equip black people to respond to the growth and change happening in American society. Booker T. Washington, whom Burroughs deeply admired, was one of the early proponents of industrial education for African Americans. During the early twentieth century black thinkers heavily debated over what might be the most effective educational model for the race. While thinkers like Washington and Roscoe Conkling Bruce emphasized industrial or vocational education by arguing that black men and women needed to perfect a trade that would give them value in the society, others like Du Bois and Cooper argued in favor of classical education and liberal arts. Although a proponent of vocational training as the most efficient means of equipping black women to respond to concrete needs in society, Burroughs believed that both industrial education and classical education were vital for producing a well-rounded individual. Her own educational background reflected the viability of both philosophies.

> We believe that an industrial and classical education can be simultaneously attained, and it is our duty to get both. We are anxious for our girls to learn to think, but it is indispensable that they learn how to work. They may not have it to do, but to know how for themselves is far better than trusting it to someone to know for them.[83]

Burroughs was realistic enough to admit that "a large percent of any race comes under the laboring class."[84] As she understood it, even if history assigned blacks to the bottom, this position was only temporary until such a time as they lifted themselves up through dignified labor. "We must realize," she maintained, "that we have to begin at the bottom; that if we would develop a full-grown race we would begin low. . . . The black race is God's race and I believe whatever we ask He will give to us."[85] Burroughs did not consider "the bottom" to be a position of defeat, rather, she saw it as a platform for opportunity. She was deeply critical of "educated parasites and satisfied mendicants" who sought what she called "ready-made jobs."[86] She believed that black people should put their "brains to work," and call on "courage, industry, ingenuity, initiative, dogged determination . . . and put up a fight for his life."[87] Fighting for the life of the race meant preparing black people to compete as equals in a rapidly changing America.

Although she advocated for the professionalization of domestic work, her goal was not to create a fleet of sycophants. Rather, her objective was to transform the masses into an army of skilled artisans who would not only be prepared to respond to concrete needs in society and the world, but also be willing to find ways to till "uncultivated fields."[88]

Central to black progress, though, was space to thrive uninterrupted. Burroughs was adamant that blacks should be given enough room to thrive and work out their destinies. While she believed that white people could participate in black uplift, she vehemently rejected white interference with progress. In "Twelve Things Whites Must Stop Doing," she made her meaning clear: "Stop putting all kinds of barriers in the way of the progress of the Negro race, and then declaring that America's high purpose is to build 'one nation indivisible, with liberty and justice for all.'"[89] Black America, she maintained, had enough resources to create a successful community. For Burroughs, the movement for self-determination demanded that blacks translate their aspirations into concrete plans and be given enough freedom to fulfill them. She told white America:

> We don't want your teachers, we have our teachers; we don't want your furniture, nor your clothes, we have plenty of clothes; we don't want your doctors nor your preachers; we have our doctors and our preachers; we don't want what you have earned; all we ask of you is a man's chance. What we ask is fair play and to be let alone.[90]

The tone of Burroughs's social and political writings reveals a woman who was deeply critical of anyone she considered to be an enemy of progress: white or black. In calling the race "up" from lethargy, she emphasized group politics and cooperative economics. She discouraged the race from "fussing" over trivial matters that did not translate into a change in the material condition of the community. "Instead of whining about what the white man is doing to him," she said, black people ought to supplant whining with work. Burroughs was particularly scathing in her rebuke of black leaders who sought self-aggrandizement as opposed to community enrichment. She decried these leaders as "leeches and parasitic toms" and called for their disposal. "They have sold us for a mess of pottage. We got the mess, but not the pottage. The question, 'What am I going to get out of it?' must get out of our thinking. This race would have been one hundred years advanced if it had not been for this thought uppermost in the minds of our so-called leaders."[91] The reader will notice that Burroughs spent the majority of her time speaking to black people about black people. She did not consider herself to be a racial translator who articulated black problems to white inquirers. She communicated with her community by relying upon cultural cues that they could understand. She understood herself to be fundamentally invested in the community, and in many ways she saw her role as moving her people toward race pride and black consciousness.

"Only God and Negroes Can Understand Negro Philosophy": Cultural-Logic, Black Consciousness, and Black History as Pedagogical Vision

Nannie Helen Burroughs's works have been largely seen as significant to the fields of education, women's history, and the sociology of religion in particular, but never philosophy. She has never been considered a philosopher or as someone whose thought might generate the kinds of questions that interest philosophers. This is precisely because, until now, a gathering of her works has never been produced that might allow a portrait of her thought to emerge. Thus what remains missing in the literature on Burroughs is an engagement with her work as a contribution to black philosophy. Reading Burroughs into this canon will open up new possibilities for study and allow something different to be said.

As has been discussed, Christianity was the infrastructure through which Burroughs articulated every major idea in her life. Whether it was social or political, she tied everything to her duty as a Christian. A discussion of her philosophy, then, will necessarily have to take into account this metaphysical component. Burroughs declared: "Negroes are wonders in spite of their million shortcomings. Only God and Negroes can understand Negro philosophy."[92] By this she meant to propose "negro philosophy" as an expression of the world and lives of black people and the unique set of cultural values that emerged from their experience. According to Burroughs, "Negro philosophy" was precisely the set of values that allowed black people to thrive despite the assaults upon their humanity. What were these cultural values? Burroughs listed them as the ability to "forget and forgive," "wear the world as a loose garment," "smile and grin; giggle and laugh and sing amidst our greatest tragedies," and to have the capacity for "misery and happiness." It was also "an optimism that is mysterious and magnetic. That optimism is our most valuable inheritance."[93] She called these values, "Negro art—the art of living without looking like you have been beaten in the game of life."[94] These were the cultural values that Burroughs believed gave black folks their identity, not the oppressive conditions they faced. The collective dignity of black people could never be nullified so long as these cultural values were sustained. At the 1905 proceedings of the Women's Convention, Burroughs articulated this in terms that are more layman than philosophical. Nevertheless, it speaks to her idea that cultural identity emerged from within the race and not from without:

> Men and women are not made on trains and streetcars. If in our homes there is implanted in the hearts of our children, of our young men and of our young women the thought they are what they are, not by environment, but of themselves, this effort to teach a lesson of inferiority will be futile.[95]

In essence, Burroughs interpreted the historical experience of black people as the reservoir from which emerged a unique cultural value system that spoke to their ways of *being* and *doing* in the world. This reservoir of experience is what philosophers Tommy Curry and James Haile call cultural-logic.[96] In other words, cultural-logic is the cultural expression of black people as the methodological process for generating knowledge and value. Thus, as a cultural-logical expression, Burroughs's "negro philosophy" is literally a creative self-representational act. In other words, it is the self-telling narrative that speaks to the way black folks create their world and their "selves" in the world. As Haile and Curry contend, cultural-logics offers a new way of doing African American historiography because it suggests that historical blacks already possessed a sense of dignity within themselves that was not dependent on whether or not it was recognized by the white world first. It is this dignity out of which risks and courage were manifested.[97] Burroughs's formerly enslaved grandmother, Maria Poindexter, provides an appropriate example. It was her grandmother from whom Burroughs absorbed the folk wisdom of her people. Poindexter's attitude toward slavery reflects the kind of "world" valuing and dignified self-valuation that was already present in black people even during enslavement. Poindexter told her granddaughter:

> Yes, honey, I was in slavery, but I wasn't no slave. I was just in it, that's all. They never made me hold my head down and there was a whole pa'cel of Negroes just like me; we just couldn't be broke. We obeyed our masters and mistresses and did our work, but we kept on saying "deliverance will come." We ain't no hung-down-head race; we are poor, but proud.[98]

Maria Poindexter did not need to be told by her "masters" what freedom meant or what dignity looked like in order to already *be* dignified in posture and free in mind. The metaphysical component to this self-valuation is that *value* was given by God, not man. She told Nannie:

> hold your spirit up inside, chile, hold your spirit up and that helps you to hold your head up. Don't let your spirit down. . . . I used to hold my head up so high that sometimes they would say, "Maria why don't you look down at the ground?" I would say "Look down at the ground? I ain't

no groundhog, I am looking up at God because that's what He made me for." Honey, they slaved my body, but they didn't slave my mind. I was thinking high, myself, and some day we colored folks is goin' to live high.[99]

This belief in the ability of black folks to create themselves in the world is what guided Burroughs's life work. It explains why she emphasized black self-determination through vocational training, and why she detested blacks who sought to submerge their blackness in "playing white." She urged black people to start thinking black as the first step to rescuing "his soul from the bondage of that death."[100] Her call to "stop thinking white" was in fact an appeal for black consciousness and a rejection of cultural assimilation into whiteness. It is important to note here the difference between Burroughs's conception of political assimilation and cultural assimilation. On the one hand, Burroughs believed that black folks ought to assimilate into the American political sphere by using the language of the founding documents as the foundation for black civic empowerment and patriotism. On the other hand, she believed that black folks had a distinct spiritual and cultural way of being in the world that needed to be preserved, valued, and expressed. Burroughs argued:

> When the Negro learns what manner of man he is spiritually, he will wake up all over. He will stop playing white, even on the stage. He will rise in the majesty of his own soul. He will glorify the beauty of his own brown skin. He will stop thinking white and go to thinking straight and living right.[101]

Even when Burroughs seemed most critical of her race, she was so precisely because she believed that the race descended from a superior civilization. She challenged blacks to live up to the intense ambitions of their ancestors. At the spring gathering of the members of the Association for the Study of Negro Life and History (ASNLH) in 1924, following the noted philosopher Alain Locke's lecture on new possibilities in African studies, Burroughs declared that black Americans were the descendants of a superior civilization in Africa. While she considered the enslavement of Africans to have been part of God's mysterious workings, she believed that this dire experience was the platform through which blacks would inject new meaning into western civilization.[102]

> Every race must preserve its tradition. Without such it must suffer from lack of inspiration. A record must be kept and it must be known. We must know that which is considered good and that which is regarded as the contrary. The Negro should not feel ashamed of slavery; for, after all, the slave got more out of it than the man who held him a slave. The Negro was taking over a civilization. He could do this very easily because he was the heir of a superior civilization in Africa. In taking over the better elements of modern civilization so much more easily than the other races which have come into contact with it, the Negro was merely demonstrating his capacity for he had had a civilization in Africa. He had already made contributions to art, ethics, science, and government.[103]

Burroughs's call to understand American blacks as the progeny of an ancient and superior African civilization reflects the general disposition among race-centered thinkers in the early twentieth century. Proponents of this view extended the geographical boundary and timeline of African American history and shifted the understanding of blacks as not merely the descendants of slaves, but as the heirs of magnificent Africans. Like Drusilla Dunjee Houston, who published *Wonderful Ethiopians of the Ancient Cushite Civilization* in 1926, Burroughs believed that black people were held in low estimation because the truth about them was hidden. At the fall meeting of ASNLH in 1927, Burroughs again emphasized "the duty the Negro owes to himself to learn his story and the duty the white man owes to himself to learn of the spiritual strivings and achievements of a despised but not an inferior people."[104] Following Houston, Burroughs's insistence on knowing black history was part of her "pedagogical vision" not only "to shape black identity from cradle to grave" but also to fix white ignorance through a truth that could be verified archaeologically, geographically, and historically.[105]

In the ancient history section of her pageant, *When Truth Gets a Hearing*, which was performed by students and ran from 1916–30, Burroughs called upon the impact of ancient African women as a way to establish "the role of Black women as creators in history." She wrote about Candace, Queen of Meroe, a wealthy metropolis of the ancient kingdom of Kush (what is modern day Sudan) and the Queen of Sheba.[106] As part of her school's curriculum, all women matriculating through the National Training School were required to take courses in black history.[107] As Alana Murray notes, Du Bois and Carter G. Woodson worked in collaboration with Burroughs and Cooper to "create an alternative black curriculum that would support the intellectual growth of African American children."[108] As the principal of a school that primarily drew its financial support from the black community, Burroughs "had the freedom to implement a school vision that used black history to support and develop the identity of African American girls without fear of reprisals."[109] The efforts, though, to endow black children with historical awareness earned Burroughs and others the attention of the Military Intelligence Division (MID), a branch of the U.S. Army and a precursor to the Central Intelligence Agency. In 1917, the MID "considered the study of black history potentially anti-American" and began monitoring the executive council of the ASNLH and the organization's *Journal of Negro History*.[110]

The initiative Burroughs took in conjunction with other race leaders to challenge traditional historiographical frames of black history and to expand the point of origin for black identity foreshadows later movements in black studies and Afro-centricity. Scholars like Cheikh Anta Diop, John Henrik Clarke, Molefi K. Asante, Maulana Karenga, Jacob Carruthers, and Ivan Van Sertima would carry forward the urgency to locate African-descended people on their own terms by reclaiming classical African knowledges and value systems as the framework through which New World Africans ought to understand the world.[111]

Understanding Burroughs as what Lewis Gordon calls "a philosopher of existence" follows 1) how she wrestled with the contradictions raised by the lived condition of blackness; and 2) how she emphasized black thinking as the foundation to a culturally affirming black consciousness that could be articulated through a black-centered pedagogy.[112] This culturally affirming consciousness would be expressed through her involvement with the International Council of Women of the Darker Races (ICWDR). Through this organization she would find an outlet for a Pan-African perspective that took into account the experiences of various "darker races." Burroughs would serve on the education committee of the ICWDR. One of the missions of this committee was to advise schools on materials and courses of study on black history.[113]

More could be said about Burroughs as a philosopher and her contribution to black studies, but it will suffice to end here. The way remains open to think about Burroughs across various disciplines and genres.

Rendering the Text: Purpose and Organization of the Text

The absence of Nannie Helen Burroughs from the canon of early-twentieth century race thought did not make sense to me in view of her massive manuscript collection at the Library of Congress. Her exile from print did not fit with the wide popularity she experienced during her lifetime. Sarah Bair points out that Burroughs "did not enjoy the privilege of her educational philosophies being published . . . [and] she did not write a theoretical treatise, or a major report, or a textbook."[114] Perhaps this might account for the fact that Burroughs has been largely overlooked as a thinker, but I think the answer is simpler. There simply has not been a demand to know about Burroughs. Despite being prodigiously talented and above average in wit, Burroughs lived an understated lifestyle and she rejected unnecessary attention. Furthermore, she never married, and she never had children; thus she did not have any biological heirs to advocate on her behalf.

As a scholar of African American intellectual history and philosophy, I am concerned with the ways in which black thinkers thought and theorized across space and time. This book grew from several primary questions: Who was Nannie Helen Burroughs, the thinker? Where does she fit in the broad network of African American historical thought (and consciousness)? Why has she been excluded from the pantheon of classical black thinkers, and how might we account for her in view of those traditions? What traditions did she embody, challenge, and extend? What can be said about Burroughs that has not already been stated? My attempt to answer these questions revealed that there was no resource inventorying the ideas with which she wrestled or the solutions she articulated to address the needs of her time. This early civil rights pioneer was simply missing in the literature. Although the bulk of her work preceded what some scholars take to be the launch of the modern civil rights movement with the Montgomery bus boycott in 1955, Burroughs's speeches and writings helped shape the discursive environment for later civil rights activists. In fact, Martin Luther King Jr. respected her as an elder and a friend of his parents, calling her "one of the leading voices in the Negro race today."[115]

Until now, the inability to pick up a book and read what Nannie said in her own words meant that we would be left to interpret her through secondary and tertiary sources. This book does not claim to be exhaustive; there are any number of books that could have been written and that remain to be written about Burroughs. A work on her educational thought alone would stretch across several volumes. What this project aims to do is serve as a conversation starter, to offer a preliminary directory to her thought on a variety of topics concerning God, sin, respectability, the role of the church in society, the nobility and supremacy of black womanhood, racial uplift, education, group politics, and social justice. More than anything, Burroughs was clear on what "the Negro must do" and what "whites must stop doing."[116] Her insistence on black self-determination and her belief in the conservation of race reveals her as sympathetic to the black nationalist conversations of her time. However, unlike the black nationalist thought promoted by Henry Highland Garnett, Martin R. Delany, and Marcus Garvey, Burroughs's race-first politics did not necessitate the removal of African-descended people from their geographical and ancestral claim to America.

Burroughs was a prolific writer and speaker who could be folksy and prosaic at once. Her words could be razor-sharp and redeeming. She was strict and disciplined by nature and that tone can be felt through her writings. She does not give the impression of being especially sentimental or introspective although she was deeply religious. To be religious and introspective are not always compatible. Although committed to working out her own personal salvation "with fear and trembling" as a Christian duty, Burroughs likely would have considered focusing on herself as narcissism.[117] She was community-focused, other-centered, and self-effacing. Burroughs never spoke about herself frivolously or casually. She always spoke in terms of her work and her God. Even if she did mention a personal anecdote, it only served as a segue to some broader point about work and God. Even while her more than sixty-year career as a public intellectual guaranteed that she would have something to say on a variety of different issues, she always spoke from the position of a Christian missionary and an educational evangelist for the race.

This book restores to print her most famous works and rescues from obscurity lesser known works previously only accessible through the Nannie Helen Burroughs Papers at the Library of Congress. Specifically, this volume brings together six decades of documentary material including speeches and writings, editorial articles, and excerpts from conventions and conference proceedings. The documents are organized under three genres: religious thought; social, political, and race-centered thought; and popular thought.

Part 1, "Things of the Spirit: Religious Thought," takes nine of Burroughs's most significant theological reflections and organizes them under two main themes: "Reflections on Baptist Theology, the Bible, and Paganism" and "The Role of the Church in Society." These writings reflect Burroughs's thinking on the relationship between God and man; the social role of the black church; the elevation of womanhood through Christianity; and the unity and equality of all human beings. The Judeo-Christian philosophy of history to which Burroughs subscribed identified sin as the foundation for human strife and named Jesus Christ as the conduit through which humanity would be redeemed. Christian theology served as the dominant infrastructure through which she articulated every other major idea in her life.

Part 2, "The Way Up and Out: Social, Political, and Race-Centered Thought," consists of the bulk of documents contained in this volume. It is arranged under five themes demonstrating the range of Burroughs's ideas on social service, women's suffrage, womanhood, racial uplift, respectability, education, group politics, leadership, race work, racism, social justice, racial violence, and the meaning of democracy. Together these pieces cover sixty years of Burroughs's thought and illustrate Burroughs's race-first attitude, her insistence on impeccable decorum, and the scathing intra-cultural critique she levied against those whom she considered enemies to racial progress. Her insistence on thinking black reflects her belief that black peoples should retain their cultural integrity. Burroughs's race-first philosophy called for a disposal of the antiblack values that equated Americanness only with whiteness.

Part 3, "The Figure of Nannie Helen Burroughs in Popular Thought," considers Burroughs as she existed in popular thought. Understanding Burroughs in this context is vital to any account of her intellectual history. This section traces Burroughs's national persona as enumerated through popular writing, bringing together key pieces written by journalists from her time.

A note on the text: In some cases, I have made certain grammatical corrections to the original text in order to ensure continuity and fluidity. I have made an effort to give details on names mentioned by Burroughs and to provide additional historical context where possible. Each subtopic includes an introductory note to that section.

As the first edited and annotated volume dedicated to Nannie Helen Burroughs, this work does not claim to be absolute, but it does aspire to be inspirational. This book aims to bring readers into the mind of a woman who should be considered one of the greatest thinkers of the twentieth century. If I have missed anything, grace will have to suffice. Perhaps Nannie phrased it best, "Aspire to be, and all that we are not, God will give us credit for trying."[118]

PART ONE

THINGS
OF
THE SPIRIT

Religious Thought

REFLECTIONS ON BAPTIST THEOLOGY, THE BIBLE, AND PAGANISM

As her essays "What the Bible Is and What It Does for the Human Race" and "Woman's Day" make clear, Burroughs's belief in Christian living as the highest form of civilization and the Bible as the indisputable justification for the oneness of humanity was the foundation upon which she established her life's work. The religious writings she produced flowed out of the relationship she saw between theology proper (the study of God and His will) and missiology (the commission given through God's Word to evangelize and proselytize the world). The pieces contained here demonstrate her thinking specifically on Baptist doctrine, the Bible, and the peril of paganism. In her essay "What Baptists Believe," Burroughs outlines the denominational doctrine that formed the core of her theology. This documentary reader begins with Burroughs's articulation of Baptist theology because it establishes how she would weave theological discourses into her social and political thought featured in part 2. These works also demonstrate her engagement and familiarity with earlier nineteenth-century texts, namely, *Beacon Lights of History*, vol. 3, *Ancient Achievements* (ca. 1885) by John Lord and the missiological treatise, *Crisis of Missions, Or, the Voice of the Cloud* (1886) by Arthur T. Pierson. Although she does not give credit to these writers, in "Woman's Day," Burroughs quotes extensively from Lord's essay, "Cleopatra: The Woman of Paganism" and Pierson's chapter, "Removal of Barriers."[1] Burroughs believed that whereas paganism's emphasis on vanity and carnality led women toward degradation and immorality, Christianity served as the *enlightenment* by which woman was elevated to "proud equality with man in mind, heart and spirit" ("Woman's Day"). Burroughs's 1950 woman's day missive championing the uplift of Christian womanhood should be understood as carrying forward the creed concretized by Frances E. W. Harper at the 1893 World's Congress of Representative Women. In her speech, Harper declared that the nation stood "at the threshold of woman's era, and woman's work is grandly constructive. In her hand are possibilities whose use or abuse ... [will] send their influence for good or evil across the track of unborn generations."[2] Like many women of her time, Burroughs founded her ideal of womanhood on the example of biblical women. In "Woman's Day," she regards as the paragon of Christian service the Samaritan woman at the well whose testimony of her encounter with Jesus empowered her to transform her town and community. Burroughs saw Christianity as empowerment for service. Together, these essays are expressive of Burroughs's belief that zeal alone is insufficient without knowledge. She believed that faith was impossible to quantify without a clearly articulated doctrine that outlined the fundamentals of salvation, transformation, and identity. She maintained that all Christian workers should know *what* to believe and *why*.

~

What Baptists Believe

From Nannie Helen Burroughs, *Handbook for Red Circles, Young Matrons, Young Women's Leagues, and Crusaders* (Washington, DC: Women's Convention Auxiliary, National Baptist Convention, 1933), 82–84.

> *Hold fast the form of sound words, which thou hast heard of me, in faith and love which is in Christ Jesus.*
> —II Timothy 1:13

BIBLE

Baptists believe that the Holy Bible was written by men divinely inspired, and is a perfect treasure of heavenly instruction; that it has God for its author, salvation for its end, and truth without any mixture of error, for its matter; that it reveals the principles by which God will judge us; and therefore is, and shall remain to the end of the world, the true center of Christian union, and the supreme standard by which all human conduct, creeds, and opinions should be tried.

GOD

Baptists believe that there is one, and only one, living and true God, an infinite, intelligent Spirit, whose name is JEHOVAH, the Maker and

Supreme Ruler of heaven and earth: inexpressibly glorious in holiness, and worthy of all possible honor, confidence, and love, that in the unity of the Godhead there are three persons, the Father, the Son, and the Holy Ghost; equal in every divine perfection, and executing distinct but harmonious offices in the great work of redemption.

Man

Baptists believe that man was created in holiness, under the law of his Maker; but by voluntary transgression fell from that holy and happy state; in consequence of which all mankind are now sinners: not by constraint, but choice: being by nature utterly void of that holiness required by the law of God, positively inclined to evil: and therefore under just condemnation to eternal ruin, without defense or excuse.

Salvation and the Freeness of Justification

Baptists believe that, the salvation of sinners is wholly of grace; through the mediatorial offices of the Son of God; who by the appointment of the Father, freely took upon Him our nature, yet: without sin; honored the divine law by His personal obedience, and by His death made a full atonement for our sins; that having risen from the dead He is now enthroned in heaven; and uniting in His wonderful person the tenderest sympathies with divine perfections, He is every way qualified to be a suitable, a compassionate and an all-sufficient Saviour.

Baptists believe that the blessings of salvation are made free to all by the Gospel; that it is the immediate duty of all to accept them by a cordial, penitent, and obedient faith; and that nothing prevents the salvation of the greatest sinner on earth but his own inherent depravity and voluntary rejection of the Gospel; which rejection involves him in an aggravated condemnation.

Baptists believe that the great Gospel blessing which Christ secures to such as believe in Him is Justification; that Justification includes the pardon of sin, and the promise of eternal life on principles of righteousness; that it is bestowed, not in consideration of any works of righteousness which we have done, but solely through faith in the Redeemer's blood; by virtue of which faith His perfect righteousness is freely imputed to us of God; that it brings us into a state of most blessed peace and favor with God, and secures every other blessing needful for time and eternity.

Regeneration
Baptists believe that, in order to be saved, sinners must be regenerated or born again; that regeneration consists in giving a holy disposition to the mind; that it is effected, in a manner above our comprehension, by the power of the Holy Spirit in connection with divine truth, so as to secure our voluntary obedience to the Gospel; and that its proper evidence appears in the holy fruits of repentance and faith and newness of life.

Faith
Baptists believe that Repentance and Faith are sacred duties, and also inseparable graces, wrought in our souls by the regenerating Spirit of God; whereby, being deeply convinced of our guilt, danger, and helplessness, and of the way of salvation by Christ, we turn to God with unfeigned contrition, confession, and supplication for mercy; at the same time heartily receiving the Lord Jesus Christ as our Prophet, Priest, and King, and relying on Him alone as the only and all-sufficient Saviour.

Baptism and the Lord's Supper
Baptists believe that Christian Baptism is the immersion in water of a believer, unto the name of the Father, and Son, and Holy Ghost; to show forth, in a solemn and beautiful emblem, our faith in the crucified, buried, and risen Saviour, with its effect in our death to sin and resurrection to a new life; that it is prerequisite to the privileges of a church relation, and to the Lord's Supper; in which the members of the church, by the sacred use of bread and wine are to commemorate together the dying love of Christ; preceded always by solemn self-examination.

Sabbath
Baptists believe that the first day of the week is the Lord's Day or Christian Sabbath; and is to be kept sacred to religious purposes, by abstaining from all secular labor and sinful recreations; by the devout observance of all the means of grace, both private and public; and by preparation for that rest that remaineth for the people of God.

What the Bible Is and What It Does for the Human Race

From Nannie Helen Burroughs, *What Do You Think?* (Washington, DC, n.p., 1950), 41–45.

1. It reveals God as no respecter of person.
2. It stands for a fair chance for every man.
3. It reasons with man.
4. It reveals God eternally at work in this world.
5. It warns against sin and promises eternal life.
6. It teachers the way to Christ and to abundant life through Him.

The Bible teaches the truth about race and race relations. It does not quibble. It is the one book that teaches from the beginning to the end, that humanity is one. "God is the Father of all." —Matthew 23:9. "God made of one blood all nations of men." —Acts 17:26.

> "He saw me ruined by the fall,
> Yet loved me, notwithstanding all,
> He saved me from my lost estate;
> His loving kindness, O how great."

The Bible gives an elevated conception of mankind. It does not put the stigma of inferiority on any race. It declares that in His sight "there is neither Greek nor Jew, circumcision, nor uncircumcision, barbarian, Scythian, bond nor free." It shows by human conduct and character, that all mankind is alike in all essentials, regardless of superficial differences. All mankind is born alike, sin alike (sin is sin), suffer alike, crave for creature needs alike, die alike, and receive Heaven's just rewards alike.

It is the specific purpose of Christianity to teach the fact of the oneness of the human race and work for the salvation and unification of mankind the world over—to practice Christ's way of life.

The Bible makes it clear that no race is put on this earth to dominate any other race. It teaches that it is the duty, and it should be regarded as a high privilege of individuals, groups, or races that are blessed above others with education, the religion of Christ Jesus, or with things material to share their gifts and advantages in a constructive, practical way with those who have not. By this we mean, that it is the business of the fortunate not to put any stumbling blocks or barriers in the way of the less fortunate—it is their business to point the way to opportunities for self-help and development without the spirit or semblance of condescension.

"The Bible stands alone in human literature in its elevated conception of mankind." God made man "a little lower than the angels, and crowned him with glory and honor." —Psalm 8:5. We touch heaven when we lay our hands on a human body. "It is the miracle of miracles—the great inscrutable mystery of God"—"Man is fearfully and wonderfully made." —Psalm 139:14.

The Bible tells and shows us how sinners may become saints. It exalts man's mind, making him his own free agent. No one can be highly educated without a working knowledge and genuine appreciation of the Bible. Only by the application of its teachings can social and civil ideals receive the breath of life, and enduring power. Only the application of the teachings of the Bible can change the moral and social state of the world.

It imparts to the souls of men new enlightenment and new powers. It is the only book that provides one way of life for all classes, and for all human conditions.

It teaches us how to bring human liberty into a working relationship with the Divine law, and thus bring peace on earth. It offers an effectual remedy for all the evils that drag mankind down.

Man's highest faculties and noblest views are developed and refined by its benign light of revelation. It makes of each human being a flower in the garden of humanity. It drops into each soul the dew of heaven—sympathy, kindness, love, so that when that soul is shaken (moved) by the wind, it lets fall some dew drops to the roots of others in the garden of humanity and each soul thereby, becomes a nourisher of others.

There is no hope for the world unless humanity as a whole is educated in the spirit and principles of the Bible.

Woman's Day

From Nannie Helen Burroughs, *What Do You Think?* (Washington, DC, n.p., 1950), 1–4.

Woman has had two days. One pagan—one Christian. In her pagan day, woman bewitched by vile indulgences, studied bewitching charm and many lewd vices. Cleopatra, of Egypt, represents the pagan type.

Egyptian and African blood flowed through her veins. She was dark, transcendently beautiful and absolutely irresistible. She attracted and ensnared Caesar in the midst of his triumphs. After Caesar's death, Anthony could have ruled the world had he not become so madly infatuated with Cleopatra. She held him in her grip, and deceived and ruined him. Under paganism, woman pulled man down. Cleopatra was only a type. There were hundreds like her. They had cultivated intellects—they were brilliant, and attractive; but, as immoral as they come. They sat in high places. Men sought their society and left their virtuous wives at home while they indulged in pleasures that were grossly demoralizing.

In Pagan days, the women who wanted to attract men appeared in public places with braided, decorated hair and loud dress. They talked loudly and displayed their jewels. That is why Paul advised the women of Corinth who found the "New Way" to dress soberly and keep silent. He did not want the new converts to Christianity to be mistaken for the dissolute class. Do not blame Paul and call him an old bachelor. Blame the lewd women of that day and thank Paul for trying to protect the decent women from improper advances and encroachments.

In Pagan days, wives were not the companions of their husbands. They were their menials and domestic slaves. Men were under the influence and control of outside women who appealed to their lower ungodly appetites.

Paganism taught the inequality of the sexes. In that day, woman could not rise above the condition in which she was born. Only the upper class was educated. All others were deprived of education or consideration. Woman had no resources. No value was set on moral beauty. She never dreamed of improving her condition. She was given in marriage without her consent. She had only a body. Paganism crushed her soul. Are you surprised that many of them committed suicide? Their lot was cold, hard, and hopeless.

"One of the most noticeable characteristics of Paganism is that immorality seems to have been no bar to social position. Some of those who were most attractive and sought after were notoriously immoral. Aspasia, whom Socrates and Pericles equally admired, and whose house was the resort of poets, philosophers, statesmen, and artists, and who is said to have been one of the most cultivated women of antiquity, bore a sullied name.

Sappho, who was ever exalted by Grecian poets for the sweetness of her verses, attempted to reconcile a life of pleasure with a life of letters, and threw herself into the sea because of a disappointed passion. Lais, a professional courtesan, was the associate of kings and sages as well as the idol of poets and priests. Agrippina, whose very name is infamy, was the admiration of courtiers and statesmen. Lucilla, who armed her assassins against her own brother, seems to have ruled the court of Marcus Aurelius."[3]

For centuries woman was "degraded to the level of cattle, for which she was bartered, or the donkeys with which she was associated as a burden bearer, unwelcome as a babe, untaught as a child, enslaved as a wife, despised as a widow, unwept as dead, denied all social status and individual rights and even a soul."[4]

Such was woman's first day, and millions of them in non-Christian lands still live and labor and are bowed down under customs, cares, burdens, and duties of heartless slavery and gross neglect of their immortal souls.

Christianity's day came. Jesus brought it. It gave woman a soul, and lighted her face with supernal smiles; warmed her heart with lofty sentiments, turned her caresses into spiritual fervor; gave her divine enthusiasm for lofty friendship, and made her a sublime symbol of devotion, courage, fidelity, and grace that stands by the cross and rallies from disappointment, sorrow and pain, and becomes an evangel of matchless devotion and power.

Christianity sat the music of heaven ringing in her soul and made her home a little piece of paradise, fenced off on earth with happy children to rise up, and call her blessed. It put her feet in the path of service and lifted her head up to show her proud equality with man in mind, heart and spirit.

She established schools, and enriched and endowed hospitals. She inaugurated and maintained charities, taught school—secular and Christian, went to the slums to lift up the fallen—to carry the message of salvation to those who had it not—lifted men up in mind and soul until, woman's mere "physical beauty paled in their estimation before the brilliancy of her mind and the radiance of her soul."

By her personal Christian magnetism she drew man in until he craved home and family life, "friendship, intellectual banquettings and religious aspirations." Yes, woman did that. The end is not yet. Her day is here. Her long range objective is to make education universal, suffrage without sex, industry without boycott, justice without alloy, and the religion of Jesus Christ without adulteration.

That is Woman's task for her day. She will work until the humblest woman is lifted up through salvation into service; until the soul of the humblest is bathed in the glory of the Lord, and her face shines with the radiance of heaven.

"Woman's Day" means woman's opportunity to do what the woman did who talked with Jesus at the well. She "went to town."

Are You a Colored Baptist?

From Nannie Helen Burroughs, *What Do You Think?* (Washington, DC: n.p, 1950), 50–53.

We never have been able to understand why we should classify Baptists by the color of their skins. We hear and read many times of there being a certain number of white Baptists and a certain number of colored Baptists in a given state or convention. Why the distinction? Who cares about outside color? Perhaps the classification is made because these race varieties are usually organized into different churches, associations, and conventions. This must be the reason, but the word "colored" is used to designate those of only one particular race. We have never heard anyone speak of Red Baptists when referring to Indians, or of Yellow Baptists when referring to Chinese.

But we have often wondered if we might not classify Baptists by the color of their souls. Then we could not speak of white Baptists and colored Baptists alone, for we should have to be more specific. The list might include Red Baptists, Green Baptists, and Yellow Baptists as well as Black Baptists and White Baptists. Christianity knows no color. If "color" in religion means anything it must mean a quality of mind and soul. It means pure in heart—nothing else matters.

Red Baptist—They are always fighting or looking for a fight. They are anarchists; they are savages; they are men and women of war. They would raise their red banner of revolution over every Baptist camp. No matter what the government is, they are against it. No one is free from their tomahawks of criticism, no honored head is secure from their scalping knives of jealousy and envy. They even declare that a good fight is a good thing at times for a church or a denomination. Like Job's horse, they can smell the battle from afar and their quivering nostrils greet every new undertaking with a snort of derision. The keynote of the New Testament they find in the word "contend," and they do it earnestly. They are RED.

Green Baptists—They do not know much. They do not know why they are Baptists. They do not know what their denomination is doing. They do not know what the program of their own church or Young People's Society is for the year. They do not read their denominational paper. They do not know how to lead a meeting or to teach a class or to serve as an officer in any department of the church. They do not know where our denomination does missionary work, the needs of the fields, nor why they should give anything for the support of the enterprise, they are GREEN.

Blue Baptists—They are always discouraged. They can see no hope for the Lord's work. They believe the world is getting worldlier, the young people getting worse, and things are not like they used to be. They are sure the church is doomed, Christian faith must perish, and Christian effort is useless. Christian stewardship is merely waste, Christian organization is only a burden, and all is vanity, so what's the use? Oh, they are BLUE.

Yellow Baptists—When the bands are playing, the crowds are cheering, and everything is going our way, they are on their toes. But when the struggle is hard, when the line that ought to be advancing is being pushed back, they lie down, they quit the game. If the Baptist Church in the community to which they have moved is the biggest and most popular church in town, they transfer their membership at once. But if the new church is weak, or if their business associates belong to another denomination, or if their social set does not go to church, they keep their church letters in their trunks, or they do not send for them at all. They do not even report to the pastor or to any of the members of the church that they are Baptists. If they attend the church once, they choose a seat near the rear, hurry out quickly at the close and complain that the church is not sociable. If the work of the Sunday School class or the Young People's Society is flourishing, they ride on the band wagon, but if the attendance is small and the need of leadership and effort is great, they stay away. If someone hurts their feelings, they quit. Perhaps they take everything the church has to offer, but assume no responsibility and contribute nothing for its support. They may even say or think that if they do not do their part or give their part someone else will do it or give it for them. They are YELLOW.

Black Baptists—There are not many of them; we are thankful for that. But there are some in whose souls there is an eternal night. They have no spiritual vision, no moral insight. How and why they ever came to be Baptists it is hard to tell. They are the Judases of the modern church. They betray their Lord and sell his cause for money, for pleasure, or for selfish personal advancement. They bring disgrace upon the church and upon the auxiliary organization to which they belong. They discredit the church in the eyes of the world. They bring suspicion upon the professions of all good Christians and they bring suffering and shame upon the whole organization to which they belong. They are bad, not because of weakness, but because of meanness. If you have never known this kind of a Baptist, thank the Lord for that. They are BLACK.

White Baptists—But we believe the great majority of Baptists are white Baptists. Their souls are clean. They may make mistakes now and then, but they are mistakes of the head rather than of the heart. They belong to the great multitude whom John saw in his vision, the multitude that had washed their robes and made them white in the blood of the Lamb. The Spirit of Christ has entered into their own spirits, transformed them, controls them, and has become one with them. They are the people upon whom the Young People's Society, the Sunday School, the church and the denomination depend. Their money supports the Baptist work, their prayers sustain the Baptist work, their intelligence promotes the Baptist work, and their efforts continue the Baptist work.

All Baptists are Colored. The color of a Christian's skin does not matter, but the color of their souls is most important. Most of them are WHITE or are getting that way.

THE ROLE OF THE CHURCH IN SOCIETY

As a proponent of early twentieth-century Progressive Era social reform and the black social gospel, Burroughs understood Christianity as empowerment for service. At its best, her religious writings demonstrate the way in which she sought to apply theology to society. Even though Burroughs has not been traditionally considered part of the social gospel movement proper, her work and writings locate her within that tradition. Throughout her life, Burroughs maintained that the church possessed not only a spiritual mandate but also a social function. According to Burroughs, the church must be guided by two goals: progress and perpetuity. Burroughs believed that the church not only would be advanced through consecrated lives but also should seek to ameliorate the quality of life for all people in society. In this way, she imagined a socially active church. Burroughs admonished, "all of this talk about race progress is only whistling in the dark to keep away ghosts" if the church did not address the "vast undone" ("Human Waste and Human Responsibility"). Although Burroughs operated through the particular platform of the Baptist church, her emphasis on church service was a universal call to all believers irrespective of denomination. In calling the church to address social issues, Burroughs also adamantly rebuked "gospel racketeers" whose "worn-out stunts of gospel-selling acrobats" obscured the principles of repentance, grace, forbearance, justice, humility, courage, faith, hope, love, devotion, and unselfish service ("How to Hitch Your Old Time Religion to New Conditions"). Burroughs's call for a rebirth of the church as a social engine is consistent with the views found in W. E. B. Du Bois's *The Negro Church* (1903) and Carter G. Woodson's *The History of the Negro Church* (1921). Her disappointment with gospel racketeers also mirrors some of the criticism offered by Ida B. Wells-Barnett and Fannie Barrier Williams. Burroughs detested idle Christians. She was clear that *doing* and *being* were sublime and most important to God.

In her essay "Definite Work That Uplifters Should Do," Burroughs's reference to biblical Ephraim as a symbol for the Negro masses is telling. Whereas the biblical story of Noah's curse upon the descendants of Ham dominated pro-slavery and pro-segregation interpretations of Genesis 9, Burroughs reverses this trend by appealing to an alternative symbolic genealogy in Ephraim.[5] In the biblical account, Ephraim, the second son of Joseph, first appears in Genesis 41. Ephraim means fruitfulness in Hebrew, and he was named such because his birth coincided with Joseph's prosperity in the land of his affliction (Egypt). Whereas primogeniture of inheritance (or the right of succession belonging to the firstborn son) was an important Judaic institution, the younger son Ephraim was esteemed more highly than his elder brother, Manasseh. Ephraim was blessed by his grandfather, Jacob, to receive a greater inheritance than his brother. The tribe of Ephraim would be the most important member of the kingdom of Israel. By casting the Negro masses as "Ephraim" Burroughs clues the reader to the divine mission and purpose that she believed black people possessed as both the progeny and progenitors of a superior civilization. If Ephraim was the religious typology used by Burroughs to represent the Negro collective as special and favored, she would extend this line of reasoning concerning the superiority of black civilization as the metaphysical foundation for her philosophy of race.

In her essay, though, in framing the Negro collective as biblical Ephraim, she appeals to Hosea 4:17: "Ephraim is joined to his idols." Burroughs warns, "Ephraim (the Negro masses) is either 'joined to his idols,' or he is joining too many cults." The church, she maintained, must do something "compelling" to turn the masses of black folks away from the cults that might hinder Christianity's influence and lead Negroes on the "downward way." Burroughs was concerned that the minds and hearts of black people were "empty of the things of the spirit and the vital things of life" ("Definite Work That Uplifters Should Do"). To combat this, she believed, the mission of the church must be to tackle the problem of "human waste, laziness, and degeneracy." If the church failed, she argued, "Hell will have to be enlarged to make room for Church members who like sin, idleness and evil so much that they cannot resist the temptation to . . . walk hand in hand with the devil's best imps down the road to perdition" ("Human Waste and Human Responsibility"). Burroughs's religious thought reveals her belief that God would cause the nation to prosper because of Negroes in general and the church universal in particular. For Burroughs, a "down-to-earth" plan that enlightened black people and challenged the nation was needed.

༄

Exporting Christianity and Cultivating Race Prejudice

From Nannie Helen Burroughs, *What Do You Think?* (Washington, DC: n.p., 1950), 20–22.

The missionary fires in most of our churches burn very low, because an overwhelming majority of our church members know something "ABOUT" Jesus Christ, but do not know Jesus Christ. We have our lamps, but we have no oil; if we have oil our lamps are not trimmed; if they are trimmed they are not burning; if they are burning they are under a bushel. If you are looking for foolish virgins don't look in the Bible, look in our churches.

The world needs light. It is walking in darkness because the church is filled with foolish virgins. The leadership is not spiritually wise. God does not call the blind to lead the blind—nor cowards to preach His gospel.

The average person who joins the church does not even know WHY he joins and the average leader does not know or does not tell him why. There are great congregations that shout and sing and pray and wear out several churches and kill off a dozen or more preachers, but actually do not know what it's all about. They think that the business of the church is to play on their emotions and keep them feeling good.

On the other hand, there are great cultured congregations that are simply wise in their own conceit. Their attitudes are entirely unchristian. Therefore, they join the church but do not join Jesus. They say the Lord's prayer, but do not *pray* it. They give to missions at home and abroad, but *do not live missions at home.*

For every nine talkers and singers and prayers, the Churches have only one DOER of the WORD. For every one member that has the right

Christian attitude on Race Relationship, the Churches have nine members who do not believe that God made only one race.

The majority of our churches are worth about as much to the cause of Jesus Christ in the communities as the theatres. Investigate conditions around your Church. What real vital social, moral and spiritual effect is your Church having upon the lives of the people who live within a radius of four or five blocks? Check up on the attendance of the people who live right in the door of your Church, and above all, check up on the apparent moral effect which your Church has on their lives.

Now what is the attitude of the Theatre? For one thing, Negroes can go to most of them without being gazed at in wonderment. This is not true of the majority of the churches. Unless Negroes are invited for a planned meeting, they dare not turn up at a white church for worship.

Many white denominations send missionaries to other races, but they do not allow other races to worship under the same roof with them without special arrangement. Do you wonder why the missionary fires burn so low? We are not applying the Christianity of Jesus Christ in our own lives nor in the communities in which our churches are located. We are trying to export the Christian religion through self-sacrificing missionaries and use a homemade brand of Christianity in our churches. Begin at Jerusalem!

How to Hitch Your Old Time Religion to New Conditions

From Nannie Helen Burroughs, *How* (Washington, DC: Progressive National Baptist Convention, 1992), 84–85.

The majority of our Churches need Christianizing, Spiritualizing, Evangelizing. That's all; and they need all three badly. Either one without the other two is head without heart, body without soul, or faith without works.

The triumvirate gives us a sound sense of God—sincere devotion to Christ a clear sense of the fact of human brotherhood—a sacred sense of human values—a clear, devoted, active and unselfish sense of Christian service.

We cannot become Christians and we cannot carry on the program of Christ at home, nor abroad, unless representatives of the Christian Church prepare, believe, teach, practice, and propagate these moral, social and spiritual ideals.

The progress and perpetuity of all our work—local, national and state—depends absolutely on the spiritual and moral quality of our leadership. The Christianity of Christ never grows old. It is as new today as it was two thousand years ago.

Unfortunately, this is the day of racketeering, even in religion. But the Christian religion is not a racket. Its principles—of repentance, growth in grace, forbearance, justice, humility, courage, faith, hope, love, devotion and unselfish service—are unchangeable. They are the same yesterday, today and forever. There is no substitute for them. They are divine.

Racket is not righteousness. "Rousement" is not religion. Christians cannot be built up on racket. They GROW on the sincere milk of the Word.

There is only one way by which man can get what God has in store for him, and that is to "do good and to walk uprightly." We cannot whoop nor shout men into righteousness. They themselves must "grow in grace and in knowledge."

We hear much about "soul-stirring sermons" and not enough about soul-searching sermons. Many of our churches are on a dead hunt for consecrated dimes. That's just another racket.

The majority of our "Gospel racketeers" seem more determined to clean out the peoples' pocketbooks than they are to teach them how to clean up their lives. The Church can grow and glow on consecrated lives, but we have yet to find one that is growing or glowing on so-called consecrated dimes. God isn't going to let designing men get away, successfully, with a scheme that is only a concoction of theirs to hoodwink His humble followers.

If the challenging gospel of Jesus Christ is preached and the people are properly trained, taught in doctrine and developed, they will give without being tricked into it. The fact is that the people have supported our churches generously, but the churches, with few exceptions, have actually fallen down on their end of the responsibility of building the people up in the fundamentals of living.

Leaders must teach the people how to live, by living themselves. Teach them how to do, by setting the example. Teach them how to give, by giving. That's what Jesus did. Our churches need a leadership of "livers," and the people will become congregations of "givers."

Thank God, "racketeering" is short lived. Those who try it soon run out of gas, and have to go somewhere else or do something else to attract the people, or sharpen the jaded appetites of a congregation that cannot be entertained or aroused any longer by the worn-out stunts of Gospel-selling acrobats.

The people stay away from church because they are sick and tired of "old soup warmed over." When the racketeers run out of racket and "rousement," the people will begin to sing "My Soul Wants Something That's New." The Gospel is always new when it is hitched up to new conditions. The leaders who can glorify Jesus, in their everyday living, will see their churches moving forward to higher heights of service and deeper depths of spirituality.

The Church Began in the Home

From Nannie Helen Burroughs, *How* (Washington, DC, Progressive National Baptist Convention, 1992), 83.

The Christian Church was made possible by a home. Had not Mary and Joseph prepared the proper home with its spiritual environment, certainly God would not have entrusted his Son to them.

The Christian church began in a home. An upper room that was a standard part of Oriental home architecture was the place of the first meeting.

For the first two hundred years of its existence the Christian Church met in the homes of its members. There was no other place for the Christians to assemble. Paul preached his first sermon in a private house, and he used homes to start his Church organizations around the world.

The Church got its roots into the community and into society through the homes that were opened to it and were willing to be used by it.

Today, the Negro church is the greatest single force for the advancement of the race. It needs capable leadership that it may more adequately fulfill its mission as the moral and cultural emancipator of Negro people. We need missionaries and social workers trained properly to interpret the Bible and the application of its principles of everyday living to our times.

∽

Definite Work That Uplifters Should Do

From Nannie Helen Burroughs, *What Do You Think?* (Washington, DC: n.p., 1950), 23–24.

The so-called Negro masses are not being reached or influenced in appreciable numbers, by our "uplift" or "missionary" organizations in urban or rural communities. In fact our "uplifters" and "missionaries" seem to major in self-uplift or outworn platitudes that have neither eyes, heart, nor feet. We seem to lack whatever it takes to "compel them (the masses) to come in." For that reason Ephraim (the Negro masses) is either "joined to his idols,"[6] or he is *joining too many cults*. Something "compelling" must be done to turn the masses back from the downward way that leads to moral and social destruction.

The churches, for the most part, except the cults and new gospel camps, are practically empty on Sunday nights and, that is not all, the minds and hearts of our people are entirely too empty of the things of the spirit and the vital things of life. What shall we do? Study the situation in our own community and then—

1. Go to the people and teach them through Christian centers directed by qualified men and women.
2. Prepare and publish leaflets and books that speak a language that they can understand and offer a challenge that only the demons among them can resist.
3. Enlist the children and young people in a "Glorify the Best I Have" crusade.
4. Make simple, clean every-day living attractive and contagious.

5. The slogan for a five-year crusade among the masses should be "all together for all."

You say "my church is in debt or we cannot attempt a home mission program like that." Well, we must attempt a vital program or something much less passive and more constructive. A church that is satisfied with the ungodliness around it is not serving God, and is a liability to the community.

Every church should attempt a definite program that projects itself into the community, even if it must be done on a small scale and without the cooperation of other churches. It should be an all for all drive. The cults will catch your members if you do not cultivate your field by everyday service. Our "uplift" and missionary programs must become burning bushes in order to light up dark lives and dark places. Our churches are not doing what they can and should do. It would help the churches as much as it would help the people, if they would clean up their buildings, keep them clean and get to work teaching the people how to live—how to make the very most out of what they have.

This is the joint task for our "uplifters" and the churches. Suppose we spend the time we use in criticizing the cults in cleaning up our own churches and cultivating our own church membership.

~

Human Waste and Human Responsibility

From *Eleventh Annual Message of Miss Nannie H. Burroughs, President of the Woman's Convention Auxiliary to the National Baptist Convention, U.S.A, Inc., San Francisco, California, September 9* (n.p., National Baptist Convention, 1959), 23–24.

From the way it looks on our city streets these days, Hell will have to be enlarged to make room for Church members who like sin, idleness and evil so much that they cannot resist the temptation to join, straight out, sinners in their dens, brothels and dives and walk hand in hand with the devil's best imps down the road to perdition.

Ask the world who are these who neglect their children, husbands, wives and homes and outdo the leading sinners in every evil known to the wicked? Or go to the streets and witness the heartbreaking scenes. Rome at her lowest was not any worse than American slums today at their best. If the Christian ministry and Church member cannot be moved to tackle this problem of human waste, laziness and degeneracy then what good is our brand of Christianity and what is the Church for.

Placing the blame, passing by on the other side of the street, moving away and simply talking about conditions is no means of escape from the wrath to come.

Too much money has been put into our churches for them to serve only a handful of people while nine-tenths of the race is going to waste through downright indifference and neglect by those who make their living looking superior as they make their living off of those about whose condition and status they care little or nothing.

The Negro masses can and must be reached, enlightened, enlisted, challenged and inspired. All of this talk about race progress is only whistling in the dark to keep away ghosts. It is glorifying the petty done and ignoring the vast undone.

If teachers, parents and race leaders had vision, intelligence, interest and deep concern for the people, they would unite in a down-to-earth plan and program that would not only wake Negroes up all over, but would challenge this nation to assume the full responsibility of proving what a democracy can do if and when the leaven is put in the whole lump.

We submit to you that suggested "IDLE HOUR WORK SHOPS" for young people would be a splendid starter. Is there a Christian anywhere in this nation who would underwrite one shop as an experiment? It would pay in human dividends. In God's name, Come on! Let's do something. Millions are, even now, on their way to nowhere but to the dogs.

PART TWO

THE WAY UP AND OUT

Social, Political, and Race-Centered Thought

ON BLACK WOMANHOOD, SUFFRAGE, AND THE NOBILITY OF LABOR

Black women's writings during the late nineteenth and early twentieth centuries emphasized both intellectual enlightenment and the elevation of black womanhood to a position of respect in American society. In keeping with the tradition laid out by nineteenth-century thinkers like Josephine St. Pierre Ruffin, Hallie Quinn Brown, Josephine Turpin Washington, and Fannie Barrier Williams, Nannie Helen Burroughs used her pen and voice to rebuke the negative epithets historically imputed to black women. From an early age, she foresaw her role as upholding the "'holy grail' of finer womanhood," one composed of pious, clean, and industrious living.[1] The motif of the holy grail insinuates that womanhood is inherently sacred and wondrous. Burroughs maintained that black womanhood ought to be protected, cultivated, and enlightened. She believed in instilling black women with the kind of courage and self-determination that would enable them to translate their drudgery into community-building enterprises for the race.

Burroughs officially emerged as a public figure at the 1900 National Baptist Convention in Richmond, Virginia. She was a twenty-one-year-old firebrand with the kind of grand vision that not only made her a marvel to behold but also caused friction between her and some of the convention's male leaders.[2] At the 1900 meeting, members proposed the establishment of a Women's Convention, and Burroughs was elected as its corresponding secretary. The Women's Convention offered Burroughs a level of national notoriety that perhaps would not have been achievable through the local domestic science teaching position she had originally envisioned as her calling.

It was her first public speech, "How the Women are Hindered from Helping" that defined what would become Burroughs's major life agenda: the uplift and education of black women and girls. Burroughs encouraged black women to bring honor to the race by adhering to true religion, honesty, cleanliness, chastity, and industry. Her idea of the holy grail of finer womanhood was puritanical and distinctly Victorian. At her National Training School, women practiced a modest dress code and were required to have a Bible. Without guidance, idle women, she admonished, would fall into immortality and inevitable prostitution. In her 1915 article, "Black Women and Reform," Burroughs made the case for black women's suffrage and emphasized the dignity of all labor. She considered black women to be superior in morality precisely because they had historically carried the moral destiny of two races. In "The Negro Woman Is a Mighty Big Woman," Burroughs wrote, "Believe it or not, to have been the 'mammy' of one race and the mother of another and to have enough patience, understanding and love to go around, without stint, is a rare social achievement and distinction." What might prove alarming to contemporary readers is that Burroughs did not interpret the antebellum mammy stereotype as particularly damaging. Rather, she saw *mammy* as a historical "distinction" that gave black women "more influence for good in the heart and home of white Americans than any other woman has ever wielded." On the whole, Burroughs interpreted "Negro" history in ways that sought to make sense of her people as the victors of their historical experience. Throughout her sixty years in public service, Burroughs would continue to make an argument for the professionalization of domestic work. She warned against laziness and idleness because these, she believed, would inevitably destroy the black home.

How the Sisters Are Hindered from Helping

From National Baptist Convention, *Journal of the Twentieth Annual Session of the National Baptist Convention, Held in Richmond, Virginia, September 12–17, 1900* (Nashville, TN: National Baptist Publishing Board, 1900), 196–97.

We come not to usurp thrones nor to sow discord, but to so organize and systematize the work that each church may help through a Woman's Missionary Society and not be made poorer thereby. It is for the utilization of talent and the stimulation to Christian activity in our Baptist churches that prompt us to service. We realize that to allow these gems to lie unpolished longer means a loss to the denomination. For a number of years there has been a righteous discontent, a burning zeal to go forward in his name among the Baptist women of our churches and it will be the dynamic force in the religious campaign at the opening of the 20th century. It will be the spark that shall light the altar fire in the heathen lands. We realize, too, that the work is too great and laborers too few for us to stand by while like Trojans the brethren at the head of the work under the convention toil unceasingly.

We come now to the rescue. We unfurl our banner upon which is inscribed this motto, "The World for Christ. Woman, Arise, He calleth for Thee." Will you as a pastor and friend of missions help by not hindering these women when they come among you to speak and to enlist the women of your church? It has ever been from the time of Miriam, that most remarkable woman, the sister of Moses, that most remarkable man, down to the courageous women that in very recent years have carried the Gospel into Tibet and Africa and proclaimed and taught the truth where no man has been allowed to enter. Surely, women somehow have had a very important part in the work of saving this redeemed earth.

Every religious organization in the world is trying by a special effort to raise a stated sum for the great religious campaign which will mark the opening of the 20th century. This money will be necessary to push forward the work which they must undertake. The Christian world is no longer contented at conquering by piecemeal. They have at last decided to make one last triumphant entry into heathen lands, and with one stroke slay the common enemy. The implement to be used is money for the support of men and the purchase of land to build houses of worship. We have decided to help in this campaign, and have apportioned the amounts as follows: 10 woman's conventions to give $25.00 each; 20 woman's associations and district conventions to give $5.00; 1,000 missionary societies to give $2.00 each; 2,000 women to give $1.00; 300 children's bands to give 50 cents each; 15,000 pastors to pray for a great uplift in woman's work at home and abroad.

Praying the Great Head of the Church to bless all the departments of our national work, we are yours for the highest development of Christian womanhood.

The Colored Woman and Her Relation to the Domestic Problem

From *The United Negro, His Problems and His Progress: Containing the Address and Proceedings of the Negro Young People's Christian Congress, Held August 6–11, 1902*, ed. Irvine Garland Penn and John Wesley Edward Bowen (Atlanta, GA: D. E. Luther Publishing, 1902), 324–29.

You ask what is meant by the domestic problem. It is that peculiar condition under which women are living and laboring without the knowledge of the secrets of thrift, or of true scientific methods in which the mind has been awakened, and hands made capable thereby to give the most efficient services. It is a condition of indifference on the part of our working women as to their needs to how we may so dignify labor that our services may become indispensable on the one hand and Negro sentiment will cease to array itself against the "working girls" on the other hand. It is a question as to how we may receive for our services compensation commensurate with the work done. The solution of this problem will be the prime factor in the salvation of Negro womanhood, whose salvation must be attained before the so-called race problem can be solved.

The training of Negro women is absolutely necessary, not only for their own salvation and the salvation of the race, but because the hour in which we live demands it. If we lose sight of the demands of the hour we blight our hope of progress. The subject of domestic science has crowded itself upon us, and unless we receive it, master it and be wise, the next ten years will so revolutionize things that we will find our women without the wherewith to support themselves.

Untrained hands, however willing, will find themselves unwelcomed in the humblest homes. We may be careless about this matter of equipping our women for work in the homes, but if we are to judge from the wonderful progress that recent years has brought in the world of domestic labor we must admit that steps must be taken, and that at once, to train the hands of Negro women for better services and their hearts for purer living. All through the North white imported help is taking the place of Negro help. Where we once held forth without a thought of change we find our places filled by those of other races and climes. The people who had to have servants declared that they wanted intelligent, refined, trained help, and in the majority of cases we were not ready to give them what they needed. Our intelligent Negroes, even though they may not have bread to eat, in many cases shun service work, when the fact is evident that ignorant help is not wanted by the best class of people in this country. The more thorough and intelligent the help the better.

What will this crowding from service mean to Negro women? It will mean their degradation. Our women will sink beneath the undermining influences of insidious sloth. Industry is one of the noblest virtues of any race. The people who scorn and frown upon her must die. While little heed may have been paid to the demand for better help and the supplanting of Negro servants by Irish, Dagoes[3] and English may have been unnoticed by all of us, yet it is time for the leaders to sound the alarm, ere we are rooted from the places we have held for over two centuries. The time will come when we will stand as helpless as babes, as dependent as beggars without the wherewith to sustain life, unless we meet the demands squarely.

Our women have worked as best they could without making any improvements and thus developing the service into a profession and in that way make the calling more desirable from a standpoint of being lifted from a mere drudgery, as well as from the standpoint of compensation received.

The race whose women have not learned that industry and self-respect are the only guarantees of a true character will find itself bound by ignorance and violence or fettered with chains of poverty.

There is a growing tendency among us to almost abhor women who work at service for a living. If we hold in contempt women who are too honest, industrious and independent, women whose sense of pride is too exalted to be debased by idleness, we will find our women becoming more and more slothful in this matter of supporting themselves. Our "high-toned" notions as to the kind of positions educated people ought to fill have caused many women who can not get anything to do after they come out of school to loaf rather than work for an honest living, declaring to themselves and acting it before others, that they were not educated to live among pots and pans. None of us may have been educated for that purpose, but educated women without work and the wherewith to support themselves and who have declared in their souls that they will not stoop to toil are not worth an ounce more to the race than ignorant women who have made the same declarations. Educated loafers will bear as much watching as ignorant ones. When the nobility of labor is magnified, and those who do labor respected more because of their real worth to the race, we will find a less number trying to escape the brand, "servant girl." We are not less honorable if we are servants. Fidelity to duty rather than the grade of one's occupation is the true measure of character. Every gentle virtue will go down before a people and their endeavors come to naught when they forget that the foundation stone of prosperity is toil. What matters it if we do rise from pots and pans? They tell us we came from apes and baboons, and we have made it this far. Further, if God could take a crop of apes or baboons and make beings like us He is God indeed, and we can trust Him to raise us from servants to queens. If we did come from these ungainly animals of the four-footed family, we got here nearly as soon as the people who didn't have so far to come.

What matters it if our women, by honest toil, make their way from the kitchen to places of respect and trust in the walks of life? Are they less honorable because they have been servants? Are not the women who by thrift and economy, with everything operating against them in their own race, and low wages, that mighty power before whom the poor of earth must bow, struggling for mastery, work their way to the front, more deserving of praise, more worthy of recognition and respect than scores of "parlor ornaments" who, by methods, have maintained some social standing, and hold in contempt the "unfortunate servant girl"? There are women at service who would eat their meals off the heads of barrels or dress after the fashion of John the Baptist in the wilderness before they would sacrifice their high-toned moral character, simply to shine in the social world by virtue of their idleness and ability to dress well. It is not the depth from which we come, but the heights to which we soar. The incomparable water lily grows out of the slime of black lagoons, and heaven itself consists not in location but in nobility of the character of its population. It matters not where nor how lowly the station, pursue the unswerving way of industry and victory or defeat will decide our fitness for the places we seek.

Again, if we scorn women who have character and are honest enough to work to preserve it and accept into our company women who have no character and will not work to secure it, are we making the race any more moral? This pulling aside of our silken skirts at the approach of the servant women has materially affected the morals of Negro women. How many of them have abandoned honest labor in which they could have given character and tone to the service rendered by our women, and to satisfy their ambitions for social recognition have resorted to idleness in order to gain the smiles of a class among us who will receive any woman who can dress well without working at service to pay for it.

Scorn the servant women? No, never. Rather scorn that class of women who have resolved not to work and hang out of doors and windows, hold up corners, or keep the neighborhood astir with demoralizing gossip. Scorn young Negro women who flirt and loiter about the streets at the sacrifice of their good name and the name of Negro womanhood. But honor and praise to the women who have learned that all labor is just as honorable, just as honest, as the person who is doing it. Have not all of us been servants? God made us all servants the very day He dismissed Adam from Eden. "By the sweat of thy brow shalt thou eat bread."[4] What mean these women who are eating bread and are not sweating, either, by scorning the women who are obeying the divine injunction?

Young women from rural districts flock to great cities like New York, Chicago, Philadelphia, Boston, Baltimore and Washington in search of employment. Not only are they unprepared to serve but are woefully ignorant of the new social conditions into which they must be thrown. The white women in these large cities conduct guilds and other organizations that employ attendants to meet the trains and be on the alert for the white servant class that may be coming in seeking work or homes. Christian homes and churches are pointed out to the new-comers. The strong arms of Christian women are thrown about them, and while they are far from home and loved ones, they have the assurance that they have friends who will be ever mindful of them and their interests.

What are the results of this wholesale abandonment of working women? Nine cases out of ten the girls who come from the country fall into the hands of ill-disposed Negro men or keepers of some "back way boarding house" of the famous "furnished rooms" character. Thousands of our women are today in the clutches of men of our own race who are not worth the cost of their existence. They dress well and live on the earnings of servant girls. Negro men can aid us in the solution of the problem by becoming self-supporting rather than live on the earnings of women who often get less than ten dollars per month. Not only does this increase idleness among us but weakens the moral life of women. Negro women can help solve their own problem by applying to these lazy men Horace Greeley's[5] doctrine, "Root hog or die."

The solution of the servant girl problem, then, can only be accomplished—first, by making it possible for these girls to overcome their ignorance, dishonesty and carelessness by establishing training classes and other moral agencies in these large cities and maintaining one or more first-class schools of domestic science. Second, by employers demanding the trained help from these classes or schools and paying wages in keeping with the ability of the servant to do the work. Third, by giving to women who work time for recreation and self-improvement. This constant all-day "go" has made service a drudgery. If servants had hours for rest and improvement, like other laborers, they would come to their work with a freshness and intelligence that is now absent.

Emphasize the importance of preparation for service work. Let Negro women who are idle find work, stick to it and use it as a stepping stone to something better. Let us cease reaching over women who are servants and have character enough for queens to queens who haven't brains and character enough for servants. By becoming exponents of the blessed principles of honesty, cleanliness and industry, Negro women can bring dignity to service life, respect and trust to themselves and honor to the race. Then in deed and in truth we can mount up as with the wings of eagles, soar above the mountains of virtue and hide our heads among the stars. If anybody is to be scorned, scorn those women who will not honestly toil to raise themselves and are pulling us from the throne of honor and virtue.

Not Color but Character

From *Voice of the Negro* 1, no. 7 (July 1904): 277–79.

Many Negroes have colorphobia as badly as the white folk have Negrophobia. You say this is not true. Then, what does wholesale bleaching of face and straightening of hair indicate? From our viewpoint it simply means that the women who practice it wish that they had white faces and straight hair. It simply says that they don't like their color and hair, and yet the first poor white boy who comes along singing "Coon, Coon, Coon, I wish my color would fade," these same bleachers and straighteners feel like chasing out of town.

There is no denying it, Negroes have colorphobia. Some Negro men have it. Some Negro women have it. Whole families have it, and somebody tells us some Negro churches have it. Saviour, keep us from those churches, please. Some social circles have it, and so the diseases spreading from men to women, from women to families, from families to churches and from churches to social circles. The idea of Negroes setting up a color standard is preposterous.... Has it ever been shown that fair Negroes are better morally than black Negroes? If so, I wish we all were fair. No, it has never been shown, nor ever will, as long as we present in the majority such superior types of manhood and womanhood found in thoroughbred Negro men and women throughout the world.

The fairer some Negroes are the better they think themselves, without any thought of an ounce of character to go along with it, and enough good common sense to know that color is no badge of superiority of mind nor soul. There are men right in our own race, and their number is legion, who would rather marry a woman for her color than for her character. These same men criticize such women as Hannah Elias[6] of New York, for mixing up with [Senator John R.] Platt, and yet would receive with open arms the fungus growth produced by virtue of their illicit relations. The white man who crosses the line and leaves an heir is doing a favor for some black man who would marry the most debased woman, whose only stock in trade is her color, in preference to the most royal queen in ebony.

I have seen black men have fits about black women associating with white men, and yet these same men see more to admire in a half-white face owned by a characterless, fatherless woman than in faces owned by thoroughbred, legal heirs to the throne, with pure souls and high purposes in life. We do not say that black women are not as virtueless, in many cases, as their fairer sisters, nor that because a woman is fair she has no character, or because she is black she has no character, for character is no respecter of color, for there are thousands on both sides who are worthy of the name woman; but we do mean to say that many black men have not learned this fact any more than many white men have not learned that all the virtue, refinement and culture are not locked up in white women.

The man who puts color as the first requisite in his choice of an associate invariably gets nothing but color, but the man who puts character first, always gets a woman. Of course, we are so fortunate as to be able to satisfy the most fastidious. We can give women with color and character, women with character, but not color, and women with neither character nor color. But it must be understood that some fair faces own fair souls, and some black faces own fair souls. There is character in ebony as well as in marble.

Many women who bleach and straighten out make as their only excuse that it improves the appearance. A true woman wouldn't give a cent for a changed appearance of this sort—a superficial nothing. What every woman who bleaches and straightens out needs is not her appearance changed, but her mind. She has a false notion as to the value of color and hair in solving the problem of her life. Why does she wish to improve her appearance? Why not improve her real self? Will the changed appearance enhance her value as a woman? Is her mind made brighter and her life straighter because her face is brighter and her hair straighter? The race is not half so bad off for women with whiter faces as it is for women with whiter souls. If Negro women would use half the time they spend in trying to get white in trying to get better, the race would move forward apace, but the production of more white Negroes, whether home-made or born that way, that does not bring to the race more character and worth, are unwelcome guests that may be excused at any time.

Putting in modern improvements may enhance the value of a house, but putting on modern improvements by straightening hair and bleaching faces will not enhance the real value of any woman.

It is not the whiteness of face and straightness of hair that has made the name "Anglo-Saxon woman" a synonym of purity. It is the straightness of life and the whiteness of soul that has made her the woman.

Verily, verily I say unto you, that the women who spend most of their time improving their outward appearances are invariably the very women who are preparing themselves to darken their characters and make more crooked their lives.

Many black men have provoked this state of affairs by laying down a color qualification. Black and white men must be taught that the race has clean-minded, pure-hearted women of every color who have never bowed to Baal,[7] and never will.

Further, our men have permitted many encroachments upon the moral life of the race by not entering manly protests against all who insist on having social equality of the wrong sort. White men offer more protection to their prostitutes than many black men offer to their best women. A Negro dare not so far forget himself as to insult them, and yet these same white men who will die for the vilest of the vile among their own women, dare attempt to walk with impunity into our most sacred confines. It must be here said to the credit of the majority of our men, that they are publicly gentlemanly. They respect the women of both races. A Negro man will give up his seat on a car as quickly for a white woman as he will for a woman of his own race.

In extending ordinary courtesies due every man to every woman, the white man has not allowed his manhood to go beyond his race. That is a mighty poor manhood after all. A man who is truly a gentleman, respects a woman, not because she is white or black, as the case may be, but because she is a woman, and he had been early taught that there is a certain amount of respect due every woman.

No Negro woman, however good, however refined, is considered by the average white man as much worthy of his respect and protection as the lowest of low of his own race. Our women need the protection and genuine respect of men; if not unto them, unto whom shall we go?

Whenever the men of any race defiantly stand for the protection of their women the women will be strengthened more and be saved from the hands of the most. But when the womanhood of a race is unprotected by its manhood, it is written that that race has no premium on virtue and whosoever will may come.

If white men do not respect the women enough to confine themselves to their race, socially, Negro women should think enough of themselves and of our good men to see that no encroachments are made upon us. It is contrary to the lays of our moral code for any race or people to grow morally strong under such circumstances, and it is criminal for any woman of our race to tolerate for a moment such relations with men who have no more respect for black women than the door-keeper to Dante's Inferno has for St. Peter—men who believe that the women of our race can be bought, sold or bartered to satisfy their lusts. It is the duty of Negro women to rise in the pride of their womanhood and vindicate themselves of the charge by teaching all men that black womanhood is as sacred as white womanhood.

The encroachments we had to tolerate before the war[8] and during the war are pardoned, but we live at the high-noon of the brightest day of liberty of soul and body. God help us to so live that we may raise the standard higher and higher until the name "Negro woman" will be a synonym for uprightness of character and loftiness of purpose. Let character, and not color, be the first requisite to admission into any home, church or social circle, and a new day will break upon ten million people.

Black Women and Reform

From *Crisis* 10 (August 1915): 187.

The Negro Church means the Negro woman. Without her, the race could not properly support five hundred churches in the whole world. Today they have 40,000 churches in the United States. She is not only a great moral and spiritual asset, but she is a great economic asset. I was asked by a southern white woman who is an enthusiastic worker for "votes for (white) women," "What can the Negro woman do with the ballot?" I asked her, "What can she do without it?" When the ballot is put into the hands of the American woman the world is going to get a correct estimate of the Negro woman. It will find her a tower of strength of which poets have never sung, orators have never spoken, and scholars have never written.

Because the black man does not know the value of the ballot, and has bartered and sold his most valuable possession, it is no evidence that the Negro woman, therefore, needs the ballot to get back, by the wise *use* of it, what the Negro man has lost by the *misuse* of it. She needs it to ransom her race. A fact worthy of note is that in every reform in which the Negro woman has taken part, during the pasty fifty years, she has been as aggressive, progressive and dependable as those who inspired the reform or led it. The world has yet to learn that the Negro woman is quite superior in bearing moral responsibility. A comparison with the men of her race, in moral issues, is odious. She carries the burdens of the Church, and of the school and bears a great deal more than her economic share in the home.

Another striking fact is that the Negro woman carries the moral destiny of two races in her hand. Had she not been the woman of unusual moral stamina that she is, the black race would have been made a great deal whiter, and the white race a great deal blacker during the past fifty years. She has been left a prey for the men of every race, but in spite of this, she has held the enemies of Negro female chastity at bay. The Negro woman is the white woman's as well as the white race's most needed ally in preserving an unmixed race.

The ballot, wisely used, will bring to her the respect and protection that she needs. It is her weapon of moral defense. Under present conditions, when she appears in court in defense of her virtue, she is looked upon with amused contempt. She needs the ballot to reckon with men who place no value upon her virtue, and to mold healthy public sentiment in favor of her own protection.

Miss Burroughs Plans a "New Deal" to Conserve Girlhood of the Race

From *Pittsburgh Courier*, August 26, 1933, 7.

While many are talking about charting new courses for Economic Recovery, we are concerned about charting a new course for Child Conservation. To that end, the National Training School for Women and Girls is opening a new department for little girls between the ages of 8 and 12. This new feature is added to meet a crying need of mothers who are compelled to leave their little children and go out to work every day. Only the Recording Angel knows how many thousands of promising little children actually go to waste every year because "there is nobody home."

The public school can only turn the children in at nine and turn them out at three. Thousands of children are left to shift for themselves from that time on, and they are shifting from bad to worse. Mothers are distressed over this condition. Many are the women who have said to us "I work with my heart in my mouth." Only today we received a letter from a mother in Philadelphia who says "I have to work all day and worry about my daughter, who is eleven years old." A woman cannot work and worry and at the same time give satisfaction on her job.

Above all, the race cannot move forward unless children are given a fair chance to grow up decently. As badly off as the Negro race is for leaders and home-makers, we cannot afford to stand by and see little girls going to waste without doing something about it. Writing essays and delivering high-sounding speeches about social conditions will not solve the problem. We must provide a place that will take the place of the mother and the home.

The economic plight of the Negro woman is tragic. During this depression she is bearing the economic burden of the race almost alone. She has the longest hours and she gets the lowest pay. Her home is either neglected because of her enforced absence or it is crowded with relatives and roomers because of financial conditions. Children are living in social and moral surroundings that make it impossible for them to have a ghost of a chance to grow up decently.

We propose to give the little girls who are sent here to be trained and properly educated an environment such as a real home offers and an atmosphere that is healthy, happy, and wholesome. For this new work we will have the best teachers that can be found. Negro Protestants do not have schools for little children—boys nor girls. We burden Catholic institutions with our protestant children, and some of us have the temerity to try to cast aspersions on that denomination for their vision and vigilance. I hold no brief for the Catholic Church but if we protestants were doing our duty half as well, we would not lose so many young people from the churches every year. We should provide an institution of character of our own, or we should extend a rising vote of thanks to any denomination, individual, or organization that does.

We are going to teach the child everything that it should know, from the care of its body, to the value of its soul, so that it will grow in physical, mental, moral, social, and spiritual grace. All we ask is that you send us children who are sound in body and mind—not incorrigibles—and that the parents provide simple, comfortable clothing and be able to pay the very reasonable fee. Children between the ages of 8 and 12 may remain the year round.

For this new department we are particularly anxious to have children with unusual talent for music. There will be no extra charge for music lessons. We believe this plan is inspired and out of this noble experiment will come a new and finer womanhood. Give us the child before it goes wrong and we will give you character and culture glorified.

Remember while we are doing this special work, we shall continue to do our academic and trade courses for girls of junior high school, high school and junior college grades in a bigger and better way.

***

Negro Women Must Make Future Brighter, or Continue an Economic, Social Slave

From *Pittsburgh Courier*, January 14, 1939, 7.

The Negro woman "totes" more water; hoes more corn; picks more cotton; washes more clothes; cooks more meals; nurses more babies;

mammies more Nordics; supports more churches; does more race uplifting; serves as mud-sills for more climbers; takes more punishment; does more forgiving; gets less protection and appreciation, than do the women in any other civilized group in the world. She has been the economic and social slave of mankind.

Nannie H. Burroughs, the world's most scintillating Negro woman leader, makes the above statement on the threshold of 1939.[9] [—*Pittsburgh Courier*]

Call this a picture of the past if you will. The one of today is not any brighter unless, and until the Negro woman resolves to make it brighter. Today she is fighting a new and different fight. She is now in hopeless competition with the machine, with modern household appliances; with white women, who are also in the low economic brackets; and with white men, who are grabbing the few jobs that heretofore "belonged" to Negro men, who might assume their responsibility but for the fact that white men have grabbed the jobs that Negro men used to have, and finally, Negro women have to compete with the ever present and various shades of prejudices. The Negro woman is, therefore, forced to fight harder than ever to keep the wolf from her door, and she is fighting give classes of competitors.

It would seem that in the fact of these facts, that Negro schools would insist on offering the kind of training that would fit the oncoming army of Negro girls to meet their five competitors with new strength of character, skill, and courage. It does not require the wisdom of Solomon to understand that those who are interested in the future of Negro women and girls had better offer types of training, far more practical, useful, thorough and modern than is now offered or the economic plight of the Negro woman, and automatically of the Negro home of which she is the backbone, will not only be tragic, but death dealing.

Publish this from the housetop . . . from now on, the Negro woman must not sit and wait for white women to fight for freedom and opportunity for women in the hope that if the situation for which women is improved, that Negro women will automatically benefit. Never. It just doesn't work that way. As one class of white women moves up, there will always be another class of white women, lower down, who will step into the places made vacant.

In keeping with the true American spirit, and above all, in keeping with the definite command of Almighty God to the human race to "go forward," the Negro woman must purpose in her heart that she is going to emancipate herself.

Negro Women and Their Homes

From Nannie Helen Burroughs, *What Do You Think?* (Washington, DC: n.p., 1950), 77–80.

Negro women will have to become MORE INTERESTED in learning Domestic Arts and Household Management. Too many of our homes are going to pieces, physically and morally, because the majority of our women "hate" cooking, and the everyday arts that are essential to the making of clean, happy homes.

Cooking and homemaking are man's greatest need and basic civilizer. They are the only SERVICES that can draw and hold man to his hearth. Why so many women, who want and go after husbands and homes, eschew their essential duties is a question to which wise men should try to find the answer. A woman, who wants and goes shopping for a husband and a home, bargains for home duties and responsibilities that cannot be ignored or neglected, without irreparable damage to herself, her home and society.

Everyday home duties simply cannot be hated or neglected without dire consequences. Why all of this contempt for home duties, anyhow? Basically, cooking and the kindred occupations are arts and vocations as cultural as nursing, teaching or medicine.

Homemaking does as much or more to promote health, happiness and longevity, as all of these professions combined. Civilized men simply cannot live without cooks and well-kept homes. Women, who have homes and children and neglect home duties and responsibilities, are our greatest social and moral liabilities.

It is senseless to talk about building a race, fit to stand up and carry its own load, in the kind of a civilization that is now in the making, when millions of our women are actually too lazy to get up and prepare simple breakfasts for their children to go to school on. Happy, healthy families cannot live out of cans and on poorly prepared meals.

As a result of the Negro woman's aversion to and ignorance of the art of homemaking, we waste and throw away enough food and money to run our homes, according to standards, at half of the present cost.

To know how to manage a home, properly, cuts cost and eliminates drudgery. The majority of our women, who are responsible for homes, are actually guilty, before God, for criminal negligence. Their children are fed irregularly and improperly. The children's bodies and clothes are dirty, hair unkept and the street is their home—all day and until late into the night. The streets are teeming with neglected Negro children. God's little ones going to waste!

Ignorance and laziness are the cause of most of the bad living and bad acting in the homes of the masses. The masses do not know and the classes are playing an "escape" game. White exploiters are reaping a harvest. Homes are fast becoming dens of iniquity. Nobody is bothered about the souls of the victims.

The influence of the Negro church, right in the midst of blighted homes, is absolutely nil. Moving people into "projects" is not the answer. PEOPLE ARE NOT PROJECTS—they are people and must be treated accordingly. Yes, it is a longer way round, but making homes and keeping them clean is the shortest way to the highway of life.

The only way to remedy this shocking and death dealing condition is for churches and all missionary and educational organizations to get together and map out a simple, practical, long range program of teaching challenge and guidance so as to popularize the beauty and benefits of homemaking in a way that women will understand and do their duty. There is no other way.

If this is done, intensively and continuously, the next generation will be benefitted and saved. Why should women and men sit around all day and let their children and their homes go to ruin? Men will never take the initiative in doing anything about it. It is up to women to put on a home saving campaign that will result in a real reformation.

Ideas and ideals have power: interest has influence. Put these to work in the field of homemaking and the masses will hear, understand, desire, believe and be saved.

There must be definite improvement in Negro home life. Every teen-age girl should be taught the fine art of homemaking, even if she belongs to the class that is able to have its cooking done.

The women, who earn their living as cooks, should take training and become professionals. Household engineers—if you please. The field is still open—but, if Negro women, do not learn the art, they will surely lose out in another occupation (we have lost several) that, in the world of tomorrow, will be highly paid, standardized professions.

Right now, ship loads of foreigners are on their way to America to take any kind of work they can get—to go into cooperative (small scale farming), and thus give their children a chance to grow up in wholesome environments and become stalwart citizens.

Wake up! Negro women, and rank your children and your home with the best (simple, clean livers) in this land. We can do it if we stop sitting around—wasting time, watching a new world pass us by.

Get up! Learn how! Clean up! Go up!

∽

The Negro Woman Is a Mighty Big Woman

From Nannie Helen Burroughs, *What Do You Think?* (Washington, DC: n.p, 1950), 59–60.

"A man is no bigger than he treats his fellowman." Believe it or not, to have been the "mammy" of one race and the mother of another and to have enough patience, understanding and love to go around, without stint, is a rare social achievement and distinction.

The Negro woman apparently possesses matchless maternal tenderness, affection and devotion. In the days of slavery hers was a most difficult role.

She held the reins in the home of her mistress. She not only had personality and power but she had tact and influence. Influence is greater than power. She was no tame imported "governess." She was a "home grown governor." In her unique, difficult and delicate dual relationship, she wielded more influence for good in the heart and home of white Americans than any other woman has ever wielded.

Her word was law and gospel in many Southern homes. She certainly "did something to" white America ... something to their hearts ... and to their deepest emotions. They will never get over it.

She dominated her situation and she did it with such dignity, grace, effectiveness, love and suavity, that nobody questioned her wisdom, judgment nor authority. Her rich social contribution to American life can never be properly evaluated, nor can it be paid for by simply telling patronizing "Mammy stories," or chiseling her statute in cold marble.

The Negro "Mammy" gave to white children the tenderest love. It went deep and abides. Those who are the direct or indirect beneficiaries of her love and sacrifice are debtors to the race that produced her. Hers was a quality of devotion that cannot be paid for in dollars and cents—money cannot buy what she gave. The only way that white Americans can express their appreciation of her is by dealing justly with her progeny. "Mammy's day is Gone With The Wind."

The day for mutual respect and appreciation is here. Capable Negroes should be given a fair chance on the stage to do something more than play the role of "Mammy." The two races must enter into a new relationship. A new relationship requires a new adjustment. The Negro passes from the role of servants of a race into that of sharer of responsibilities and opportunities in a common cause in a common country.

White and black Americans of today should make their adjustment as gracefully and as graciously as "Mammy" made hers in her day. Each race has and has always had something that the other needs. "Mammy" gave love to white Americans and white Americans should give justice to her offspring and not a stone.

Each race must learn that a man is no bigger than he treats his fellow-man. Measured by that high standard "Mammy" was "A Mighty Big Woman."

UPLIFT, PATRIOTISM, RESPECTABILITY, AND EDUCATION

During the early twentieth century, the United States emerged as a world industrial power. As urbanization and industry expanded, poverty metastasized across the industrial North. Thereto, technological advances and the massive influx of European immigrants threatened to displace black Americans as the nation's default laborers. In response to immigration, Burroughs challenged black Americans to develop creative ways to make themselves more preferable than immigrants as the nation's laboring class of choice. Burroughs was not anti-immigrant in the sense that she despised diversity; however, she was adamant that the influx of foreign peoples would disrupt the flow of opportunities that might otherwise go to black Americans. This is representative of her race-first or race-centered politics.

Thereto, the social progress solution she envisioned did not singularly revolve around industrial education. While Burroughs believed that industrial education represented an important part of progress, it alone would not suffice as the only remedy to solve the problems faced by black folks. She admonished black people to forsake materialism in deference to the cultivation of spiritual gifts. Whereas white Americans, she maintained, cultivated "things of the flesh," the greatest contribution black people could make to American society would be through "gifts of the spirit" ("With All Thy Getting"). She believed that black people should devote their spiritual gifts to the development of an authentic Christianity in America, one that would spiritualize American life. It bears noting that in particular Burroughs's article "With All Thy Getting" demonstrates an interesting fusion of discourses. The paternalistic language used by Burroughs to describe blacks as "a child race" reflects some of the dominant ethnological discourses of the nineteenth century that labeled Africans as an inherently infantile race of people in need of saving.[10] At the same time, she upheld the era's racial gifts thesis and the concept of race conservationism. Her emphasis on the spiritual gifts of black folks specifically follows the black ethnological theories of the nineteenth century that regarded African Americans as "the Redeemer Race."[11] Burroughs believed that through spiritual gifts, "the Negro... must ransom [America]." She reminded her readers that blacks were not only superior Americans but also "eminently superior in knowledge concerning the truth about races ("How Does It Feel to Be a Negro?"). In her view, black people had a future in America that would be defined according to their intelligence, industry, courage, chivalry, patriotism, and spirituality.

∞

Industrial Education—Will It Solve the Negro Problem?

From *Colored American Magazine* 7, no. 4 (March 1904): 188–90.

The Negro Problem is a problem of color, and not of fitness. Industrial education is not a skin changer, and could not, therefore, solve a problem that is but skin deep. By industrial education I take it that you mean the development of that part of the mental and physical man that will respond to all or some special phase of manual labor. Industrial education will solve but one phase of the problem, and the Negro must have all phases of the problem solved in order to secure the key to the situation.

Before anyone can assume that industrial education alone will solve the Negro problem it must be proved first that the Negro's mind, feelings, tastes, habit, interest and enthusiasm naturally adapt him to this particular branch of learning. This being proved, systematic development and cultivation along industrial lines would make him the man intended by his Creator. But it has yet to be shown that the Negro is outside of the law of evolution, and needs a special law for his development. Since he is within the pale and it has taken all kinds of education to solve the problem of other races within those confines, it will take the same kinds of education to make him a better man and a better citizen, the same man and the same citizen, equal to any, inferior to none.

Secondly, it must be shown that the Negro can do everything else well except manual labor, and with this happy adjunct his salvation along all lines will be complete. It must also be shown that he cannot simultaneously attain two kinds of education. For if he can, the law of economics would suggest that he do so. The Negro is surely not the one-talent fellow of Bible fame, and the demand should not be made upon him to yield a one-talent result. God used the same constructive timber in making Ham that He used in making Shem and Japheth, and His "whosoever will" Gospel will reclaim the one as quickly and as surely as it will the other.

Those who outline a specific course of study and attempt to confine him to one field of labor must remember that his capacity, his ability, his ambition is as varied as to quality and quantity as the capacity and the ability of each individual of any other race, and the educators of the Negro race must prepare to meet the demands of individual inclinations, feelings and tastes, as far as it is possible.

It has never been shown that the Negro's mental power must be cast in an industrial mold in order to fully respond to the biddings of his mind and the pleadings of his heart; nor have we evidence to show that the Negro makes a better citizen and a better man with an industrial education than with any other kind; nor has the Negro any evidence that an industrial education will secure for him an even break in the race of life. Is the Negro to spend years fitting himself as a laborer of skill, and then be forced to work for unskilled prices or starve? Can any race be saved morally, spiritually, intellectually, and industrially, by directing its energies along one line? Verily, verily, I say unto you, unless the Negro is saved, not in part but wholly, he cannot see the kingdom of earth nor reign therein. The very best thing, as I see it, is for him to do as he has been doing for the past thirty years—take his chances and follow the other race in every avocation from the bootblack to the college chair, from the coal cart to congress halls.

It takes as much and as many kinds of education to solve the Negro problem as it took and is now taking to solve the white man's problem. It takes as much education to make the Negro a man as to make the white man a man. To say that it takes less would be to say that the Negro by creation is superior. A well educated Negro is worth as much to any community as a well educated white man, and wherever he has been given a chance to prove his worth, his loyalty, or his manhood at home or abroad, he has never been found wanting. If the Negro can be made a good citizen by having one kind of education, a white man can also, and this enormous expenditure of government funds and gifts of philanthropists for all branches of learning is useless. In the educational world as elsewhere the Negro asks no special favor nor any specific remedy to cure his malady. He asks that the same laws protect him, the same facilities be offered him, and the same chances be given him as other men, and he will move up to the flag, and will not ask that the flag be brought back to him.

If industrial education will save the ignorant Negro, the same gospel will save the ignorant white man, and you have only to look around to see that one is as bad off as the other, and it is the salvation of all its citizens at which this republic must aim.

General education is as necessary for the formation of character and correct notions of life as general exercise is essential to systematic physical growth. The reformation of any people is not abiding unless the mass of that people build upon the broad, general platform of individual preparation along general educational lines. Then, if there is in that mass those in whom the love of the classics extinguishes all other loves, they should have seats in the best colleges in the land, and to keep them from these colleges because the mass cannot go would be as criminal as to incase a prospective giant, and make a pygmy of him, or to dwarf one child because the other one cannot grow.

The Negro, as a mass, is neither fitted by creation nor can he be fitted by training to ply at one profession or trade. There are thousands of Negroes who would make first-class professional men who couldn't farm, shoe horses, or invent a device as an improvement to the haymower if the race problem is never solved. There are hundreds of Negro women who would make first-class clerks, stenographers, book-keepers, musicians, and teachers, who couldn't maintain themselves by cooking, washing, ironing, sewing and working on a farm if the race problem were never solved.

A large percent of any race comes under the laboring class. There need be no special legislation, discussion nor training to put them there. Circumstances over which they have no control put them there, and necessity which knows no law keeps them there. The Negro is not an exception to this rule.

The Negro must write some books for himself. They must not all be upon one subject. The Negro must make some music for himself, and all must not sing along the same line.

The Negro must do some high thinking for himself, but all must not think the same way.

Industrial education alone would never have produced our Banneker, our Douglass, our Bruce, our Langstone, our Blyden, our Scarborough, our Fortune, our Roscoe Conkling Bruce, nor our Booker T. Washington.[12] Had these bright lights, that have helped to illumine the hall of fame, marched by any other route than by the one they traveled, they would have perished in the middle-passage.

The progress of the Negro has been rapid and pleasing because all have not hoed corn and picked cotton. While some have been in the field, others have been at the desk. While some have been at the anvil, others have been in the college chair.

At what trade did Frederick Douglass work to become one of the greatest orators the world has ever heard? At what trade did Booker T. Washington work to build Tuskegee? What trade did Roscoe Conkling Bruce ply to march off with the honors of Harvard? At what trades have the thousands of teachers, preachers, doctors, and lawyers worked to open up the understandings, save the souls, and give ease to the enfeebled bodies of the thousands who have come unto them?

Have not these men and women, from Phillis Wheatley and Frederick Douglass to the last leader in any calling, been great factors in the solution of the race problem?

If the Negro had tried all other kinds of education and failed, I might say, try industrial education; but he has not been found wanting in any of the branches of knowledge nor incompetent in any calling, but to the admiration of his friends and to the humiliation and regret of his enemies, he started in the School of Adversity and never stopped until he stood as Valedictorian of Harvard, and has yet to be heard to say, "My cup runneth over."

If the object of the American people is to make the Negro a better man and thus a better citizen, he must be dealt with as a man, and given a man's chance to choose for himself such callings as appeal to him individually.

Why talk about a Negro problem when he has not propounded a single question to the American people as to his ability to do or to be. He has never asked whether he could learn reading, writing, spelling, arithmetic, geography, history, Latin, Greek, geometry, physics, music, painting, drawing, medicine, or law. He has never asked which would be the more conducive to his growth and happiness in this country, hoeing corn or studying a little science from a book. He has never asked if he may stay here or take ship for another clime. He has never asked whether he is a man or a missing link. He read in his Bible that "out of one blood God hath made all nations for to dwell upon the face of the earth," and he said, "that means me, too." It has never been a question, therefore, with him as to where he came from, where he belongs, or where he is going, for he believed this Bible assertion, and felt that since he came from where other races came, must dwell where other races dwell, that with like course of action, he would go where other races go.

"You may talk about the Negro,
You may make his faults infinite,
But you cannot turn a wheel,
That the Negro isn't in it."

∽

The Negro Home

From *Outlook,* September 15, 1926, 84–85.

The Negro home is suffering from the "outs." Too many Negro mothers "work out," and too many trifling Negroes "hang out." In a physical and moral sense it can be truthfully said of two-thirds of our places of abode that "there is nobody home."

For various reasons, and often without any good reason at all, Negro mothers are away from their children all day and a part of the night. As a result, the race is teeming with Topsies. To two-thirds of the race their homes are not homes; they are places in which to eat, sleep, and store furniture. Why are we out when we should be in?

First, because of economic circumstances. Colored men are given those occupations in which the pay is the lowest. Their income is not sufficient to support their families.

Second, we are a wasteful people, and we sacrifice essentials for frills. When our women learn to waste less and put essentials first, they will not have so many bills to help meet and can stay at home and rear their children properly.

The third reason is that the masses have sight without sense. They work around white people, see how they live and act, and they try to ape them without ever stopping to think. They do not realize that the white race laid its economic foundation securely before it began to joy ride or play golf, and that every door of opportunity is open to white people.

In the language of Booker T. Washington's old colored lady, "the white race has been whar it's gwine." We are just starting. The Negro sees the white man during his hours of relaxation and play. He likes the way he "carries on," and he decides to try the same stunts. He forgets that the majority of those whom he serves during their hours of relaxation have worked hard and long, and have established themselves and their homes, and can afford to forget their business for a few hours or a few months. The idle class of white people that give all of their time to pleasure are not worth aping.

The Negro does not stop to think. He has splendid sight, but not enough common sense.

The Negro home is being demoralized because we have staged a perpetual performance to practice and display what we pick up from the bad examples set by the most ordinary type of people for whom some of us work.

Our fourth observation is that the Negro does too much "hanging out" for the moral and physical good of his home. We have a National Association of Exterior Decorators—Negroes who hang out. They are our greatest liability. They grease up our fronts, wear out our grass, break down our fences, and run down our neighborhood; use their homes as broadcasting stations and their mouths as loud-speakers. They keep the ambitious ones of the race from getting where we are going.

Unfortunately, we cannot see through glass. We cannot see across the street unless we throw up the window and poke our heads out. Negro communities are infested with window watchmen. They are that class that throw up the windows and poke their heads out in order to see—nothing. Go to any thickly settled community if you want to "see the headline." Have you seen it in Harlem and other centers? Look up at the windows; it's there.

We are fighting segregation, but we cannot make very much progress until we put our Exterior Decorators to work hanging up instead of hanging out; cleaning up instead of greasing up; building up instead of breaking down. Some of the time that we spend in abusing white people for not allowing us to live in first-class neighborhoods should be devoted to the very practical duty of teaching interior decoration to our Exterior Decorators. They do more to keep us out of desirable neighborhoods than anybody else.

Fifth, our homes are suffering because we want to "keep up with the Joneses" in our own race. We spend entirely too much money to get things because other people have them, instead of spending the time developing ideals and standards because we need them. Then too many women do not want the responsibility of housekeeping and caring for their children. This burning desire to "work out" is their alibi for not making homes for their families.

The sixth cause of the deterioration of the Negro home is ignorance. The Negro is not getting enough intensive teaching of the fundamental things of life.

Every Negro girl should be given a thorough course in the fine art of house-keeping and home-making. We should learn and apply the ideals and standards essential to the making of clean, orderly homes.

Seventh, the majority of us are just too plain lazy to keep our homes properly. We do too much sitting down after we get up. We do too much talking "about" and walking "out" when we should be setting our houses in order.

We have not learned that high ideals and industry are essential to the making of homes. There is no substitute for them.

With All Thy Getting

From *Southern Workman* 56, no. 7 (July 1927): 299–301.

"The Negro race is a child race." This fact was often repeated by the late Booker T. Washington. A child race ought to be taught to put first things first. The cultivation of divine gifts—things of the spirit—is first in the building of individuals and races.

The Negro is highly endowed with things of the spirit—love, forbearance, gentleness, meekness, forgiveness, hope, song, faith—but he is not cultivating them. Gifts of the spirit are made to races for three fundamental purposes: to enable them to lift themselves, by their own boot straps as it were; to lay secure foundations on which to build materially; and to make valuable contributions to world progress, independent of, but conjointly with, other races.

The first thing for a race to learn is the value of gifts of the spirit and how to use them. These gifts develop moral stamina, self-respect, independence, and courage within, and secure respect from without. Thus panoplied, races face great tasks and march to battle unafraid.

The Negro has undermined his spiritual and moral vitality, by cultivating an insatiable love for the material at the expense of higher virtues. As a result, he sits apathetic and paralytic before his great moral tasks. The fact is, the Negro and his credulous friends have done too much bragging about his material progress. He brags about what he owns, but he goes to others for what he needs. The time spent in bragging should have been given to the development of qualities of soul. Despite his bragging "something" inside of the Negro tells him that he is not putting on the right armor. Despite his superficial display of things material, he heads the receiving line before philanthropists for gifts for his uplift.

Complete absorption of thought, time, and strength to the acquisition of material things spells moral death and spiritual death to any race. The Negro in his puerile state of mind is conjured into believing that things—houses, land, bank accounts, second-hand knowledge, and rights—will get him a place of power in this material civilization. *They will not*. He cannot catch up with the Anglo-Saxon materially, but he can catch up with him spiritually and morally.

If progress is to be measured in physical materials and dollars and brains, in themselves, the Negro will be—by comparison, for centuries—contemptibly poor. Why, there is an automobile manufacturer in Detroit and a mail-order house magnet in Chicago who could buy everything which the race owns and then have enough money left to keep on producing cars and mailing clothes. One rubber-tire manufacturer in Ohio has done more by the use of his brains to keep the Negro moving physically, than the Negro has done for himself in that particular. But where is the Negro going and what is he going to do when he gets there? That's the question.

Despite the fact that the race is travelling at high speed materially, it cannot get within hailing distance of the race that has a thousand years lead of him in material things. The Anglo-Saxon, on his own nerve, initiative, and inventions has stopped riding and gone to flying. The Negro has no plane, but he can soar in spirit. That is what the Anglo-Saxon did first. That is how he got the plane. The Negro must use his brains to supply some vital needs. This civilization is in great need of gifts of the spirit, but has no material want which it cannot satisfy. In fact, America will destroy herself and revert to barbarism if she continues to cultivate the things of the flesh and neglects the higher virtues. The Negro must not, therefore, contribute to her doom, but must ransom her.

Furthermore, it will profit the Negro nothing to enter into ungodly competition for material possessions when he has gifts of greater value. The most valuable contribution which he can make to American civilization must be made out of his spiritual endowment. He must do it in self-defense, and in defense of America. She needs it. Without it she will never dispense justice, and will be consumed by her own folly and wrath. The Negro has helped save America physically several times. He must make a larger contribution to her spiritual salvation. Who knows but that the divine purpose for bringing him into this country was that, in due time, he might make just such a contribution.

The tragedy in this problem-solving enterprise is that the Negro is not being taught the tremendous achieving power of his virtues. He is not being taught to glorify what he is. When he learns that he has the leaven that is needed in this American lump, he will put it in. In other words, he will proceed to use his spiritual powers and give new meaning and proper evaluation to the Beatitudes, and at the same time, give new impetus to the development of a real Christian civilization.

When the Negro learns what manner of man he is spiritually, he will wake up all over. He will stop playing white, even on the stage. He will rise in the majesty of his own soul. He will glorify the beauty of his own brown skin. He will stop thinking white and go to thinking straight and living right. He will realize that wrong reaching, wrong bleaching, and wrong mixing have "most nigh ruin't him" and he will redeem his body and rescue his soul from the bondage of that death.

The final values of races are computed almost entirely in terms of high ideals and noble purposes lived up to. Jesus told his ambitious, materialistic disciples that the kingdom—the glory which they craved—is not here and it is not there—it is within you. In other words, it is not what you have but what you are inside of yourself, that counts.

I believe it is the Negro's sacred duty to spiritualize American life and popularize his own color instead of worshiping the color (or lack of color) of another race. It can be done in Negro life, in pictures, in plays, in books, in spirit, if the Negro would spend as much time glorifying his own character as he now spends imitating the color and foibles of the white race. The Negro can become the most beloved and the most lovely race in the world. His happy spirit and varied hue make him the very spice of life among other races. No race is richer in soul quality and color than the Negro. Some day he will realize it and glorify them. He will popularize black.

The Negro can actually use the bathtub, the Bible, and the broom—weapons and emblems of health, righteousness, and industry, and make of himself and his environment things of loveliness and beauty. It is within him—within his grasp—within his power—within his group. If he uses them religiously, the race will "rise and shine."

God wants to help the Negro work out his own salvation. The Negro need not be skeptical as to the outcome, because the Almighty is at His best when He is working with an individual or race to prove that the weapons of His warfare are not carnal, but spiritual. If I were a Negro preacher, looking for a text for a timely sermon to preach to the entire race, I would paraphrase and analyze Solomon's wisdom-getting advice and make it read:

> "Get education—but with all your getting—get common sense.
> Get clothes—but with all your getting—get clean.
> Get houses—but with all your getting—get homes.
> Get stores—but with all your getting—get standards.
> Get your rights—but with all your getting—get right."

Preachers, teachers, leaders, welfare workers ought to address themselves to the supreme task of teaching the entire race to glorify what it has—its face (its color); its place (its homes and communities); its grace (its spiritual endowment). If the Negro does it, there is no earthly force that can stay him.

From a Woman's Point of View

From *Pittsburgh Courier*, September 27, 1930, 6.

Eleanor R. Wembridge,[13] referee of the Juvenile Court of Cuyahoga county, Ohio, contributed a real human interest article on "Negroes in Custody" to the "American Mercury" of September. Miss Wembridge discusses the behavior of Negroes in court and the spirit of the Negroes in rage.

She does not understand how the Negro can take his medicine—court medicine—with a smile, get over what hurts him, like a child, and wear rags that make him look like odds and ends left over from a rummage sale, and withal hold his head high, look you in the face and "strut." Miss Wembridge cannot understand how people can be in trouble in rags, and happy. Of course, she cannot understand. Negroes are wonders in spite of their million shortcomings. Only God and Negroes can understand Negro philosophy. We forget and forgive; we wear the world as a loose garment; we smile and grin; giggle and laugh and sing amid our greatest tragedies. Negroes have a marvelous capacity for misery and for happiness.

It is all due to the fact that for 250 years we were the leading actors in America's greatest social tragedy—slavery. We made the best of what we had, where we were and sang "There's a Better Day A-Coming." We smiled and sang and called our oppressors "honey" when our backs were aching and our hearts were bleeding. We had to play the part. In other words, we had to make a noise like we were happy—"make 'tend." You know acting became very real to us and it will take 250 years for the Negro to get through "making 'tend like." That is why Negroes will become America's greatest actors. Negroes do not know any better, yet. The fact of the matter is that Negroes are superior Americans because they really major in the pursuit of happiness. That is the Negro's valuable contribution to American life and America needs that contribution.

Miss Wembridge wonders why Negroes in rags—in odds and ends—and in custody do not behave like white people. Well, there are two reasons:

First of all, white people thus panoplied are a sorry, woe-begone pitiful looking lot. They look too banged up for Negroes to even want to look at them and they certainly do not want to look like poor whites. Negroes, even in slavery, had an aversion to being bossed by poor whites.

Secondly, Negroes lived in rags and in custody for 250 years and they took their medicine hopefully. They wore their jeans gratefully.

My grandmother was what she proudly called an "F.F.V. Slave." They tell me that she was a most remarkable woman. She was a seamstress and a philosopher. They tell this interesting story of her attitude towards slavery. She would say: "Yes, honey, I was in slavery, but I wasn't no slave. I was just in it, that's all. They never made me hold my head down and there was a whole pa'cel of Negroes just like me; we just couldn't be broke. We obeyed our masters and mistresses and did our work, but we kept on saying 'deliverance will come.' We ain't no hung-down-head race; we are poor, but proud." That proud Virginian would say "hold your spirit up inside, chile, hold your spirit up and that helps you to hold your head up. Don't let your spirit down." She said, "I used to hold my head up so high that sometimes they would say, 'Maria why don't you look down at the ground?' I would say, 'Look down at the ground? I aint no groundhog, I am looking up at God because that's what He made me for.' Honey, they slaved my body, but they didn't slave my mind. I was thinking high, myself, and some day we colored folks is goin' to live high. Walk together, children, don't get weary; there's a better day a-coming in [t]his here land."

The framers of the Constitution could not have had a clearer vision of the future of America. "There's a great day a-coming in dis here land." That's why Negroes can hold up their heads and "strut" in rags, that's why their songs begin in trouble and end in hallelujahs. The Negro has a future in America. He feels it in his bones.

Slavery developed in us an optimism that is mysterious and magnetic. That optimism is our most valuable inheritance. Negro slaves sang, laughed, "strutted"; they worked and waited on their masters and on the Lord. Deliverance came and they just can't keep from being happy because "there is a better day a-coming" when we get right down to work for it as did our fathers. Let us not lose their spirit, even if we are in rags and in the custody of the court and of American prejudice. Laugh and sing and work. Deliverance will come and other Americans like Eleanor Wembridge will "stand second to none" in their admiration for the magnificence of Negro art—the art of living without looking like you have been beaten in the game of life and are mad at the whole world.

Manhood, Patriotism, Religion, Going Out of Style among Negroes

From *Pittsburgh Courier*, March 12, 1932, feature.

Races are built on intelligence, industry, courage, chivalry, patriotism and reverence and any individual life that is worth living is also built out of the same fundamentals. In spite of this fact, the majority of Negroes are teaching their children not [to] have any manners (chivalry), any patriotism nor any religion.

Those who are not actually teaching their children to eschew these essentials are not stressing the fundamental value of them. Some children are incidentally exposed to some of them, but these virtues are not contagious. One must be inoculated with them and they must be propagated. Unless these six factors actually function—hit on all six—

the life of the individual becomes six cogs in the social wheel. It becomes a limp, a lag, and a lean, a leaf, a lie, a lose—six cogs.

All individuals and races that get anywhere exercise, magnify, exalt and glorify intelligence, industry, courage, chivalry, patriotism, and reverence. The Negro is getting some kind of education, but intelligence alone is worthless. Intelligence must be driven by five horsepower.

The individual or race that excels in all six of the fundamentals listed is a superior individual or race. Did you note the word all? Jesus Christ, the greatest of teachers, said: "Teach them to observe all things."

Negroes are trying to get somewhere with a little second hand knowledge and without the other essentials. It cannot be done. Intelligence has to be pushed by industry and pulled by courage, stimulated by patriotism, ornamented by chivalry and sustained by reverence. Our race has actually come to the place where we are not teaching young Negroes to observe anything. They are licensed to do as they please just so they do not please to be well mannered, chivalrous, industrious or religious. They are encouraged to eat, drink, and be merry.

"You are in the world on a picnic, have a good time—start anything and don't stop until you get ready."

That gospel is a long way from "teaching them to observe all things." You say chivalry has gone out of style—that this is the age of sex freedom—grant it. But a race that has not passed through the period of training in fundamentals cannot jump over those fundamentals. The six essentials here listed must course through the blood of the race. If we haven't them, we must get them because we cannot long abide in any civilization, nor can we make an enduring contribution to that civilization without them. Without them we are headed toward self destruction. Our Niagara Falls are just ahead.

Teach manners—no, never. Manners have gone out of style. Chivalry? What is that? Negro boys have been so neglected in the matter of teaching manliness that nine-tenths of them are actually too lazy to tip their hats. The majority of them drag their hand up to their eyebrow and salute ladies with one finger because they are too lazy to do doff their hats. We have an army of drag. If they decide to condescend to get up and give ladies seats they do it so ponderously that one thinks they have lodestones tied to them. They seem to be ashamed to be polite, to be on their feet in a minute. They sit in automobiles lazily and let women pull in and out instead of doing the Chesterfieldian act. There are men far past middle age who are like knights. They put these dullards to shame—if this new brand has sense enough to be ashamed.

This new brand does not stand up like men. They lean and slouch. They shamble and swagger instead of walking cleanly. They are very smart, you know.

Negro men are entirely too idle and they are entirely too satisfied at being idle. They are doing too much sitting down, hanging out and hanging around. Men cannot be made under those conditions, they are unmade.

The manhood of the race is going to weeds—going to waste. Go up and down the street to Negro ghettoes and see for yourself. Social deterioration has set in. Mothers and fathers are responsible for much of the laziness and lack of manliness. They have not taught their sons to be industrious and chivalrous.

Then too, young and old women ruin men. They ruin good men and make bad men worse. They run after them, support them and let them sling them around as if they were rags. Men have no incentive to be gentlemen when ladies are so scarce and women are so common.

Chivalry is developed by the social chase but it cannot be developed when men are chased. Every year is leap year now.

There are women who can do a great deal to turn the race around and help it to face in the right direction. Have they heart interest enough to do it? The work will engage them the rest of their days. Our social problems are staggering, but it is up to us to solve them.

But what about patriotism? What is it good for anyhow? It is good to make men. It is like music. A man that hath not patriotism "in his soul is fit for treason, strategy and spoils. Let no such man be trusted." Negroes are teaching their children to be indifferent towards their country. The flag means nothing to them. Some Negroes do not sing America. They justify their attitude on the ground that their constitutional rights are abridged and denied, that they are disfranchised, lynched and segregated; that this is not a government of the people, by the people and for the people, that it is a government of some of the people. All of these charges are true, but don't forget this is the land where our fathers died as well as the land of the pilgrims' pride. The fact that no President or Congress of the U.S. has ever attempted to live up to their oath of office in enforcing the Constitution is a travesty on the white man's sense of honor and integrity and not a justification for the Negroes to lose their love of liberty. That gross violation of oath is a greater reason why Negroes should keep the ideal of liberty and equality before their children. Men never win liberty by giving up and going into their tents and sulking—they win by keeping up the fight. No man is a real man who is not a patriot of the first water. Patriotism puts iron in the blood, fire in the soul, nerve in the arm, strength in the ankle bones, and stamina in the backbone. It makes a man "a man for a' that and a' that."

Millions of people are glad to see us sulking in our tents instead of taking a broomstick if we haven't a flag, as did the heroic woman, and march up and down the streets that are just as much ours as they are any white American's who fell on Bunker Hill or stood in Flanders Field.

If the young Negro becomes a rebel, America will lose much, but his race will lose much more. The young Negro should take the position that he is not going to give up America, he is not going to give up the flag and he is not going to give up any of the ideals for which the flag stands. His fathers toiled and fought to get freedom and the price which they paid is too dear to sacrifice to prejudice and injustice. When the Negro puts up a real fight—business [w]ill pick up.

Give up and sulk or become indifferent? Never! It gives too much comfort to the enemy. In any conflict always find out what your enemies want you to do and don't do it. Yes, boost George Washington. We fought with him. Why not tell the world? Don't let any man take your crown or get your goat.

> "Your flag and my flag
> Will be our flag some day."
>   until the hills answer."

Make it come true or report [to] God the reason why. This is the year to talk patriotism. This is the year of jubilee. Talk American ideals. That's what they are for. When they become real you stop talking about them and enjoy them and find some other ideals about which to talk.

Brag about the father of our country. We have some mighty bad ones, but it is our duty to honor them.

There are somethings that are sacred. Reverence them, cultivate your spiritual life. Get religion. You need it. Whatever it is, get it. Take it from me, it is a grand and glorious inside feeling, a longing for happiness and peace. It is something that the world cannot take away from you. It is the food on which Faith and Hope are fed. It is the unshaken belief that you are the master of your fate, and Christ is the captain of your soul.

When you feel that way you are a match—eventually—for whatever comes.

Now, what have I said? It is this—cultivate chivalry, patriotism, reverence, industry, courage, and intelligence. Engage in the profitable business of making men to match our mountains. Hit on all six. Don't miss.

∞

Bathing Is a Personal Right; Smelling Is a Public Offense

From Nannie Helen Burroughs, *What Do You Think?* (Washington, DC: n.p., 1950), 138–41.

"Every dog has his day; every season its fad and every cause its week." The days or weeks are sponsored by certain groups, organizations, trades or professions.

The purpose of these special days or weeks is to disseminate information, popularize and promote fundamental ideals and principles in the interest of certain causes.

For the moment we shall pass over the fact that our Churches are over doing the Woman's Day racket. Woman's Day can and ought to be made a day of great significance, enlightenment and challenge, but it has degenerated into vulgar rivalry, in money raising and cheap bally-hoo speech-making. Somebody will have to take it upon themselves to redeem that day. It can be done.

If Solomon were with us, he would declare that of the naming of days and weeks there is no end—just as he said about "the making of books."

But let us talk about a week instead of a day. Let us talk about the one week we have set apart and designated as "Health Week." The purpose of Health Week is to emphasize the physical, economic and social value of cleanliness and all of the instrumentalities for adding to man's length of years and cultural development. Of course, bearing down on principles and ideals for one week or one month in a year is better than not bearing down at all; but the "masses" (and even some of the "classes") will not begin to take these values seriously until these ideals are made a definite part of a progressive and continuous program of education.

Proper care of the body, from head to foot, is a daily duty. This fact has to be taught, and the majority of our children, and grown-ups too for that matter, do not know the value of body cleanliness. Many people who are face, hands and nails conscious have body odors that bear unmistakable evidence of carelessness.

They lose friends and jobs, because they are physically offensive. Nobody should go around smelling. Of course, bathing is a PERSONAL RIGHT, but body odor is a PUBLIC OFFENSE.

Our public schools should employ Health teachers. Teaching health is just as important as teaching reading, writing and arithmetic.

You say the home should teach children how to care for their bodies. True, but our homes have fallen down on so many of their everyday jobs that the schools will have to assume more responsibility for teaching the fine art of caring for the body, or the masses will simply go on smelling and adding to the bad health record of the race. If children were properly instructed, we would soon see great improvement in the health record of the race.

But back to the adults. We're a laboring class of people. Our work requires daily contact with dirt, grime and heat. Our bodies are exercised by lifting, pulling, hauling, digging, plowing, slinging and "busting." We're cooks, maids, laundresses, ditch diggers, track hands, street sweepers, field hands, cart drivers, etc. . . . Even the white-collar workers are compelled to take their daily dip in order to keep fit.

In plain, United States English, every man, woman and child should have a definite understanding with a bath-tub once a day. It's a sin against common decency not to have an all-over, at least every other day. Installment bathing is alright as a morning and evening supplement to the all-over, but it is not a substitute for it. Plain talk? Yes, but when people are ignorant or when they become careless, willful or indifferent about a thing that is as far-reaching as health, it is time to speak plainly.

Too many of our everyday laborers not only neglect their bodies but they go to work entirely too dirty and ragged. Too many of them buy new over-alls and wear them out without ever washing them. Too many of them get out of the ditch, and get on the street-car, and plank themselves down by the side of daintily dressed women, and become offended if the woman seems to want to protect her dainty dress.

It is bad enough to be physically offensive, but it is worse to have the audacity to add to that offensive language and conduct.

Our churches can do a great deal to improve the health and manners of the masses. Yes, we understand that too many people do not have bath-tubs, that too many of our homes are not comfortably heated. These are terrible handicaps, but wash basins and the washtubs are available in the poorest homes, and we can learn how to use them just as effectively for the cleansing of our bodies as we do for our clothes. Bath-tubs are among our recent inventions and improvements.

There are people who will say, "We have made marvelous improvement." Yes, we have, but we have facilities for speeding up our health and cultural program, and we should do it and stop being satisfied and stop making excuses as long as we are behind in our ideals.

Civilization is a matter of standards and the people who excel in the use of the bath-tub are the most highly civilized. Let's take it on at any cost—even if we have to use a basin and bathe on the installment plan.

How Does It Feel to Be a Negro?

From Nannie Helen Burroughs, *What Do You Think?* (Washington, DC: n.p., 1950), 81–84.

Well, that depends entirely upon what kind of a Negro you are from the neck up and from the heart out.

There are only five kinds of human beings and a Negro—like any other kind of human—falls into one of the five classifications.

The Satisfied—The class in any race that is satisfied with things as they are, "good enough" and are too indifferent to make any improvement in spite of the fact that they see people all around them improving and getting ahead.

The Callous—The class that has become hardened by neglect, association, environment or habit.

The Impossible—The class that knows but does not care and will not do—"joined to their idols." They are the "immovables" in the social order.

The Unenlightened—The class that simply does not know but will respond to teaching.

The Sensitized—The class that has a quality of mind that makes them susceptible to, capable of and responsive to improvement, development, mental, moral and spiritual growth.

But, first of all, why should a Negro feel any different from any other human being since all men are biologically, physiologically and sociologically the same? His needs, desires, appetites, impulses, longings and weaknesses are the same as all other human beings. In some Negroes, those basic, inalienable, inner qualities lie dormant, suppressed, or inactive but they have them in the same native proportion as other men.

But what has happened is this. For centuries pseudo-scientists, writers, teachers of youth, molders of public sentiment, newspapers, magazines, and the stage have used every means at their command in an effort to prove that the Negro is innately and inherently different—that he is mentally inferior, morally depraved, physically offensive, socially corrupt and industrially incompetent and lazy.

For centuries he has been the object of persecution, exploitation, misrepresentation, discrimination, defamations, humiliation, segregation, malignment, and the victim of studied and organized injustices of every conceivable and ungodly kind.

He is used, betrayed and abused. He is the victim of relentless race prejudice. He is held up before the world as a brute and rapist. He is killed without trial; beaten without reason; shut out in spite of law; robbed of education, in spite of the Constitutional pledges of equality in a democracy. He is denied work because of his color; made the buffoon and butt of vicious jokes because of his race and color. He is ridiculed and burlesqued for commercial purposes. He is portrayed as a confirmed pilferer, petty thief and loafer. He is shut out, shunned, tolerated or despised.

I shall try to define the feelings and reactions of the Sensitized Negro. The other four classes are either objects of contempt, ridicule, exploitation, charity, pity, or education.

There are degrees of sensitization. How deeply one feels depends upon how delicate, responsive or how highly developed are his inherent, moral and spiritual qualities. A Moral Negro's natural appetite, impulses, emotions, desires, longings and weaknesses are the same as are other normal human beings because he is biologically and sociologically the same as any other man in any other race. Therefore, the feelings of a normal, decent aspiring Negro run the gamut of basic human emotions. We are constantly forced into unnatural and therefore uncomfortable situations. How do we react?

At times we feel wounded, hurt, disappointed, disgusted, resentful, sick of it all. At other times we feel skeptical, outraged, robbed, beaten. We chafe, hate, overlook. Then again we feel like ignoring, defying and fighting for every right that belongs to us as human beings.

The flame of our burning soul leaps higher. We feel like praying, forgiving, working, but never taking less than what is due us. When we read and understand the plan, purpose and promises of God for the human race, we feel that God is on trial and not the Negro. We feel that if we do not let any ungodly attitude or treatment break our spirit that God will work out through us some of the rich promises which He has made to those who do their full duty, put their trust in Him and walk uprightly.

We look down at our lashed body, bleeding feet and ravished souls.

"Stony the road we trod,
Bitter the chastening rod."

We move staggeringly slow through relentless race prejudice, age old, and as "black as a pit from pole to pole." We look with eyes of faith beyond our human tragedy and see God, who "is no respecter of persons" sitting high and exalted and we hear His voice saying "Lo I am with you." We try again. The voice of God sets our unconquerable soul on fire. We sing, "I feel like going on," and we go.

Every noble impulse within us is awakened, charged and supercharged with divine fire. We feel like a man among men. We do not care what men think, do or say—with God on our side we feel that we are their match. We know that in the last round, character and not color—right and not race triumphs.

We stand up and put our faith in the ultimate triumph of justice over the world, the flesh and the devil. We feel like living and working in a way that will discredit every lie that has ever been written, told or implied about the innate inferiority of the Negro.

We feel superior to those who devise ways and means of wronging and outraging us. We feel that our divine mission in the world is to join other noble souls who are working to build a Christian social order in which respect for human personality will be the dominating virtue. We feel eminently superior to those who waste their lives trying to "keep the Negro in his place," or trying to break his spirit or penalize him because God saw fit to make him black.

Wrong attitudes grow out of ignorance. Being a normal, decent aspiring Negro makes you feel that it is your duty to help educate the ignorant in both races, by right living, and helping to teach the truth about races.

"Must Uplift the Masses"

From Nannie Helen Burroughs, *What Do You Think?* (Washington, DC: n.p., 1950), 92–95.

The vital problems and basic needs of the Negro masses are— Improvement and transformation of character and conduct. Proper training for and right attitude towards work. Improvement in home and community life.

To these three basic needs all preachers, missionaries, teachers, professional men and women and welfare workers should unite, plan and work intensively and continuously until the masses feel and are affected and influenced to move upward and forward on the highway of life.

Only by the sincere interest and united and definite action, on the part of all who preach, teach, guide or advise the masses, is it possible to save the people from further demoralization and self-destruction. Anybody with eyes can see the undone state of the masses. They have broken down INSIDE.

Their neglected minds must be touched by real teachers with the live coal of faith in themselves; their callous hearts must be softened by the devoted spirit of leaders who know how to stimulate their pride. They need leaders who are past masters in the fine art of making people SEE WHAT THEY ARE and believe in what they may BECOME.

The people's imagination must be fired with a desire for the better way of life. The Negro problem has become too acute, far-reaching and involved for weak, selfish leaders to make any progress towards its solution. It is going to require strong men and women of great faith, real love, and charity that vaunteth not itself, to deliver the masses from the body of their death.

Right now, the character, conduct and environment of the masses are enough to stagger the faith of the strongest, as to the possibility of satisfactory improvement in this generation. Only God and everybody who loves Him enough to help Him save souls can do anything worthwhile with this problem in this century. Base American race prejudice on the one hand, and blind race leaders on the other, have produced nearly nine million men and women, right here in a so-called Christian nation, who are much worse off mentally, physically, morally and socially, than the so-called uncivilized in Africa or pagans in China or India.

This job of uncivilizing Negro masses is being done by civilized people right here in a civilized land. It is useless to waste time calling names and fixing blame. The situation is tragic. Negro preachers, teachers, and professional people must unite and work together. NOW IS THE TIME.

There is no reason for waiting. The blue print for transformation can and should be made while the world is getting ready to live as becometh men. No other time will ever be as propitious as now.

There are some white friends and agencies that will help mightily, but it is the specific duty of Negro leaders to unite and go ahead, regardless of who helps or who doesn't. If the leaders in the field of religion, education and health do not tackle the task—who can or should?

We took the caption for this editorial from the well-known columnist, Joseph D. Bibbs, and now we shall quote from his column in the "Pittsburgh Courier."

Mr. Bibb said, "Professional groups and enlightened members of the colored race should fully realize that a profound duty is imposed on them in facing changing conditions.

Colored Americans now need the inspiration and guiding influence of the members of their race, who are highly and especially trained, almost as much as they were needed amid the terrible times of the Reconstruction. Physicians, dentists, lawyers, ministers and enlightened colored people, who are now waxing fat from services sold to the less informed members of their race, owe a positive and affirmative duty to these people. That duty exceeds the rendering of expert; professional service. The teeming thousands of colored people, who are beset by the multiplied problems of living decently, should be ministered to by those who are receiving their unstinted patronage. Every colored professional should be public spirited. Under the American system, the classes are judged by the masses. The masses of colored Americans must be uplifted."

It sometimes seems that the big men of our race have lost sight of the potency and effectiveness of the "gospel of little things." Everyone knows that the colored Americans' public conduct is sub-standard. Everyone knows that he talks too loud, dresses too flashily and gaudily, and that he is unmindful of the little niceties of life. Everyone knows that the colored American is sadly in need of knowledge of correct social amenities. Here is a job that the colored professional can and should address himself to—the improvement of the conduct and decorum of his people. He owes them that duty.

Instead of entering into constant and continual harangues and dissertations about the injustices of the white man, it would be of far more value for the "cream, culture and wealth" of the race to set about to improve the less fortunate.

Every decent Negro in America should be "all out" for a simple, practical program that will engage all who highly resolve to help the masses lift themselves from the filth that has bogged them down.

The world that has been told that the Negro is impossible is making a beaten path to the door of America. What will life in America or the new world social order be, if our leaders fail the masses in this hour of destiny? Preachers, teachers and professionals—NOW IS THE TIME—for you to tackle this stupendous task. Tomorrow will be too late.

∞

The Only Way to Victory

From Nannie Helen Burroughs, *What Do You Think?* (Washington, DC: n.p., 1950), 88–89.

Today, the American Negro must think about his future more seriously than ever before. He must prepare to take his place in the industrial scheme of things. He must contend for his rightful opportunity to do his full duty as an American citizen. He must insist on assignment or appointment to places or positions in the Federal Service on the basis of ability. He must take pride in doing his work superbly well. He must keep his mind and his eye on the future, and he must prepare now to enter the new day that will come in America and in all the world when this cold war is over.

The leaders in every home, every school, and every church should become voices in the wilderness, urging Negroes—young and old—to "awake, shake thyself from the dust; make your paths straight; put on thy strength; prepare for the day after the war." Preparation for that day must not be superficial. It must not be put off. The next period in American life will be directed and dominated by men and women of initiative, ingenuity and skill. It will be a period in which

"New arts shall bloom of loftier mould
And mightier music fill the skies."[14]

Unless the Negro is prepared, he will be easily dislodged by foreigners. By skill and skill alone can he press his claim to economic justice.

The Negro is in eminent danger of being displaced by aliens from battle scarred, war ravaged Europe. Now is the time for every Negro to make an opportunity to learn a useful trade. He should prepare to meet competition by building stronger bodies; cleaner lives; higher ideals;

straight thinking; more dexterous hands and high and more resolute purposes.

From now on, White Americans are going to take their obligation or opportunity to aid aliens very emotionally. They are going to take aliens into their homes, churches, communities, labor organizations, shops, factories and employments of all kind. They are going to lavish every consideration upon their newly found love and forget all about the Negro's proved loyalty to this nation.

The fact is that even now, many Americans would rather employ known white Communists than to give Negroes equal opportunities for work in all fields.

America would rather trust her known white enemies than to trust her tried and true Negro citizens. When men passionately desire to build a nation, *they put first things first*. They give up prejudice and superficial differences of all kinds. At the crisis of the Civil War, when victory depended on national unity, Abraham Lincoln towered to unexcelled greatness when he said, "I would hold McClellan's horse if it would bring victory to the Union."

The only way that democracy can survive on this planet is for Britain and America to stop their undemocratic practices—NOW AND FOREVER. They must "lay aside every weight." Race prejudice is a millstone about the neck of this nation. May "God give us a nation that is strong enough to build an International Order of Brotherhood."

∽

Up from the Depths

From *Rhetoric of Racial Hope*, ed. Roy L. Hill (Buffalo: University Press, State University of New York, 1976), 49–52. Speech written January 25, 1954.

Having been introduced by Rev. T. O. Fuller, then President of Howe Institute, Bron Bones said, "like a black goddess of liberty who had come to bring messages of peace and love to her oppressed people, Miss Burroughs arose amid loud and continuous applause, standing like a statue . . . she was a picture to behold." When quiet had been restored, Miss Burroughs spoke as follows:[15]

It would be the greatest pleasure of my life if Wendell Phillips, William Lloyd Garrison, Frederick Douglass, Charles Sumner, Harriet Beecher Stowe and Henry Ward Beecher[16] were here tonight witnessing this magnificent scene of black professors, teachers and pupils in one of the grandest institutions of learning in the South.

The man who wrote this piece of poetry seems to have written it for me and for this occasion. The poet expressed the deepest craving of my heart when he wrote, "Lord, plant my feet on higher ground." This should be the sentiment of every teacher, student and leader of the race with which we are identified. Look upon this great audience tonight and be not discouraged. Two thousand years ago our Anglo-Saxon friends were eating from the skulls of their ancestors in the hills of Europe, notwithstanding which fact today they are the most powerful people in the world. The same thing that made the white race great will make the black race great.

We must realize that we have to begin at the bottom; that if we would develop a full grown race we would begin low. Take the character of Jesus Christ: note the humble position which he occupied. At no time was he weighed in the balance and found wanting. God took David from the low position of a shepherd boy and made him King. Paul, one of the greatest and most intelligent characters in the Bible, on his way to Damascus, got so high that the Lord had to knock him down.

Did you ever plant flowers and corn and return and find the roots growing upward? No, for they grow downward. Did you ever know a man to invest his money in mountains unless for gold, silver and coal? These grow in the earth and they must be digged from it. Did you ever hear of a man who went to gather pearls, looking for them on the top of the water?

You ask me what made the white race great and I will tell you that the great secret was love, the blessed gospel and the art of commencing low. The Bible is the stepping stone to greatness. For, in as much as the Bible has been a great help in elevating the Anglo-Saxon race, it will aid in elevating this race of ours. The black race is God's race and I believe whatever we ask He will give to us. No one can go to the top alone; the man who attempts to climb to the top alone will certainly fall. Some of our enemies say we are kin to monkeys and therefore will never reach the highest heights of civilization. If we can produce from monkeys a Frederick Douglass, a Bruce, a Langston and hundreds of others I might mention, we should be encouraged to continue the well begun work of preparing ourselves for every duty performed by other citizens of our country, regardless of what our enemies say.

I was in the city of Philadelphia some time ago in the white women's convention and was invited to answer in a lecture this question, "What does the black race of America want?" The conclusion of my address was as follows: "We don't want your teachers, we have our teachers; we don't want your furniture, nor your clothes, we have plenty of clothes; we don't want your doctors nor your preachers; we have our doctors and our preachers; we don't want what you have earned; all we ask of you is a man's chance. What we ask is fair play and to be let alone."

Talk about dividing the fund for education: that white men are paying for our education. Our education was paid for in advance by our mothers and fathers, our great-grandmothers and our great-grandfathers.

There is a great noise about the race problem—there is no race problem—it is simply a problem of justice and injustice. The Governor of Mississippi says the Negro is immoral, that education is not the thing for the Negro; that it is a curse and unfits him for farm work. If it is a curse, it is a blessing.

No, they don't want you to love education, but they do want you to love the jail, the workhouses and the penitentiary. The Negro can go into any jail in the United States and there is no color line. He can go into any penitentiary and on any farm and there will be no color line, but he cannot go into any place of amusement or any schoolhouse. It has been said that the Negro has begun to want and demand typewriters and stenographers. The Negro is not beginning to want, but he had been wanting and now he has them.

In Georgia there was a white man from the North visiting a school and when he was about to leave he asked the children what did they want him to tell the people when he returned home. One little boy said, "Tell them that we are risin'."[17] Another little boy raised his hand and said, "Mister, don't tell them people that we are coming, tell them that we have already come."

The Negro is making wonderful progress and that is why you hear so much about the race problem. They know that we are getting near them. They realize more than we that we are coming. Beneath the black skin of the Negro there is as much intelligence and morality as there is beneath the white skin of the blue-eyed and flaxen headed Anglo-Saxon. There is no field of labor, science or literature in which the Negro has not held his own.

While we are enumerating our wonderful progress we must not forget some of the stumbling blocks that impede our onward march. The Negro race often reminds me of popcorn. You know when you pop corn in a skillet, when it beings to pop, if you do not put a lid on it, it will all pop out. I guess the American prejudice is the lid to keep us in the skillet.

We have several ways of getting away from the race; some are bleaching out and others are straightening out. When we have almost bleached out, we straighten out the rest. I am sorry we are colored as we are. I am sorry all of us are not black.

When we would get out, prejudice tells us to get out and pop with the rest.

The white man and the Negro are like the fable. Once a white man had a house which was said to be haunted, so he said to a Negro, "John, there are spooks in that house and if you can stay there you may have it." John said, "Yes sir, boss." We all like to have houses of our own. When John quit work he was very tired and he took a few quilts and spread them on the floor and fell upon them and there he went to sleep. About twelve o'clock he heard a great noise. He uncovered his head and began to look around and there was a great deathlike figure standing over him with his finger pointing down on him. He covered up again and decided to keep one eye out the next time. So he did, and there stood that same deathlike figure with that same finger pointing down on him. He began to think of the convenience that the carpenter had made whereby he might make his escape. He jumped up and made his way out of the house and ran about a mile and when he sat down to rest there was that same spook, and the spook said, "Tain't nobody here but you and me, didn't we have a run?" The Negro says, "Yes, and 'tain't half what it is gwine to be."

Yes, we are living in a dark period and it is going to be worse for a while, but I believe that God will lead his people through. When the clarion note is sounded, let the Negro go forth.

Negro soldiers have borne a conspicuous part in every war in which their country has engaged. The magnificent charge up San Juan Hill by our black boys in blue challenged the admiration not only of the American people, but liberty loving people throughout the world, as well. A race so true to its flag as we have been, remembering God and His teaching, will in the end be more than conquerors.

What we want as a race is justice and fair play.

GROUP POLITICS, LEADERSHIP, AND RACE WORK

Burroughs never praised her community without simultaneously offering scathing criticism that cut deep to the marrow. If she injured a few feelings along the way or crushed a few egos, she did not mind. Her leadership style did not allow for commendation without identifying areas for improvement. Likewise, her strict and disciplined personality did not suffer gladly leaders she called "educated parasites" that took advantage of the least of these ("Educated Parasites and Satisfied Mendicants"). Her tone, though eloquent and folksy, was neither sensitive nor particularly diplomatic. In the early 1930s, she blasted corrupt Negro leadership whom she accused of not laying "the foundation for building genuine patriotism.... Nearly all of our political leaders are of the type that 'get theirs.'" ("Writer Asks How Dems Election Will Affect Negro"). In 1933 she issued a dramatic demand: "The Negro must unload the leeches and parasitic leaders who are absolutely eating the life out of the struggling, desiring mass of people. Chloroform your 'Uncle Toms!'" ("Unload the Leeches and Parasitic 'Toms' and Take the Promised Land"). Burroughs did not need to mention names in order for her blow to be felt. In her mind, uplifting the race was about reforming individual behavior and equipping individuals with tools that would enable them to be independent and self-determined. On the other hand, race work was about doing group politics and establishing an economic infrastructure that would keep black dollars within the community, thereby rendering the community viable and competitive. In her article "Why Our Dispositions Are 'Most Nigh Ruint,'" Burroughs insisted that race work was delayed when black people wasted time fussing about issues that did not translate into tangible reform. "We must not ruin our angelic dispositions majoring in fussing with ordinary white folks. They are not worth it." Fussing would need to be replaced by "actual work." Particularly during the years of the Great Depression, Burroughs was adamant about the fact that black civil rights organizations and women's clubs had a responsibility to lead with a cooperative vision for the masses. She encouraged the formation of economic allies and business unions. Even if the Depression promised economic instability and insecurity, she believed that her people had "enough of what it takes to redeem us" ("Educated Parasites and Satisfied Mendicants"). One of her more popular works, "Twelve Things the Negro Must Do for Himself," enumerates the race work to be done.

∞

Go Down Town and Meet Him

From *Pittsburgh Courier*, October 5, 1929, 2.

"I don't believe in standing around up town talking big. If that white man thinks that I am not as good a man as he is, every day in the week, I'll go down town and meet him and show him what I am." That's what I heard a Negro who was apparently courageous and wrought up say to another colored man the other day. Just what he meant I did not know, but curiosity moved me to find out. I drew "nigh" and listened because I could see that the man [who] would "go down town and meet him" was no ordinary chap. But I wondered if he would do anything besides talk after he got down there. I heard the "ins and outs" of it, but the case in point did not interest me very much nor was I convinced that what he would do would amount to anything.

Somehow I could not refrain from turning the thoughts that came to me into another channel, and I began to think on the deeper significance and economic possibilities wrapped up in that challenge to "go down town and meet him." That, thought I, is just what Negro business men will have to get courage, sense and standards enough to do—"go down town and meet him."

Have you ever thought how strange it is that the Lord calls Negro preachers to "go into all the world and preach the gospel" to NEGROES ONLY and He calls Negro business men to go into back streets and Negro ghettos and cater to NEGROES ONLY? Until Negro business men set up business in business districts and compete and sell to "whosoever will," our people will continue to spend their "sho 'nuf" money with white merchants and their pocket change with Negroes and apologize for patronizing Negro stores.

Negro business man, take this advice: Move out of Sodom and go down town, or up town—wherever the "sho 'nuf" business section is—and open up and "meet um."

It is positively pathetic, embarrassing and disgusting to see Negroes wading through department stores, drug stores and the big business sections, spending their money and lugging bundles, eating out of paper bags and can't even get a nickel's worth of anything to eat in nine-tenths of the big stores that have soda fountains, lunch counters, restaurants, and dining rooms. Some of the five and ten-cent stores have the nerve to serve whites only at their little old hot dog stands. A Negro might spend a thousand dollars in some of the department stores and faint right in the middle of the store from hunger, but he would have to stagger home to get a cup of coffee with which to revive himself.

Money talks, but the Negro's money does not talk the right way. It must ask for one hundred percent of the public service of the stores in which it is spent—that means "eats" as well as sheets. Serving patrons in a store is a public service and not a social courtesy.

It is high time that Negros were either bombarding the merchants with letters of protest and boycotting stores that will let him dress up in there but will not let him eat up in there, or it is high time that some enterprising Negroes, with high standards, were getting [text illegible] enough to conduct first-class lunch and coffee shops in the business sections of our large cities. "Go down town and meet um."

∽

Why Our Dispositions Are "Most Nigh Ruint"

From *Pittsburgh Courier*, February 8, 1930, 6.

Negroes are ruining their perfectly good dispositions fuss[ing] at, about and with white folks. They certainly have enough to fuss about every minute of the day, but this thing of majoring in fussing is too small a job for a race that has a future to work out. Furthermore, fussing cankers the heart and makes us so "cantankerous and porcupinish" that we will not be able to get along among ourselves, not even long enough to decide for which outrage to stage a real, sure-enough, honest-to-goodness, outside-of-the-race big fuss about, and how to go at it so as to win.

Twenty years ago some Negroes and some white folks (and there are some and there will be some more before long) did get together long enough to organize an anti-lynching crusade to get the bad end of the white race sufficiently civilized to stop them from tearing out Negroes' tongues, cutting off their limbs, plucking out their eyes, tarring and feathering them, saturating their bodies with kerosene oil, setting them on fire and fighting for the bones of the victims to keep as souvenirs.

After 20 years of hard work the Advancement Association[18] has reasoned enough sense into the wild end of the white race to get them to reduce their victims to 12 a year. This association stopped fussing and got down to hard reasoning. They had to do it to save the bodies of Negroes and the souls of white folk and the face of America. That's the way to do. Reason together.

But this fussing business as an indoor and outdoor sport, winter and summer, is just too engaging to allow us time to exercise our Christian graces. Something must be done about it. It is constitutionally weakening and socially demoralizing. It takes up too much time and robs too many people of a ghost of a chance to get to heaven.

Here is what we are up against. If we get on a street car we have to get in a fuss about a 5-cent seat.

If we go to the theater we have to fuss because all of us "do not choose to go to the roost." If we are perfectly decent and move into a decent community we have to fuss to get to live in our own house. If we go to school we have to fuss about what we should learn. If we go to the store we have to fuss about not being served. If we go to a hotel we have to fuss about being refused, and if we go to church we have to fuss about the un-Christian treatment which we receive. Having to fuss nearly all the time and about everything that belongs to free human beings, or that is natural for them to want, "has most nigh ruint" our dispositions and pauperized our souls. This thing of having to give people a piece of our mind to "get them told" every time you turn around or every time you turn up anywhere, outside of the penitentiary, would demoralize a saint. We are about to lose our world-wide reputation for being good-natured.

Now, here we were fussing, as usual, about our own affairs right here in America when along comes General Smuts[19] from "over home" and called our kinfolks jackasses. Poor Major Moton had to "get him told" right there on the platform.[20] It just spoils the evening—that's all. Now every Negro newspaper in the country is giving the general a piece of their minds. You know that is awful. We won't have any minds left by the time we get through giving these people pieces of it.

We did not get over that Smuts kick before Parham was put out of West Point for flunking, and now we have got to fuss about that and send him right straight back there to work that "'rithmetic." As if these two fusses at the extreme ends of the poles were not enough, up jumps Senator from the Wild West, flaunting into our faces a detestable bill, fresh from the shades of the fifteenth century, proposing national regulation of marriage and divorces, in the twentieth century, when the whole black world is organizing to fight caste, mind you.

Now we have got to fuss about that bill because right through here Negroes are having enough trouble marrying and divorcing their own, and they certainly do not propose to be further demoralized by legalized concubinage. No, siree! Here is where every Negro outside of the insane asylum will fuss in self-defense not to break into the white race. Oh, no! but to keep the white face from breaking into their race with license.

Fussing all over Africa and America about our God-given, blood-bought rights is making us so disagreeable that we cannot even get along among ourselves. We have fussed so much until it is difficult for us to have a meeting all by ourselves, and to attend to our own business without having to fuss about something.

We used to sing, grin, and wear the world as a loose garment, but this bad end of the white race is making us fuss and frown and tighten up for combat. The good end of the white race is doing its best to hold their wild ones off of us, but we know how difficult it is because we have some bad Negroes whom we have to hold off of white folks sometimes, particularly when the bad whites work up a riot. But we must not ruin our angelic dispositions majoring in fussing with ordinary white folks. They are not worth it.

Let's pool our brains and work and we will get somewhere. If we keep on fussing, the virtue of hate will poison our souls and we will not enjoy this earth and we will miss heaven. Let's stop trying to DO the bad end of the white race by fussing and OUTDO them by actual work. Let's get ahead and go ahead. THAT'S THE DOPE.

Nearly All the Educated Negroes Are Looking for Ready-Made Jobs

From *Pittsburgh Courier*, August 8, 1931, sec. 2.

The Negro masses are in a bad fix. The tragedy of it is that the majority of the well-fixed Negro class and the army of "school keepers" don't give—a dime. Their attitude toward the masses can be best summed up in the parlance of the street, "I should worry." The evils of satisfied ignorance and idleness are ripening fast.

The so-called leaders who crucified Booker T. Washington because he has the right "dope" for the masses and insisted on giving it to them, are largely responsible for the race attitude that had brought about the present condition. Dr. Washington pointed the only way up and out. He stood for the mental and manual efficiency of the masses. He urged dependent struggling masses to become small farm owners—to, "let down your buckets where you are." Cultivate the soil and by thrift and frugality educate your children, improve your homes, and see to it that your children by independent management, industrious habits, and application in the development of the essential elements of character earn their place of respect in the life of the nation.

Had the Negro race accepted Dr. Washington's gospel, we would now have a place of greater industrial efficiency, harnessed and effective power, general respect, and earned security in the economic structure of the nation. The masses under Dr. Washington's plans would develop their actual capacity and acquired common sense enough to properly evaluate their own powers for self-help.

The place for the Negro masses is in the open country and not in congested urban centers. If the laboring class of Negroes cannot make it on the soil in this country they certainly cannot make it on the pavement in the city. Most persons interested in the advancement of the Negro have been ill advised. It does not take a sage as wise as Booker T.

Washington to see that the greatest need of the Negro race today is a program of education that will fit him to hoe his own row and meet the adequate demands for skilled labor. The Negro masses should be urged to stay in the open country.

Philanthropists who want to help the race should encourage Negro settlements of land owners and home builders out in the country with schools, churches, work shops and stores equipped and managed by competent negroes. Open country communities, set up and developed by thrifty families, would surpass in concrete results anything that philanthropy has ever attempted in mass uplift and interracial cooperation in the history of America.

For fifty years Negroes clamored for higher education. Philanthropists and foundations were rather inclined to accept Dr. Washington's program. Since Dr. Washington's death there is no loud voice crying in the wilderness, but the day which he prophesied would come—the day of skilled labor—is here. Since that day has come philanthropists and foundations are quite willing to give more money for so-called higher education but what is the Negro going to do with it after he gets it. The teaching profession is crowded. The market is over-stocked. If the present rate of output keeps up Negro teachers can be secured at the five and ten cent store.

White students are going into the trades and profession that require innate ability, initiative and industry—professions and trades that lead into world conquests, world service, and courageous endeavor, while nine-tenths of the educated Negroes are looking for ready made jobs that require no initiative and industry. We have, therefore, come upon a day when educated Negroes are not looking for any jobs at all.

We might as well get down to the business of working our way out of this situation.

~

Get Ready—Winter Is Coming, Says Educator; Leaders Idle

From *Pittsburgh Courier*, August 1, 1931, sec. 2.

All the hibernators are out. Summer is here. The bread line has disappeared. The work line is getting whiter and whiter. The Negro masses are joy riding, gassing, and gadding about going nowhere to do nothing or just sitting around waiting for somebody to help them out. Ants, bees, and bugs are busy getting ready for next winter.

The novelty of the bread line has worn off. Next winter charity is going to serve the unemployed with a longer spoon with less in it.

When the American people get over the novelty and thrill of a thing they either discard it or sober up and settle down to thinking. The charity and chest leaders and donors have their hands together—thinking—bread liners look out for their ultimatum. The people of this country are not going to work for able bodied men and women. Machine age or no machine age—Eden's decree will never be revoked—nor Horace Greeley's doctrine repudiated. The former declares that "in the sweat of thy brow shalt thou eat bread," and the command of the latter is "root, hog, or die."

We might as well make up our minds to go to it. You ask what can Negroes do when the whole world is in the same fix. The Negro can do just what others are doing—call on his courage, industry, ingenuity, initiative, dogged determination, put his brain to work, and put up a fight for his life—that's all. The man who uses his head, hands, and heart can make his own bread, buy his own house, sit by his own fire, instead of standing for somebody to feed him. Idle men could scour the towns for jobs.

Negro leaders haven't interest enough in the masses to hold a job finding convention. The majority of them are too busy getting elected to places of ease, honor, power and glory. Good Lord, deliver us from these "luxurious leaders" of ours. They are our greatest liabilities. They haven't done a thing concrete and far reaching to help us out of this hole. A few of them got excited last winter, but they cooled off in March.

It was just at that time that they should have enlisted and organized the army of unemployed. The slogans should have been "Get Ready for Next Winter," "Find a Job or Make One," "Plan a Garden," "Plant in Your Back Yard, Borrow Vacant Lots," "Cultivate a Farm," "Get Ready, Winter is Coming."

People will have a great deal more respect for us if we borrow land to raise our own good than they will have if we are too plain lazy to help ourselves.

The women's clubs that are supposed to be mothering home and child could have started a nationwide "Can all you can" movement. Their slogan could have been, "Get ready for next winter." They could have put streamers in every church with the reminder that "Winter Is Coming" on them. Club women should be running garment stations (old clothes). Summer is the time to collect and remodel old clothes. People will give away more at this season than they will next winter. The "Ladies Alders," as Pollyanna calls them, could be at work making over, remodeling and repairing garments. Their slogan should be, "Repair, make over and remodel, winter is coming."

Six months from now the Negroes of this country are going to be in a terrible plight. The leaders in all organizations will be responsible. Something definite, constructive and far-reaching can be done. It takes brains, initiative, industry, unselfishness, and vision to do it.

Americans by the millions have the keenest appreciation for individuals and races that fight their moral, social, and economic battles like men. Try it, and this nation will rise up and call—even black men—blessed.

∞

Educated Parasites and Satisfied Mendicants

From *Pittsburgh Courier*, February 20, 1932, 2.

Here it is! The Negro race is in a terrible fix economically. It has two millstones about its neck—the educated parasites and satisfied mendicants.

We could deliver ourselves from our present state of thralldom if the majority of us were not too plain lazy to think straight and to act decisively.

The fact of the matter is that on the whole we have been handling our economic and social problems so pusillanimously that the race is seriously afflicted with social epilepsy and social paralysis. We have never made a serious and united effort to coordinate our thinking nor our activities. We are a race of individualists, and weak ones at that, trying to function in a highly cooperative age. We cannot do it. The Negro will have to coordinate, organize, cooperate or degenerate. Those who try to do a one man act are beaten before they start.

Men of individualistic minds were cast into the limbo a thousand years ago. The Negro will have to learn to work together or be worked. That's that.

But let's get down to brass tacks. What can he do? Some cold water mugs say—nothing. We can do a thousand times more than we are doing. Of course we do not like to see this in print, but the world knows it and we might as well get courage enough to face the truth and sense and industry enough to do something about it.

White people are spending their perfectly good money to give us all the higher education we want, but what we need is initiative and the kind of genius that turns superior training into superior service. There are new worlds to be discovered, new miracles in science to be performed, a new social order to be constructed.

The Negro can start to work in his own field. Suppose we meet the needs in the dying and showing off business—that is where we shine. Negro undertakers might form a national union and manufacture coffins. They could buy up the woods, employ workmen, build the factory on the spot. There is money in this phase of the dying business. Build a shroud factory in a metropolitan center. Furnish the whole outfit to the members of the National Union of Negro Undertakers.

Go into the greenhouse business. We could give jobs to some of these Negroes who are loaded down with degrees and cannot find anything to do. They could apply their knowledge of botany and floral culture to the greenhouse business. Of course the business would have to be located far out in the suburbs of large cities. It is not easy to get many educated Negroes far from ready-made jobs. The greenhouse business is an untouched field among Negroes. By the way, we have struck another snag. The essential materials, such as manure and soil, are offensive to nine-tenths of the ready-made job seekers. What would we do with the greenhouses? Furnish flowers for the sick, dead, marrying and graduating. What a field for a host of people who have studied botany and like to work with nature. Nature has no prejudice. She knows no race nor color. Furthermore, there is no risk in this field because Negroes are going to die if it is the last act. They invest heavily in flowers for funerals.

Is there another uncultivated field? Yes, there are dozens of them. Negro fraternal organizations spend fortunes for badges and regalia, but the time is spent parading, gripping and passwording. Fraternal organizations spend millions of dollars for printing, advertising, uniforming and showing off. They dispense charity. Nine-tenths of their members need work, not charity. The Negro fraternal organizations could combine and give employment to thousands of their own members. Why don't they do it? Ask the leaders, they know.

If the white people did not supply us with our funeral necessities, we would have to wrap our dead in sheets, drop them in holes and decorate their graves with weeds. Poor us! We have enough of what it takes to redeem us, but we give it to others and then we beg, whine and trail.

∞

Writer Asks How Dems Election Will Affect Negro

From *Pittsburgh Courier*, December 3, 1932, 2.

Not any. Because the Negro's political troubles, like most of his other troubles, are internal and not external. The race has been bled to death by its own venal political leaders. No political party can cure our ills. Races or groups make their own political advantages in the nation. But these advantages do not make the race. Races set their own goals, and hew their own way. In order to be taken seriously by other groups to be courted and counted between elections as a vital political factor to be reckoned with, the Negro race will have to produce a new brand of red-blooded political leaders. Those who have led the race have not laid the foundation for building genuine patriotism.

Would-be political leaders for the most part have not stressed and stood for vital principles, fundamental ideals and common objectives. They have not thought in terms of group welfare. They were individualists seeking their own personal welfare at the expense of all things vital and valuable for the promotion of the common good. Nearly all of our political leaders are of the type that "get theirs." In common parlance, they are political racketeers; they wax fat and the people are "bologna" fed political paupers. Groups cannot become vital factors in the body politic unless they have clear-visioned, sagacious, unselfish political leaders who make it their major duty to indoctrinate the people in the value and the spirit of their highest privilege and most vital function [of those who] as citizens have not enjoyed any such tutelage.

∽

Unload the Leeches and Parasitic "Toms" and Take the Promised Land

From Nannie Helen Burroughs Papers, 1900–1963, Manuscript Division, Library of Congress.

The Negro must unload the leeches and parasitic leaders who are absolutely eating the life out of the struggling, desiring mass of people.

Chloroform your "Uncle Toms"! Negroes like that went out of style seventy years ago. They are relics and good for museums. I don't care whether they are in the church as the preacher, in the school as the teacher, in the ward as politicians—the quickest way to get rid of them is the best way, and the sooner the better. They are luxurious, expensive, unworthy. The "Uncle Toms" are greater enemies than [Ben] Tillman or Cole[man] Blease[21] had ever been to the Negro race.

They have sold us for a mess of pottage. We got the mess, but not the pottage. The question, "What am I going to get out of it?" must get out of our thinking. This race would have been one hundred years advanced if it had not been for this thought uppermost in the minds of our so-called leaders.

No Deliverers

Don't wait for deliverers. . . . I like that quotation, "Moses, my servant, is dead. Therefore, arise and go over Jordan." There are no deliverers. They're all dead. We must arise and go over Jordan. We can take the promised land.

Die for Justice

The Negro must serve notice on the world that he is ready to die for justice. To struggle and battle and overcome and absolutely defeat every force designed against us is the only way to achieve. Men must have life, the opportunity to learn, to labor, to love. Without these fundamental virtues we cannot achieve. We must not give up the struggle until this is obtained.

No Charity

More than this, the Negro must glorify the things of the spirit and keep the things of the flesh under control. We must get a correct sense of values. When we've accomplished this—Shiloh will be here.

Human beings are equipped with divinely planted yearnings and longings. That's what the constitution meant by certain inalienable rights.

Don't Apologize

The Negro is oppressed not because he is a Negro, but because he'll take it. Negroes forget your color. Stop apologizing for not being white and rank you race.

Organize yourself inside. Teach your children the internals and eternals, rather than the externals. Be more concerned with "putting in" than "getting on." Ye have been too bothered about the externals—clothes, money. What we need are mental and spiritual giants who are aflame with a purpose.

Anglo-Saxon Has Four Loves

The Anglo-Saxon has four great loves. Love of liberty, love of home, love of women, and love of life. He'll wade through blood for these. When we make up our minds to not take substitutes for them, we'll get them.

But we're not going to get them as individuals. The day of individualism is past. We'll get them as a great race or group.

Crusade

We're a race ready for crusade, for we've recognized that we're a race on this continent that can work out its own salvation. A race must build for nobility of character, for a conquest not on things, but on spirit.

We must have a glorified womanhood that can look any man in the face—white, red, yellow, brown or black—and tell of the nobility of character within black womanhood.

BOW DOWN TO WOMEN

Stop making slaves and servants of our women. We've got to stop singing, "Nobody works but father." The Negro mother is doing it all. The women are carrying the burden.

The main reason is that the men lack manhood and energy. They sing too much, "I can't give you anything but love, Baby." The women can't build homes, rear families off of love alone. The men ought to get down on their knees to Negro women. They've made possible all we have around us—church, home, school, business.

Aspire to be, and all that we are not, God will give us credit for trying.

☙

Twelve Things the Negro Must Do for Himself

From Nannie Helen Burroughs, *Twelve Things the Negro Must Do for Himself* (Washington, DC: n.p., 1950).

> If The Negro Would Try
> *The Negro race has never tried to do very much for itself. The race has great possibilities. Properly awakened, the Negro can do the so-called impossible.*
> —Carter G. Woodson

1. The Negro Must Learn to Put First Things First. The First Things Are: Education; Development of Character Traits; A Trade and Home Ownership.

The Negro puts too much of his earnings in clothes, in food, in show and in having what he calls "a good time." The late Dr. Kelly Miller[22] said, "The Negro buys what he WANTS and begs for what he needs." Too true!

2. The Negro Must Stop Expecting God and White Folk to Do for Him What He Can Do for Himself.

It is the "Divine Plan" that the strong shall help the weak, but even God does not do for man what man can do for himself. The Negro will have to do exactly what Jesus told the man (in John 5:8) to do—Carry his own load—"Take up your bed and walk."

3. The Negro Must Keep Himself, His Children and His Home Clean and Make the Surroundings in Which He Lives Comfortable and Attractive.

He must learn to "run his community up"—not down. We can segregate by law, we integrated only by living. Civilization is not a matter of race, it is a matter of standards.

Believe it or not—Some day, some race is going to outdo the Anglo-Saxon, completely. It can be the Negro race, if the Negro gets sense enough. Civilization goes up and down that way.

4. He Must Learn to Dress More Appropriately for Work and Leisure.

Knowing what to wear—how to wear it—when to wear it and where to wear it are earmarks of common sense, culture and also an index to character.

5. The Negro Must Make His Religion an Everyday Practice and Not Just a Sunday-Go-To-Meeting Emotional Affair.

6. The Negro Must Highly Resolve to Wipe Out Mass Ignorance.

The leaders of the race must teach and inspire the masses to become eager and determined to improve mentally, morally, and spiritually, and to meet the basic requirements of good citizenship.

We should initiate an intensive literacy campaign in America, as well as in Africa. Ignorance—*satisfied ignorance*—is a millstone about the neck of the race. It is democracy's greatest burden.

Social integration is a relationship attained as a result of the cultivation of kindred social ideals, interests and standards.

It is a blending process that requires time, understanding and kindred purposes to achieve. Likes alone and not laws can do it.

7. The Negro Must Stop Charging His Failures Up to His "Color" and to White People's Attitudes.

The truth of the matter is that good service and good conduct will make senseless race prejudice fade like mist before the rising sun.
 God never intended that a man's color shall be anything other than a badge of distinction. It is high time that all races were learning that fact. The Negro must first QUALIFY for whatever position he wants. Purpose, initiative, ingenuity, skill and industry are the keys that all men use to get what they want. The Negro will have to do the same. He must make himself a workman who is too skilled not to be wanted, and too DEPENDABLE not to be on the job, according to promise or plan. He will never become a vital factor in industry until he learns to put into his work the vitalizing force of initiative, skill, and dependability. He has gone "RIGHTS" mad and DUTY dumb.

8. The Negro Has Bad Job Habits.

He must make a brand new reputation for himself in the world of labor. His bad job habits are absenteeism, funerals to attend, or a little business to look after. The Negro runs an off and on business. He also has a bad reputation for conduct habits on the job—such as petty quarreling with other help, incessant loud talking about nothing; loafing, carelessness, due to lack of job pride; insolence, gum chewing and—too often—liquor drinking. Just plain bad job habits!

9. He Must Improve His Conduct in Public Places.

Taken on the whole, he is entirely too loud, and too ill-mannered.
 There is much talk about wiping out racial segregation and also much talk about achieving integration.
 Segregation is a physical arrangement by which people are separated in various services.
 It is definitely up to the Negro to wipe out the apparent justification or excuse for segregation.
 The only effective way to do it is to clean up and keep clean. By practice, cleanliness will become a habit and habit becomes character.

10. The Negro Must Learn How to Operate Business for People—Not for Negro People, Only.

To do business, he will have to remove typical "earmarks"; learn business principles; measure up to accepted standards and meet stimulating competition, graciously—in fact, he must learn to welcome competition!

11. The Average So-Called Educated Negro Will Have to Come Down Out of the Air. He Is Too Inflated Over Nothing. He Needs an Experience Similar to the One that Ezekiel Had—(Ezekiel 3:14–19). An He Must Do What Ezekiel Did—

Otherwise, through indifference, as to the plight of the masses, the Negro, who thinks that he has escaped, will lose his own soul. It will do all leaders good to read Hebrews 13:3, and the first Thirty-seven Chapters of Ezekiel.

A race transforms itself through its own leaders and its sensible "common people." A race rises on its own wings, or is held down by its own weight. True leaders are never "things apart from the people." They are the masses. They simply got to the front ahead of them. Their only business at the front is to inspire the masses by hard work and noble example and challenge them to "Come on!" Dante stated a fact when he said, "Show the people the light and they will find the way."

There must arise within the Negro race a leadership that is not out hunting bargains for itself. A noble example is found in the men and women of the Negro race, who, in the early days, laid down their lives for their people. Their invaluable contributions have not been appraised by the "latter-day leaders." In many cases their names would never be recorded, among the unsung heroes of the world, but for the fact that white friends have written them there.

"Lord, God of Hosts, Be with us yet."
WE FORGET—WE FORGET.

The Negro of today does not realize that, but, for these exhibit As, that certainly show the innate possibilities of members of their own race, white people would not have been moved to make such princely investments in lives and money, as have been made, for the establishment of schools and for the on-going of the race.

12. The Negro Must Stop Forgetting His Friends. "REMEMBER."

Read Deuteronomy 23:18. Deuteronomy rings the big bell of gratitude. Why? Because an ingrate is an abomination in the sight of God. God is constantly telling us that "I, the Lord thy God, delivered you"—through human instrumentalities.

The American Negro has had and still has friends—in the North and in the South—These friends not only pray, speak, write, influence others, but make unbelievable, unpublished sacrifices and contributions for the advancement of the race—for their brothers in bonds.

The noblest thing that the Negro can do is to so live and labor that these benefactors will not have been given in vain. The Negro must make his heart warm with gratitude, his lips sweet with thanks and his heart and mind resolute with purpose to justify the sacrifices and stand on his feet and go forward—"God is no respecter of persons. In every nation, he that feareth him and worketh righteousness is" sure to win out. Get to work! That's the answer to everything that hurts us. We talk too much about nothing instead of redeeming the time by working.

REMEMBER

In spite of race prejudice, America is brim full of *opportunities*. Go after them!

RACIAL VIOLENCE, SOCIAL JUSTICE, POLITICS, AND DEMOCRACY

Burroughs's social and educational work with women began almost immediately upon her graduation from high school. Her political activism was more delayed. Prior to the early 1920s, Burroughs admitted that she had never taken an active interest in national politics, at least not as a potential career trajectory. Although, during World War I, Burroughs did come under government surveillance on the suspicion that she might be a black radical. In the first fifteen years of her career as a public intellectual (the years immediately preceding World War I), the vast majority of her writings focused on race work, self-determination, and the education of black women and girls as opposed to politics proper. Burroughs's emphasis on group politics as the foundation to productive race work should not be confused with her official engagement with national partisan politics during the interwar period and World War II. Even though Burroughs's argument for black women's suffrage during the teen years broadly foreshadowed an inclination toward political involvement, in her mind the movement for black women's enfranchisement was primarily expressive of Progressive Era social reform ethics, not politics proper. Between the early 1920s and late 1940s, Burroughs's writings and speeches revealed a woman who was becoming overtly political and partisan.

The way in which Burroughs framed her relationship to the American project is endlessly interesting. Contemporary scholars will almost certainly critique Burroughs for her boundless faith in the nation's most sacred documents. An inveterate optimist, she positioned herself as an American apologist. For example, whereas Burroughs saw war as the "sum total of wrong attitudes and practices" ("The Hope of the World"), she framed the nation's involvement in World War II as an almost divine moment that would bring about the "kingdom of God" and the "divine rights of men" ("This Is the War of the Five Rs"). Her 1942 article "This Is the War of the Five Rs: Race, Room, Raw Materials,

Rights, Religion" best exemplifies her dialectical thinking in reference to conflict and progress, while the commencement address she delivered almost a decade earlier in 1934 at Tuskegee Institute demonstrates the optimism she believed was necessary in order to meet the challenges of the time.

In 1924 the National League of Republican Colored Women was founded. Burroughs was elected its president in 1928. Through this position, she became a highly sought-after speaker for the Republican National Committee's Speaker's Bureau. In 1932 President Herbert Hoover appointed Burroughs to chair a fact-finding commission on Negro housing.[23] She also participated in national anti-lynching crusades.

Burroughs's engagement with partisan politics did not mean that she forsook to interject the discourse of redemption and salvation into her writings. She was first and foremost a crusader for Christ. In her mind (and her writings reveal), there was no easy line of demarcation between the religious and the political. In the same way that Jesus Christ came to earth to provide a template for humanity to follow, Burroughs organized her life in such a way that the example she set might inspire people to pursue righteousness. She tackled antiblack racism through a moralist discourse that fused poetry and scripture with an awareness of concrete needs in society. She brought the Christian church to bear upon American politics by suggesting unequivocally that the nation would crumble unless the church preached the principles of brotherhood and the sacredness of human personality. At one point, she said that the nation's "acts and deeds of injustice" rendered it "an abomination in the sight of the Lord" ("The Hope of the World").

Despite the jabs she took at the nation for the violence and injustices that consistently erupted against black life, Burroughs understood herself to be an American patriot, albeit a protesting one. To her, black Americans were the "real" patriots. Whereas the early twentieth century saw the proliferation of black nationalist movements like Marcus Garvey's United Negro Improvement Association that conceptualized America as being fundamentally inhospitable to black people, Burroughs called America home. She was a patriot with an abiding hope in the nation of her birth to forsake injustice in deference to its most sacred promises. She believed that black people had an equal inheritance in the Bill of Rights, the Declaration of Independence, and the Constitution. Even if Burroughs admonished black people to never abandon their patriotism, she simultaneously maintained that African Americans were a unique group with their own flavor and spirit. As she argued, black people needed space and opportunity to express their difference through "cultural things" ("The Challenge of the New Day").

Burroughs's 1959 article "We Must Fight Back, but with What and How?" demonstrates the trajectory of her thought concerning civil rights activism and her rejection of Robert F. Williams's self-defense tactics. Burroughs found it difficult to square her Victorian sensibilities with any kind of militant politics that required black people to take on what she considered to be an unbecoming disposition.

∽

Miss Burroughs Replies to Mr. Carrington

From *Voice of the Negro* 2, no. 2 (February 1905): 106–7.

Mr. E. W. Carrington, in the October number of THE VOICE OF THE NEGRO, makes "An Earnest Inquiry" as to the cause of assault by black men of the United States upon white women.[24] After assuring us that he is well posted on the current history of the Negroes of the United States and the West Indies for the past forty-three years, he swings out on this question, "Why is it that we do not 'LEARN OR HEAR' of outrages committed by the Negroes of the West Indies upon the white women there?" He says the "opportunity exists." Then he asks, "Why the absence of such crime?"

In the first place, because we do not "LEARN OR HEAR" of the crime is no evidence that it is not committed. There are many heinous crimes committed in the West Indies and in the United States of which we do not "HEAR." Is there any law in the West Indies for the punishment of such crime? If so, how long has it existed? What provoked it? Why the law if no such crime was ever committed?

Mr. Carrington leaves us to surmise that he is not just clear as to the absence of the crime when he asks, "Why is it that we do not 'HEAR' of it?" The reason we do not "hear" of such crimes in the West Indies is because of the method of punishment. He tells us that the Negro there is protected by law and absolutely free from mob violence, it matters not what the crime may be. That is just why we do not "hear" of the crime. The Negro in the United States who commits such an outrage is not protected by law and he is open to mob violence. The method of punishment in the Island shields the criminal, while the reign of lynch law in the United States is wholly responsible for the publicity of the outrages. The method of dealing with the criminal and nothing more.

Stop lynching and you will seldom "hear" of such outrages in the United States. Let the people of the West Indies go into the lynching business and you will "learn or hear" of similar offenses committed by Negro men of the West Indies upon white women. There is no other civilized nation in the world except the United States, practicing lynching, and no other race except the Negro, being lynched. The exception of itself would give publicity to the act. Mr. Carrington might ask, why is it we do not "hear" of the white men of the United States committing outrages upon white or black women? Is it because no such outrages are committed? Not a bit of it. White men in the United States were the first to begin the business of outraging women. They have outraged more women of both races than Negroes will ever outrage. It was alright until the men of another race begun to make inroads upon their women, and then no law on the statute book afforded punishment sufficiently severe and they begun the enforcement of an unwritten and unknown law to punish Negroes only. Now why do we not "learn or hear" of outrages by white men? The reasons are obvious. The fact that there was punishment by law, long before the Negro begun his base operations, proves that the white man was at it. Not the absence of the crime but the concealment of it has protected him from public notice.

"Lynch him, burn him, and tell the world what a brute he is," was the command given as soon as the Negro begun committing the sin. But over the white man's sin is thrown the mantle of charity. For what? To conceal Anglo-Saxon vice and keep that race on the throne of virtue. To publish such crimes perpetrated by them upon their own women would deprive their women of that protection of which the Anglo-Saxon delights to boast and in which he wants his women to feel secure. The crime is not absent. Go to the court records. Let the thousands of white women whose mouths are shut by pride, speak out. When such crime is brought to the notice of the court, public KNOWLEDGE of it is absent because the criminal is protected by law and not hounded by a mob of civilized savages and swung up, riddled with bullets, tarred and feathered and burned to crisp. Such methods of punishment as are used upon the Negro would certainly furnish interesting reading matter for civilized people, and so the papers publish the news. Another reason we "learn and hear" of such crimes in the United States when committed by Negroes, and the motive for publication is to continue to mold public sentiment against him. The people of this country have been hunting about for the past twenty years for the most damaging evidence against the Negro to prove to the world that he is a brute, and that contact with the white race makes him pompous, and that he is dying to have social equality. These exposures are only to clinch the argument and make enemies for the Negroes.

The class of men, white and black, in the United States or anywhere else, who commit outrages upon women, have no respect for law and order. The same man who will join a mob to lynch a Negro for committing an outrage upon a white woman will outrage a black or white woman any time he makes up his mind so to do. The men who lynch have no more respect for law and order than the men who commit outrages.

This class of crime is not confined to race nor country, but is so general that all civilized nations have provided punishment by law for the offense. The Negro of the United States is the target. He is living under the scorching heat of base prejudice, hence we "learn or hear" of his bad deeds by day and by night, while his virtues are seldom mentioned.

Divide Vote or Go to Socialists

From *Baltimore Afro-American*, August 22, 1919, letter to the editor.

Unless the two great political parties—Republican and Democratic declare themselves on the Suffrage, Labor and Lynching questions, the Negro should go to the Socialist party that has already declared itself for exact justice and equality of opportunity for all, regardless of race.

For nearly sixty years, the Negro has been expecting the Republicans to assist him in safeguarding his constitutional and political rights, but that party has failed ignominiously. Every four years we are fed on campaign dope for a few months only to starve from failure on the part of that party to select the men and stand by the measure designed to give political and economic opportunity to all. We have lived on promises without [text illegible]. We are suffering and dying as a result of neglect on the part of the party to which we have given faithful and unstinted support.

Whether you know it or not, or, rather, whether you believe it or not, the Negro is either going to divide his vote among the three parties or he is going to do the desperate thing—throw his entire strength to the Socialist party.

Then, too, Negro men are going to resent the infamous insult of the Woman Suffrage Association. In their effort to secure the ballot, they have virtually promised the South to leave the Negro woman out of the equation. Negro women are perfectly willing to be left out but Negro men who have the ballot are going to see that somebody else is left out.

A Campaign of Education is going to be launched and Negro men and women will be advised to do just as I have intimated. We have three things in mind during the next campaign: to square with the Democrats for the way in which they have treated Negroes on both sides of the ocean during the past four years, to settle with the Republicans for their sins of omission—and to kill woman suffrage because it is willing to throw us over-board in order to get white women into the ship.

An Alabama suffragette asked me, some years ago, "Why, what will colored women do with the ballot, if they get it?" I replied, "What could they do without it, if white women get it?"

The Negro has an objective, politically, and the only way for him to reach it is to get with the party that will take him nearest to it and thus defeat the parties that have failed to recognize his value and his objective.

I have never taken an active interest in politics but I am planning to assist in directing the Campaign of Education to be conducted by the National Association of Colored Women. We are going to stand for anything that is 100 percent American and oppose everything that is less.

What Is Social Equality?

From Nannie Helen Burroughs Papers, 1900–1963, Manuscript Division, Library of Congress.

Sometime ago a white woman asked me the age-old question—"Do you believe in social equality?" To which I replied, "I will answer your one question by asking you three."

First: Is there such a thing as social equality?
Second: If there is, why should I not believe in what is?
Third: If there is, just what would my disbelief amount to?

She boggled. I knew she was thinking race and thinking white. "Of course, you know," I said, in an effort to help her recover, "persons of the same race are not necessarily social equals. They must have the same or similar personal tastes, natural affinity or attraction."

There are whites who are not social equals of other whites. Their individual and personal attitudes, likes and dislikes are poles apart.

Persons do not have to belong to the same race to have similar social tastes. This thing that you call social equality is made out of inborn stuff that is entirely alien to one's color or race. It is not made, sustained, nor protected by blood, birth, tradition, custom, laws, civic regulations, restrictions, nor wealth. It is built on individual personal desire for social affiliation. It is social reciprocity subject absolutely to individual desire for personal intercourse and association.

Kindred spirits crave and seek their kind. They are strongly attracted toward each other, and desire to share their inner possessions of mind and spirit. These inner urges and desires pave the way for reciprocal social intercourse and affiliation that cannot be controlled by laws. Legislation and other legally conferred rights and restrictions do not make nor keep persons from being social equals.

This woman, like millions of other people confuse *social equality* with common public privileges or *social rights*. Though unjust laws and social prejudices regulate and control the common rights of Negro citizens, no laws nor personal prejudices can ever prevent persons in any race from being the social equals of persons in any other race. It makes no difference whether they ever have individual social intercourse, they can be socially equal right on.

Franchise, travel on railroads and in public conveyances, admission to public places of amusement and instruction, and opportunities for employment are purely public rights, and have nothing in the world to do with social equality. Social equality is sentimental and purely personal. Social or public rights are fundamentally and specifically impersonal, divine in origin, and too vital and sacred to human development and happiness to be confused with social equality which is only an incidental expression of man's personal likes and dislikes. We are even mixed up on the meaning of eating in the same restaurant. Eating in the same restaurant or riding in the same street car is economic equality.

The false definition and interpretation of social equality have stultified the Negro's self respect and robbed him of practically all the common social rights that belong to him as a man and citizen. The business of denying or abridging the social rights of Negroes under the delusion that the granting of such common general rights is social equality is the height of ignorance.

We are off the trail and we should not waste time talking about Social Equality. We should work everlastingly for Social Rights, and the removal of all municipal restrictions and let morons and social odds and ends discuss the Social Equality bogy to their hearts content.

Legitimate Ambitions of the Negro

From *Missionary Review of the World* 45 (June 1922): 454–56.

The legitimate ambitions of the Negro can be summed up in one sentence: "He wants a chance—an equal chance—free and unhampered—to prove that the color of his skin is not a badge of inferiority." That he has never had the chance, that society and governments are organized to keep him from having it, is a fact as pathetic as it is pernicious and unfair. Unless all races are admitted into the International Order of Human Brotherhood on equal terms, another Gibbons will write "The Rise and Fall of Modern Republics" and will record this tragic fact—"Their civilization failed because they denied in practice the doctrine of Human Brotherhood."

Edward Everett Hale said that the watchword of the next century will be *"Together."* It is the watchword of the Book of Life. The very existence of civilization depends upon our acceptance of that doctrine. The legitimate yearnings of the Negro—his innate and lawful desire to achieve something great and good—spring from this sense of oneness in origin, equipment and destiny. Briefly, the things that he desires, and to the achievement of which he will dedicate his life are the following:

His first ambition is to have his *claim to brotherhood* recognized. Upon the recognition of this claim depends the happiness, progress, development and perpetuity of civilization. There can be no Christian civilization without good-will and this is predicated upon the unconditional acceptance of the doctrine of human brotherhood. The race name, "Negro," incidentally denotes a shade of skin and, happily, it suggests a sweetness and beauty (Nēg- rōse) of soul—a forgiving spirit. It is this rich contribution that the Negro is determined to make to civilization and that is needed in civilization. He will allow nothing so to embitter his spirit as to rob him of this endowment and privilege.

Second—The Negro wants to be *himself in color* and in distinguishing characteristics, to perfect all his possibilities, to have latitude for the unfolding of essential elements of character by which friction from individual and group contact is reduced. He wishes to contribute of the richness of his individuality, without having his claims to justice and equality questioned, ignored, abridged or denied. In other words, he claims the right to be different without being treated or necessarily considered as inferior.

Third—He wants to enjoy *justice and equality of opportunity*—equality of opportunity in preparation, equality of opportunity in service, and equality of opportunity in the enjoyment of life. He desires that merit, and merit alone, be the determining factor. He will press his claim for a chance to qualify to meet the social and economic requirements of modern civilization. His claim is not selfish. He is so related and situated as to advance, retard or contaminate the social group. If the Negro is forced to the bottom of civilization, his putrifying body will pollute the whole mass.

Fourth—The Negro is right in insisting upon the full recognition of his *political, economic and civic rights* in any government *which he is required to help build* up or support. He is right in asking for the benefit of all welfare agencies maintained by public taxes. He should not be forcibly prevented from enjoying every blessing and every privilege granted to other citizens similarly taxed. The right to enjoy public parks, public play-grounds, public bathing facilities, is his in common with other citizens. He claims that it is the duty of a democracy to help its citizens to qualify for the enjoyment of these privileges and not deny or abridge them on the score of race, color or previous condition of servitude.

Fifth—He should not be required to plan a *destiny* separate and apart from the common destiny of other citizens who have pledged their allegiance and proved their loyalty by offering their lives in times of war and their skill and industry in times of peace. It is morally and socially dangerous to allow or encourage the group to "flower out of harmony with" the ideals of its community or country. Fortunately for America the Negro has not the germ of disloyalty and radicalism in his system. Had the seed been there, it would have germinated during his long season of abuse and neglect.

Sixth—The Negro wants to be measured by *American standards and ideals*. He hears it said daily, "That is good enough for Negroes." Nothing is good enough for him that is not good enough for others. Double standards, social and moral, are dangerous and demoralizing.

Seventh—He wants to be *measured and assorted and not herded* or segregated on the mere score of color. He must be counted by the census taker to show his numerical strength, but he should be measured by society to ascertain his moral value and, according to his virtues and ideals, given place and privilege. The trouble in this whole race situation is that most people know *about* the Negro but they do not know *him*. To that end, they do not need more statistics but more clarity. The American people should be less concerned about how much color they have on their hands, and more about how much character they have—less about how many Negroes, more about their calibre. When the moral value of the man is considered, the Negro will be privileged to live in neighborhoods in keeping with his ideals and finance, ride in public carriers or patronize public hostelries in keeping with his money and tastes, and sit in public, places in keeping with his means and manners. "Birds of a feather" will then be privileged to "flock together." Segregation on the mere score of color is a relic of the Caste System, and should have no place in a modern progressive government.

Eighth—The Negro should not be singled out as *a target for maltreatment*. He wants to be assisted in finding the cause of social ills and encouraged and helped in the eradication of them. The moral reaction is upon those who mistreat the Negro. The nature of the persecutor is always brutalized.

Ninth—The Negro wants his *home and family life regarded as sacredly* as the home and family life of other Americans. He wants public sentiment as vocal and as merciless, and the law as exacting and swift in dealing with those who encroach upon his home and family life as they are in dealing with him when he is charged with encroachment and trespassing. In other words, the Negro wants to be punished only for the crimes for which he is responsible, and not for the color of his skin for which he is not responsible.

Tenth—He wants a *square deal by the public press*. While his crimes and failures are chronicled, his achievements and contributions to community progress are often either ignored or minimized. If as much publicity is given to the latter as to the former, the barriers of ignorance of his aspirations and possibilities will break down and, in the light of understanding and appreciation, the world will begin to see him as he is.

The cause of the Negro is now up for a hearing. In settlement of these ten legitimate claims to equality of opportunity and preparation—equality of opportunity in service, equality of opportunity in the enjoyment of life, liberty and the pursuit of happiness—he will accept no compromise.

Why America Has Gone Lynch Mad

From *Pittsburgh Courier*, December 23, 1933, 2.

America's lynching record is mounting. Why shouldn't it? Any industry will succeed if it has strong backing and certain contributing factors. The lynching industry has both. It has had the backing of a tremendous white public sentiment. Then, too, silence gives consent. It has had the backing of officers of the law. The mob has gone unmolested. For these reasons it is quite natural that a national state of mind has triumphed again and again over the law of the land.

One contributing factor has been the attitude of the nation. That attitude is to look down on the Negro. Such an attitude invites and encourages injustice and persecution.

Another contributing factor is the failure of the Federal government to enforce the Fifteenth Amendment. Such failure leaves two-thirds of the Negro population voteless, and therefore defenseless. It actually sets the stage for discrimination, wanton aggression, injustice and crime.

The third contributing factor is the call of the blood. Americans have been lynching human beings for nearly 50 years. Thousands of fathers and mothers have either sanctioned, attended or participated in lynching bees. They tarred, feathered, burned and roasted alive three thousand, seven hundred and eleven men and women. They brought their little children and babies to witness the orgies. They danced, shouted and laughed gleefully at the death throes of their tortured victims.

The mothers and fathers begot children, into whose veins they passed the slime of the virus of hate and a non-eradicable strain of brutality. The children born of lynchers, therefore, inherit a thirst for blood. "The fathers eat sour grapes," says the Bible, "and the children's teeth are set on edge."[25] The blood of two generations has been poisoned by the cast and deeds and attitudes of their forebears.

We have still another factor contributing to the success of the lynching industry. Many policemen, constables, guards and officers of the law, who do not actually participate in lynchings, brutalize their natures by their conduct towards Negroes. They club, shoot, beat into insensibility and murder, to vent their spleens on helpless creatures. The strain of this brutality enters the blood of their progeny and runs its course from generation to generation. The reports say that the young are leading the mobs. They are to be pitied. Their forebears did the same thing.

As long as Negroes were being lynched, the nation was apathetic, indifferent and impotent, but as soon as the mob broke into the white race—ah! Then interest picked up—the voice of the nation is heard speaking out in thunderous tones against mob violence and against anybody high or low who aids, abets or sanctions the acts and deeds of the great lynching army.

America has been in the lynching business for nearly fifty years and this is the first time the nation, the press and the pulpit have spoken out. After all, it might be a case of who is lynched, rather than the savage act itself, that arouses the nation.

The mob has been allowed to go on so long that lynching Negroes has become a tame business. Every once in a while the mob has to rack its brains to find a new thrill and now it crosses the white line. The nation is stirred.

For over twenty years a few individuals and some small organizations have been trying to stop the atrocities by education, appeal and legislation. The most effective organization now working in the field is the Association of Southern White Women Against Mob Violence.

Now that the lynchers have crossed the line, anti-lynching bills will be introduced in many state legislatures this year, and it is quite likely that Congress will try to get through a federal enactment. Put this fact down, legislation will not cure lynching. It will not be any more effective than was the Volstead Act, in curing the thirst for liquor. Men cannot be legislated into social attitudes, tastes, and social and moral conduct. They must be born, bred and developed into such attitudes and amenities. It has taken nearly fifty years to poison the blood of the nation. It will take fifty years to purge it. This nation has reached the state where its senses are seared, its ears deaf and its voice inarticulate against wrongs perpetrated upon citizens, who are human beings but not white. Passing an anti-lynching law is a gesture. When it comes to applying that law it will depend on the race that violates it.

The best thing that the federal government can do is to enfranchise the eight million disfranchised Negroes of the United States by enforcing the Fifteenth Amendment. If this is done the Negro will have the weapon with which to take care of himself. The sheriff who obeys the mob does so because the members of the mob are voters, and the sheriff is a candidate for office. He is looking for votes. If the Negro had the ballot, he too would meet at the polls, the sheriff and the members of the mob, who are office seekers. Instead of passing a new law, America had better try to enforce the one law that will make office seekers and office holders perform their duty when the mob comes to take a prisoner away from the law.

Furthermore, the nation will have to change its race attitude. It will have to stop looking down on the Negro with contempt, simply because he is not white. Stop teaching race hatred, race prejudice, and race superiority based on color. Such an attitude is dangerous and poisonous. It invites and encourages injustice and persecution. The Negro without the ballot, and the nation filled with contempt for him, are the two weak gaps in our national life through which blood-thirsty mobs will continue to enter and wreak vengeance upon the defenseless.

It is strange how some Americans who are wont to cry out against Reds and Anarchist, who come here from other lands, actually ignore the fact that the mob is composed of home-made anarchists, who are far more dangerous to the life of the nation than all the alien brands that will ever enter our ports. This nation has, by its very silence, grown an army of anarchists of its own. We have developed almost a national state of mind by which great groups of people in various states and communities can in a moment's time put the law down and elevate a crystallized sentiment that triumphs at once over the law of the land.

The nation condemns Governor [James] Rolph[26] for his endorsement of mob violence. Governor Rolph doubtless assumed the role of official spokesman for the thousands of Americans who have taken part in former lynchings. Up to this time the mob has not had an official leader, though the newspapers usually report that the "best citizens took part" in the feast. Governor Rolph is the first high official who has had the temerity to thrust himself forward as a leader of the national mob. He has dared to tell which side he is on, but what about the scores of governors, the thousands of preachers, the millions of "the best citizens," and the very highest federal officials, who have condoned and encouraged lynchings by their very silence, inaction or indifference? You will recall that the men who held the clothes while the mob stoned Stephen to death were put down as particeps criminis.

Let us sum up the five reasons why America has gone lynch mad:

1. National attitude of contempt for the Negro
2. Nullification of the Fifteenth Amendment
3. Emboldened by forty-five years of success of the lynching industry
4. National silence
5. In answer to the call of the blood bequeathed to their children, by two generations of lynchers.

This is some of the ripe fruit which the nation gathers, from teaching race hatred and practicing race discrimination for nearly a century.

Right about face, America. The national attitude is wrong. The national sense is seared. The blood of the nation is poisoned. America cannot be "delivered from the body of this death,"[27] unless the Christian Church preaches and practices the principles of brotherhood, and the sacredness of human personalities, and the nation itself, comes back to the letter and the spirit of the Declaration of Independence, and the National Constitution for which black and white have paid the price in blood, for equal justice.

It is a long way back, but it is the only way out and up, because only "righteousness exalteth a nation."[28]

∽

Race Attitude

From *National Notes*, vol. 37, no. 2 (December 1934), 5.

The Government has summoned thousands of social and economic doctors to find a cure for what hurts us.

Billions of dollars are being spent in a mad effort to deliver America from the body of this death.

Regardless of high hopes, high promises and high financing, this nation nor any other nation cannot recover from what actually hurts it until those three words become the kind of spirit and flesh that shall give the nation a "New Racial Attitude."

The nation has actually sown deliberately, willfully and gleefully in the calm what it is now reaping in a storm. The attitude of the American people as a whole is wrong.

She teaches even little children race ridicule, derision and hatred at home, in school literature, history, civics and geography; at play in games and athletics and toys and pictures; and in moving pictures.

She poisons their little minds. She teaches them to scorn and look down on any race that is not white. Races that are thus scorned and mistreated in turn seek to resent Anglo-Saxon arrogance and false assumption of innate superiority. Except these races repent, they shall likewise perish. We are all sinners before God.

The Challenge of the New Day: Commencement Address, May 24, 1934

From *Tuskegee Messenger* 10, no. 6 (June 1934): 2, 11.

We are on the most sacred spot in America and in the world. We are on the grounds dedicated to the future hopes and dreams, aspirations and prophesies of the founders of our democracy. You and I today are surrounded by the most marvelous achievement that has taken place in American history during the past seventy years. The class that returns here today after ten years on the firing line witnesses a new Tuskegee, its magnificent buildings, its marvelously improved campus, its splendid and modern equipment, its great faculty and the Commander-in-chief in the person of the President of Tuskegee Institute.

Today I shall speak to you as members of the graduating class and as men and women who are going to contribute their part to the building of a great, new, vital social order on our continent—you who are going to dedicate yourselves again to those spiritual and moral ideals which moved the founders of our country to build on this continent a government of the people, by the people and for the people, and as Abraham Lincoln said in his famous Gettysburg Speech, he entertained the hope that "a government so conceived and so dedicated shall not perish from the earth." If the saints are permitted to look from the battlements of heaven today they rejoice to witness this magnificent scene in the heart of the deep South wherein you are making the spiritual and social and economic contributions to our great republic. They must be happy today to see here in the midst of our new dreams, new hopes and aspirations this magnificent audience of white and black people who believe that we shall in deed and in truth build on this continent a Christian civilization not for blacks, not for whites but for all who shall come to our land and contribute spiritual, moral, social and economic advancement to the world.

I shall talk to you this afternoon on the "Challenge of the New Day." First of all what is the new day? The new day is the day Tennyson visioned in Locksley Hall:

"When I dipt into the future far as
    human eye could see;
Saw the vision of the world, and all
    the wonder that would be.
Till the war-drum throbb'd no longer,
    and the battleflags were furl'd
In the Parliament of man, the Federation
    of the world.
There the common sense of most shall
    hold a fretful realm in awe,
And the kindly earth shall slumber,
    lapt in universal law."[29]

As you go forth from here today I would have you realize that the things that have been prophesied, all the things that have been promised, all the things that are to be reaped in abundance in this world shall be enjoyed by you. Not by gift, but by struggle, by sacrifice, by indomitable will, by courage, by hope and by every human and spiritual effort that is possible for you to put forth in whatever fields you shall labor and find yourself. And as you go forth from here you will work for six things. You will dedicate yourselves to a new social order and to the building of it in the hearts of men. You will work first of all for life—abundant life—life promised by Him who came over two thousand years ago and said that he came that we might have life and that we might have it more abundantly.

You will work for liberty—absolute and complete freedom for all men of every nation under all suns and skies and flags. You will dedicate yourselves as did the man who fired the hearts and imaginations of the American people in the great struggle of the Revolution. You will stand forth as men and women in a new day facing a new challenge and speaking as did that famous, humble American who interpreted the hopes and dreams of centuries that are to come. Out of humble Williamsburg, Virginia, realizing the purposes for which this republic was founded, Patrick Henry stood forth as you shall stand forth and declared for our new day and for those new challenges that "it matters not the cost to other men but as for me, give me liberty or give me death." That challenge to America, that rededication to the Declaration of Independence rings and reverberates in the hearts of all men in America, in the North and in the South.

You shall work for another ideal. You shall work for love, the love of humanity, the love of the humblest—the least man and the lost man whether he lives in America or in India or in China or in Burma or in the isles of the sea. We shall work and dedicate ourselves to the end that all men everywhere shall enjoy the love of God and develop the best that is in them. And we shall not by act nor deed nor word nor association put a single stumbling block in the way of any humble struggling human being in all the world. We shall work for love.

You shall go forth and accept the new challenge not only for love but for learning. There is no substitute for learning. The hope of every hamlet and section of our America and every part of the world wherever mankind is found is that we shall give men the learning which Tuskegee represents—the learning which all great schools have. Schools that have received the sacrificial benedictions of philanthropists and the wonderful and rich contributions of the tax-payers of America and the world. It is the investment of our hopes and dreams for the generations that are to come. We shall dedicate ourselves to the great ideal that all men everywhere must know—must learn—must be given an opportunity to develop the best in them. You must dedicate yourselves—your mental powers to the fields in which you find yourselves—to science, to art, to literature.

Then you must work for another "L"—Labor. Work for it to the point that every man, high or low, will be given an opportunity to earn his bread by the sweat of his brow, to contribute to the support of his family, to purchase a home, to cultivate his own farm and like the famous blacksmith that every child knows about he can "look the whole world in the face for he owes not any man."

We must work for leisure. Having worked for life, for liberty, for love, for learning, and for an opportunity to labor, and having dedicated ourselves to the advancement of human society in whatever field we find ourselves, we owe it to ourselves and to our great social order to spend our hours of leisure away from work and toil and strife, that we may learn again what to man and what to God we owe. It will be that great period of meditation, of renewing our spiritual selves from which we may go forth into the struggle of life, into the great avenues of employment and take our place beside our brother. It is this ideal of leisure for which we shall have to battle all over our country and the world. As long as men and women are being turned out of schools like this, we shall dedicate ourselves to the great ideal of giving them a chance to devote themselves to these things for the advancement of human society, to the development of cultural things that make life worthwhile.

So we rededicate ourselves to the new day in spite of the darkness that surrounds us, in spite of the depression, which after all is not a depression only but a sort of spiritual, moral and social discipline through which we are passing. When we come out of it as individuals, as groups or as nations, if we have taken our medicine like men and women, we are going develop for the next generation whether it be twenty-five or fifty or a hundred years hence a type of man and woman stronger and more durable mentally, socially and spiritually. This discipline through which we are passing is going to be the best tonic that we have ever had, serving to tone up our inner equipment.

We are going to accept the challenge to build a new social order. We have dedicated ourselves for the past hundred years to building a material civilization and there are those who sit in this audience today who are in doubt and wonder what is going to become of us when the things all around us seem to be crumbling and failing; when bank accounts and great fortunes which were built up in the past hundred or more years have been wiped away; when the material possessions that we had, homes, farms and things of the flesh have been taken away. You stand in wonderment as to what will become of us. When we talk about the war clouds that are gathering in Europe, Russia, China or in South America, when all European territory is in a restless condition and in America we talk of the failures of the past few years, you are shocked with the facts and begin to think that all civilization is trembling in the balance and that nobody knows when the night will come. I stand here young men and young women of the Class of 1934, and say to you that what you see all about you are things material, nothing to be compared with those things moral and spiritual out of which you are going to build the new social order.

The Lord is preparing some spiritual giant, some magnetic human being to deliver the people from the bondage of this material world. We are going to be more humanitarian, more spiritual and dynamic. It is to be a civilization such as we have never known.

So this afternoon you young men and women who are soon going away sit here in doubt, and wonder whether you will get a job, whether there is a ready-made job for you in the world. I have come all the way down to Tuskegee to tell you NO! All the jobs we have had are taken. There are no ready-made jobs anywhere; but there are one hundred and twenty million jobs that can be made; and that is your job. If you can't take that challenge, if you can't go out and blaze new trails and find new avenues of employment make new roads, find new highways and discover new ways to do old things—if you can't do that, well, "look to the Lord and be dismissed."

Open your mouth and the Lord will fill it—with air.

The civilization now in the making, spiritual, moral, social and mental is yours. It is yours to make, yours to possess and yours to glorify. Men before you made the civilization of which they were a part or they gave to the world new ideas and started it off on a new trail. We have come over it for some two thousand years working on the ideals and dreams of one man here and another there, in one generation after another. We started it with that man who came to redeem this world with an individual ideal of human brotherhood, social justice and the idea of peace on earth good will toward men. For two thousand years the world has been marching toward that social ideal. We have not arrived and we are thousands of years distant from it, but we are facing in the right direction, marching towards justice, equality, brotherhood.

During these thousands of years men have waged bloody warfare for life, liberty, love, learning, labor and leisure and it is in part going to be realized by this generation; then they will pass on the torch to another generation. But we are going to witness a new heaven and a new earth right here worked out in the hearts of men. It is coming in proportion as we dedicate our faith, our courage, our hopes and our indomitable will. Young people, there is no force on earth, no handicap, no barrier on earth that can stay any race or individual who organizes its courage, its faith, its hopes, its industry and its indomitable will. You can't defeat it. You may delay it, or place a barrier around; you may block up the stream, but it will swing around the dam and join the current and continue on its way to the great ocean beyond.

I want you today to remember that there are thousands of men who dream dreams for you; you are realizing some of them today. But you do not realize it fully because you are too near to it, too much a part of it, to sense what is taking place right here in the southland. Today in spite of the prejudice, barriers and handicaps we are thousands and thousands of years, which are but a yesterday in the divine plan, thousands of years beyond the dreams of our fathers over seventy years ago. It has been a marvelous development in such little time.

It is a long way from an ox-cart to a good car hitting on all cylinders, but you have made it and you have made it in less than twenty-five years. And we are going to make more speed—I mean mental, moral, social and spiritual speed in the next twenty-five years than we have made in the past one hundred years. We are going to make it because we desire it. In the heart of every young man who sits in this audience today is the desire to be a man, to be somebody and to do something and to go somewhere. It is in the heart and it is burning as a spirit aflame. Out of that human desire we are going to create a civilization characterized by courage, faith, hope, cooperation and sympathy. We are going to get it because men desire it. It is true of every generation. Martin Luther's reformation was a success because he dreamed a dream. Yes, that is true, but there was in the hearts of millions of people of his day the desire for certain spiritual freedom. They hungered and thirsted for it and when he tacked the thesis on the door and was responsible for the calling of the Diet of Worms, it was a declaration of what men had desired for generations hence they caught it up, fanned the flame and baptized it with the spirit of their great desire. So today, we are marching to a new reformation of social and spiritual betterment in spite of difficulties. I would have you realize that in the challenge of our new day these things are going to come in America and in the world. We are going to forget this incidental thing, color, and come to the day of which Emerson wrote, "if you can make a better mouse-trap, or preach a better sermon than anybody else though you build your house in the woods the world is going to make a beaten path to your door."

What are some of things to be done? First, we have got to have better automobiles. Those out there twenty-five years from now will be objects of curiosity in some museum. They will go out of style but some mind is going to conceive new ways to build automobiles and to improve them. Some mind is going to conceive new things in medicine, new ways of keeping men well, ways of building in men the physical and moral stamina that will enable them to carry on in their work. Some mind is going to conceive a finer and better way of lighting our homes and heating our houses. We now heat them from things in the cellar called furnaces or stoves but some mind is going to conceive a way of heating homes directly from the mine without hauling coal from all over the United States and then carrying it downstairs. They are going to get sense enough to pipe it to us so we can press a button and have heat. Somebody is going to conceive a finer and better way to stay up in the air. The world will not think of the color of the skin but will accept whatever contrivance or machine or conveyance that will get one safely where one wants to go—and on time.

I want you to take the struggles, the hardships and the handicaps of this civilization and turn them into stepping-stones. That is what other races have done, black and white. Disregarding handicaps, they have decided within their own souls that they were men and could look this old world in the face, could beat down barriers and climb the rough side of the mountain. I heard an old woman praying one time. She asked, "Lord please don't take me up on the rough side of the mountain." I spoke to her afterwards and told her please not to include me in that number because that was not the side I wanted to go up on. I wanted to go up on the rough side because I knew there was some chance for me to get to the top, but if I went up the smooth side I might slip down. You young men and young women are going up the rough side of the mountain, going through handicaps and barriers; you will have to meet the struggles of this world but out of the depression you are going to come forth a new group of men and women, strong and with powerful characteristics and lasting influence.

∾

Ballot and Dollar Needed to Make Progress, Not Pity

From *Pittsburgh Courier*, February 17, 1934, 2.

The following self-pitying, sycophantic, poetic, prattle appeared in one of our papers last week.

> "What will become of us?
> Can we but know?
> Must we be treated thus
> Where e'er we go?
> Is there no law for us
> We who are weak?
> What will become of us?
> We, whom you seek?
>
> What will become of us,
> As things now are?
> Is there no help for us,
> Near or afar?
> Must we be victims of

A White man's hate?
What will become of us
Sooner or late?

What will become of us,
The Negro Race?
Must we be subject to
Every disgrace?
Shall no one lend a hand
To right the wrong?
What will become of us?
How long? How long?"

Well, Mr., Mrs., or Miss Hazel, you talk like a dear little child. You pity the Negro's condition and beg the white man to have mercy on him. Mercy? Don't you know that people who pity themselves or wince under blows are set upon and beaten by their adversaries.

You don't know the white man. In fact, you don't know human nature. It is human nature to either eschew or kick around or walk over whiners and beggars. That's why the Negro is treated thus. But you will say this is a Christian nation and it should show mercy. Would to God that it were, but it is the most lawless and desperately wicked nation on the globe. Therefore, we will have to take it as it is. So don't expect to be given quarters.

You are wasting time begging this white race for mercy. In fact, the Negro does not need mercy. He needs common sense—that's all.

You ask in a piteous tone, what will become of us? Not one whit more than we ourselves choose to become.

Figuratively speaking, there are five classes of Negroes: mud sills, door mats, stepping stones, hound dogs, and bull dogs. What will become of these five classes? Get ready to weep, Mrs., Mr., or Miss Hazel because the mud sills will be walked over; the stepping stones will be walked upon, the hound dogs will be kicked around; and the bull dogs will get what they go after.

The poet does not seem to realize that the American Negro has enough weapons in his own possession right now to use effectively to serve notice on the world that he is taking himself seriously and means to fight his battles with the only weapon he has. And, take it from me, those weapons can be used effectively.

The Negro has enough ballots in his hands and enough spending change in his jeans to get what he needs and to get him where he should go. The ballot and the dollar are the shield and the sword for any people in a democracy. If they do not learn to evaluate them and use them to protect themselves and to fight their battles, they will always be mud sills, door mats, stepping stones, and hound dogs.

When the Negro has the ballot, he has the one thing that the white man fears. When he has the dollar he has the only earthly thing that the white man worships. The ballot is the Negro's sacred, blood bought heritage; the dollar is his economic sweat bought possession. Instead of whining about what the white man is doing to him, the Negro can take his ballot and do or undo him at the ballot box. Instead of fussing about what the white man is not doing for him, he can spend his dollar where he can be employed to do something for himself. It isn't what white people are doing to the Negro that counts against him half as much as what he is not doing for himself with what he has.

Mr., Mrs., or Miss Hazel asks poetically, "Shall no one lend a hand?" No! The Negro has his two hands and from now on he will get what he wants. Fighters for his emancipation did lend hands when his hands were chained. They did not stop until they were unchained and a weapon (the ballot) was put into their hands, with which he could defend himself.

Do you recall that when Israel lived in the midst of a strong race that they complained all the time about their burdens? Finally God had a talk with Moses, Israel's great leader. Moses' excuse was that his people did not have weapons with which to fight their enemies. God asked Moses only one question, "What is that in thine hand?"—Moses said—"A rod." Jehovah commanded him to use it. The rod seemed so insignificant that Moses hesitated. Finally, he decided to obey God. Israel was delivered.

The Negro will have to do the same thing. When the Negro learns to use what he has, he will get what he needs and get it more abundantly. Not until the Negro stops spending his money with anybody and everybody who grins at him, and stops giving his ballot to men who will not give him an equal opportunity to learn and an equal opportunity to earn, in exchange for it, will he get anywhere or be anybody.

∞

Declaration of 1776 Is Cause of the Harlem Riot

From *Afro-American*, April 13, 1935.

Harlem did not have a "race" riot. It had a "human" revolt.[30]

Communistic propaganda, Red agitation and unemployment are not the causes. Nor did a colored boy, a nickel pen-knife and a screaming woman cause the uprising. Hush the voice that tells you so.

There is a world of difference between local manifestations of an uprising and its creative influences. A statement of that fact seems superfluous, but I make it because people so easily mistake the manifestation for the cause.

That was the mistake of the Pharisees whose case Jesus summed up in one sentence. He said to them: "You make void the law through your traditions." That is exactly what America has done in the case of the colored man.

Abuses Tolerated

This nation openly endorses, tolerates, and legalizes the very abuses against which she originally waged a bloody revolution.

A colored boy, a nickel pen-knife and a screaming woman were no more the cause of the Harlem uprising in 1935 than was a shipload of tea in the Boston harbor, in 1773, the cause of the Revolutionary War. The tea party episode was only the manifestation. "A long train of abuses" created the cause.

Samuel Adams feared that the colonists were being lulled into indifference to their rights. He was mistaken. The Boston tea party convinced him.

The causes of the Harlem riot are not far to seek. They lie buried beneath mountains of injustices done the colored man in every state and in every relationship, through years of "patient sufferance" on his part. In dealing with colored people, America makes "void the law" through customs—that's the deep-seated cause of the Harlem riot.

CAUSE OUT OF REACH
A few years ago there was a gigantic explosion of dynamite on the New Jersey side of New York Bay. It shattered thousands of windows in Manhattan and even broke dishes in Brooklyn, fifteen miles away. All the fire engines in the lower part of New York came out and raced helplessly up and down the streets looking for the cause of the damage. They found plenty of manifestation of the explosion, but did not discover the cause, for that was miles out of their reach.

The framers of the Declaration of Independence prophesied that uprisings would occur "in the course of human events," if people are denied those inalienable rights to which the "laws of nature and of nature's God entitle them."

Re-read their prophecy—their justification for such natural, human resentment after patient Sufferance. It is written in every American history. They declared that "when a long train of abuses and usurpations pursuing, invariably the same object, evinces a design to reduce them under absolute despotism, it is their right, it is their duty to throw off such government, and to provide new guards for their future security."

OPPOSED INJUSTICE
If that's Red,[31] then the writers of the Declaration of Independence were very Red. They told Americans not to stand injustice after "patient sufferance."

The colored man has reached the endurance limit—the point where the Declaration of Independence says it is time to revolt when the "invasion on the rights of the people seem most likely to effect their safety and happiness and obstruct the administration of justice." Yes, a long train of abuses caused the Harlem uprising.

A few days ago the daily papers excoriated Secretary Perkins for permitting deportable aliens to remain in this country. They called them Reds and enemies to American institutions and ideals. There are too many of them here, they say.

The newspapers are right. Since America manufactures her own Reds through the lynching industry and other forms of base injustice, she has a huge surplus of Reds of her own on hand.

Saves Uncle Sam's Face

It saves America's face to put the cause on alien propagandists, Communists and Reds—or on unemployment. They are good alibis, but they are not on that "long train of abuses" that actually engender bitterness and resentment.

America rewards all Reds—home-made and imported—by giving them unlimited opportunities to do anything they are big enough to do, but she seldom gives loyal, law-abiding blacks a square deal.

Day after day, year after year, decade after decade, black people have been robbed of their inalienable rights. They have been goaded, hounded, driven around, herded, held down, kicked around and roasted alive, by America's home-made Reds. In Harlem the cornered rats fought back. The worms turned over and turned around.

Cramped in Harlem

The majority of the colored people of Harlem came from mob-ruled sections, or are the victims of persecutions of various kinds. They came to Harlem seeking opportunity to enjoy life, liberty, labor and happiness. They are beginning to feel cramped and handicapped. Their hearts are hurt. They find themselves apparently pursued by the very evils from which they fled.

America's age-old attitude on the race question is the cause of the Harlem riot. That "long train of abuses" is a magazine of powder. An unknown boy was simply the match—a frightened woman's screams lighted it and threw it into the magazine of powder, and Harlem blew up.

Colored folks feel that Harlem is their last stand.

∞

This Is the War of the Five Rs: Race, Room, Raw Materials, Rights, Religion

From *Pittsburgh Courier*, January 31, 1942, 8.

This is a war for the five Rs—RAW MATERIAL, RACE, ROOM, RIGHTS, AND RELIGION.

First, RAW MATERIALS. All the progressive nations of the world want all the copper, zinc, tin, petroleum, oil, and rubber they can get in order to "keep 'em diving; keep 'em rolling; keep 'em flying; and keep 'em defending the five freedoms forever."

All men are fighting for something or against something. The clear visioned are fighting to set the stage for building a civilization that, because of its quality and strength—based on supreme values, will endure a thousand years and will then be good for a thousand more. No normal man or woman in the world can be neutral or indifferent in this undreamed-of world circling crisis. Race, room, raw materials, rights, and religion are the stakes. The fight is on all fronts, for all-out justice, for all men.

The question of race looms bigger in this war[32] than it has ever loomed before in the history of the world. It is fomenting intense race hatred. The slogan seems to be "Hate them and then you can annihilate them without any compunction of conscience."

HATE IS CHILD OF HELL

Hate can spread a conflagration that will turn this world into a veritable inferno. Hate is a child of hell. "War is hell," said [William Tecumseh] Sherman; and now we have both. But, "believe it or not," when this war is over THE WORLD WILL BE DONE WITH HATE as a part of its inner and organized equipment for endurance and security.

Nations are fighting for more ROOM. Those that have dense populations want more breathing space. They seem to choose to want to breathe in lands that are rich in raw materials. Therefore, they are not only fighting for (room) earth, but for the fullness thereof. They want land—through whose mighty subterranean veins oil flows unceasingly; and lands whose bowels bulge with coal, metals, and minerals.

GOD-GIVEN RIGHTS

Men are fighting for their God-given RIGHTS that belong to man as man. No man, set of men or governments, have a right to deny them. A true democracy is built on acknowledgment of, and granting to, every human being "certain inalienable RIGHTS, among which are life, liberty, and the pursuit of happiness." Any laws, customs, schemes, or devices for the circumvention or abrogation of these rights are not only undemocratic, but ungodly. Such laws or devices make a so-called democracy insecure; and, its development (in segregated groups) sporadic, and out of harmony with the ideals of a true democracy.

Want Real Democracy

The question for all nations that are signed up to fight to "make the world safe for democracy," is to decide whether they want a real democracy or a dual democracy. Mankind has had enough of the dual. They want the real. This war is for the purpose of correcting all those travesties of democratic principles that have given certain privileged groups in democracies the right to suspend the law, or put themselves above the law, in dealing with minority groups in so-called democracies. Any attempt to build democracies with "A house divided against itself" will fail—ignominiously.

This is a fight for the DIVINE RIGHTS OF MEN. The future of every race is definitely and seriously involved. This is a fight for freedom to build the Kingdom of God in the hearts of men on this earth. It is a FIGHT against that act of infamy that seeks to stamp out the RELIGION of Jesus Christ (or the freedom of religions), and to force upon society a man-made religion.

No weapons that are fashioned against the Christian religion shall prosper. So says Jehovah—and His followers are enlisted to destroy those weapons.

Jesus Christ came into the world for ONE SPECIFIC PURPOSE: *He came to interpret God and life to mankind.* He emphasized the fact that GOD means LOVE; and that LIFE means JUSTICE and BROTHERHOOD. The realization of the supreme purpose of the religion of Jesus Christ is at the bottom of this great war. "God moves in a mysterious way His wonders to perform."

Man wants land. God wants man. These two objectives are now poles apart. God will permit wards and destruction throughout the earth, until man puts God's objective for man, and God's eternal values first.

This war, if fought to a finish—and it must be in order to make the game (gain) worth the (cost) powder, will purge the world of more sin, and do it more lasting GOOD than anything that has happened on this planet since Jesus arose from the dead.

The position of minority groups throughout the world will be greatly advanced as a result of the conflict. Minorities will be accorded more of their fundamental rights and will be heartened to perform more of their sacred duties. Majorities will be cured of their thirst for power to be used by exploit and dominate the lives of the weak. They will take time to plan a social order built on justice and goodwill. All men will be in on the program and plan for world redemption.

The war for these great and enduring values will be a long and sacrificial one, but if from this Aceldama[33] (world-wide field of blood) comes a new world army that shall fight together to uphold justice and make brotherhood real, these millions of "dead shall not have died in vain."

Education and Justice

From Nannie Helen Burroughs, *What Do You Think?* (Washington, DC: n.p., 1950), 11–12.

Education and justice are democracy's only life insurance. Without these mere armourment is so much junk and high preachments about democracy is so much bunk.

We talk much about making America safe for democracy. The only way to make America safe for democracy is to make her what she is supposed to be in matters of justice and equality of opportunity for all her citizens.

In a democracy a man is either a citizen, an alien, a ward, or a tool. He is a citizen if he enjoys all of the rights guaranteed him by the constitution and reciprocates by doing his full duty as a citizen; he is an alien if he has sworn allegiance to the flag; he is a ward if he is cared for by the government; he is a tool if he allows himself to be used by citizens and politicians to promote themselves and keep him looking to them for creature existence.

If he accepts the position of a tool without eternal, intelligent and effective protest, he is not quite ready to live in a democracy. Men who are satisfied with less than absolute freedom and even-handed justice can never become factors in a government of men who will ask nothing more or take nothing less than what belongs to them as men.

Justice and equality of opportunity are the only two ideals in a democracy that are worth living and dying for. This nation has promised them to all citizens, regardless of race. The Negro wants them so that he, like other men, can have something that is worth defending—and depending on.

Put the Leaven in the Lump

From Nannie Helen Burroughs, *What Do You Think?* (Washington, DC: n.p., 1950), 36–38.

Democracy is like a lump of leaven which a woman took and hid in three measures of meal, until the whole was leavened. Yeast is a strange substance. Scientists do not understand it. To this natural mystery, Democracy may well be compared; for it will leaven men, give equal opportunity and bring equal results.

The American revolutionists, when they talked of "certain unalienable rights," when they justified armed rebellion by appealing to ultimate truth, and when they based their new government upon "equality," little knew how far their radical principles would carry them, but they believed it would carry the nation forward.

They believed their program would bring independence from England; but the powerful genius of equity they had invoked would not stop there. It would work "until the whole lump became leavened."

We are beginning to get some notion of the extent of the power and reach of Democracy. Simply stated, it means that every human being born into the world has a right to equal opportunities with every other human being. That is the idea that is transforming the world today. That is the meaning of the coming of Christ into the world. That is the meaning of 1776. That is the significance of 1861.

It took almost a century for Americans to see that conviction could not hold slaves. Since the Rebellion the yeast of justice has worked vigorously in the lump.

At the bottom of all labor troubles, is the yeast working for justice. Underneath all the stew of strikes and lockouts is the unconquerable desire for equal rights for all. It is not socialism that is coming, nor communism, nor any other imported scheme, but the cry of the soul of every man for justice. That is Democracy in travail.

Democracy will eventually unloose the God-given wealth of the world to all men. For wealth will never be secure until it also is democratic.

What about women? They were once bound. The "Woman Suffrage Movement" was but another indication of the working of the yeast of Democracy. It worked until the world conceded the fact that women were entitled to basic rights as a human being.

The public school system is the result of the same leaven. It means that every child brought into the world has a right to a decent training for life.

Yeast works. All social changes are the result of work. Democracy brings constant change. Democracy means continuous, progressive readjustment. Of course, that means danger. There are always those who fear change. For change threatens established things. The yeast is working today. The call to the nation to apply all Civil Rights regardless of race is fermenting and foaming furiously. The Civil Rights bill will eventually be passed.

Nothing so hates change and defends established custom as does ancient tradition. How men fought to preserve "the divine right of kings," to maintain class and caste, to uphold ecclesiastical absolutism, to keep their clutch upon inherited and unearned wealth! But little by little has the yeast of Democracy permeated this society. It will continue until the whole lump is leavened. All men in America will have an equal chance to learn and an equal chance to earn. It's coming! Slow, but the yeast is working!

Second Class Citizens

From Nannie Helen Burroughs, *What Do You Think?* (Washington, DC: n.p., 1950), 32–35.

In this very century, Negroes—who are determined to become American citizens, will have to fight a war that will win for them all of the rights for which the wars of 1776 and 1865 were fought—freedom from oppression and unjust taxation without representation, and freedom from physical slavery.

The Negro is still a slave in America because laws keep him in physical, economic and social servitude. America is as far from being a democracy in practice and in spirit, today, as she was in 1858.

She has progressed in writing words "about" democracy and in making face-saving gestures in certain places and on special occasions, but in practice and at heart she belies her own pretense of love for a real democracy. She writes and promises one thing and practices exactly the opposite.

In practice, the so-called Christian Church in America follows the same pattern in its treatment of the Negro as a brother, that the government sets in dealing with the Negro, as a citizen—and yet, the Church claims to believe in absolute separation of Church and State. Where? And in dealing with whom? The Church and State surely are together in their attitude and actions on the treatment of the Negro.

We have come to the place in American life where all who want this nation to endure must work definitely and doggedly against all legalized, traditional or accepted arrangements that make race the basic requirement for the enjoyment of equal opportunities.

Jim Crow cars, ghettoes and inequalities in education and employment are rank enemies to the development of democratic ideals and practices.

America knows, too well, that she simply cannot make self-respecting citizens in Jim Crow cars. The sole purpose of Jim Crow cars, segregation and ghettoes is to subject Negroes to constant humiliation. Every form of discrimination does something to the personality and soul of decent Negroes.

Piling Negroes up in "projects" is the latest and most vicious social millstone device for drowning the race. In twenty-five years from now, nearly everyone of the many "projects" will be in various stages of deterioration and decay. Those who built them will be rich; those who live in them will be worse off than they were when they moved in.

Home ownership—be the home ever so humble—is the first step towards a better future for all Americans. The pattern of the projects is to provide tiny rooms for Negro families to live in; run stores to serve them and "go on about your white business." Negroes who stand for it and like it are not doing any thinking.

When the Negro makes up his mind that he is through being a second class citizen and decides that whatever it takes to move up into the first class that he is going to do it or report to God the reason why, America will let him pass—perhaps reluctantly—but, she will, at least, stop setting up what she considers expedient arrangements and barriers based on race. She will learn that the Negro is working and fighting his way through to sound thorough-going Americanism.

There must come out of the Negro race a leadership that can inspire and lead the masses out of this social, economic and spiritual morass.

Negroes must work to remove every apparently justifiable excuse for dual standards. More efficient service, better conduct, and better kept homes are the only answers to America's "excuse" for not dealing justly with Negro citizens.

America's way of dealing with her citizens who are farthest behind is neither democratic nor Christian. Her very purpose is to keep the Negro behind—"prove" that he is inferior. Why try to force the American brand of Democracy on Europe, if it is unsafe to give it to thirteen million American citizens, who are entitled to it by every right and sacrifice by which men earn justice?

There are not thirteen million citizens in any land who are more entitled to justice, under the law, at the hand of their government, than is the American Negro in his own land. But laws are on the statute books to keep him from the enjoyment of basic rights or even protection as a citizen.

In America, laws are passed to actually prevent Democracy from working here. As a result we have three classes of citizens:

1. Those who are above the law. They lynch and treat Negroes as they please.
2. Those who keep within the law, but are not so keen on letting citizens of color in on equal footing or they are silent in the face of gross injustices.
3. And those who are below the law. They are Negro citizens. They have no rights that white men are bound to respect. This is American Democracy in practice at home.

From it, may the good Lord deliver us.

Slavery Was a Success

From Nannie Helen Burroughs, *What Do You Think?* (Washington, DC: n.p., 1950), 61–66.

American slavery was a success. It did not do anything FOR the Negro, directly, but it did three important things TO him.

1. It woke him up.
2. It made him work.
3. It brought him in.

An undertaking is a success if it accomplishes the purpose intended by its promoters. The purpose of Slavery was:

1. To get free labor.
2. To build up the cotton industry in the South.

But, all institutions and inventions have their by-products. Slavery was no exception.

It also happens, again and again, that the by-products turn out to be more valuable than the primary invention. Then, too, through experimentation, by-products are often various, more beautiful and profitable. That was true of Slavery.

But, how did slave holders make a success of the institution? They were dealing with people, who were unaccustomed to the climate, the people, the kinds of labor, the orderly exactions that are absolutely essential to success in any business.

The Africans, that were stolen from Africa, lassoed, brought here and sold into slavery, knew absolutely nothing about the why of all the trials through which they passed. Ten generations passed through the institution. Millions of them cried to high heaven "how long, dear Savior, O how long?"

But, it was several generations before they knew upon whom to call for deliverance. Put a peg there, and go on to answer the main question. How did the South make a success of its gigantic economic undertaking? Slavery was a business. The first requirement of successful business is that it moves on time.

Slave holders, therefore, *woke their Negroes up*. Yes, woke them up. No late when you get ready; if you feel like it or not come at all, makeshift workers. Yes, from dawn to dark, they "drove" human beings to increased production and personal happiness for the White South.

This is not a discussion of the wrongness of the institution of slavery. It is to put our finger on why the economic plan was such a success.

The Slave holders *made their Negroes work*. That is the only way that any people can succeed. Since Southerners were not going to do the work themselves, they had to get somebody whom they could make to do it for them. Human slavery was the only answer. Slaves worked everywhere—on plantation and in and around the "big house"—doing with their might whatever they were told to do. But that is not all of the secret of the success of Slavery.

Slave owners *brought their Negroes in*. No staying out all night—no, not even at prayer meetings. Between the patrols and blood hounds, slave owners brought their Negroes in. They were not particularly interested in the physical wellbeing of slaves, but they knew workers could not do a good day's work unless they had sufficient sleep. They were always concerned about the health of their slaves—for economic reasons.

Right or wrong, the South made fair success of slave labor, only because it applied the three rules, essential to success in any business:

1. Wide awake on the job.
2. Work when you work.
3. Control your habits. (Come in on time.)

But, "God moves in a mysterious way, His wonders to perform." He makes the wrath of man to praise Him. While slave owners were waking the Negro up physically, God was waking him up spiritually and morally. Those prayer meetings, with turned down pots, were harbingers of the day of upturned faces.

Those church gallery Negroes were the advance guard of Richard Allen, in the A.M.E. Church in Philadelphia, and George Liele, David George and Jessie Peters, Baptist Trial blazers at Silver Bluff, South Carolina, and Savannah, Georgia.

That army of silent Negroes on every Southern plantation, woke up mentally, and so sincerely did they desire to throw off the shackles of ignorance, that as Edwin Embree[34] puts it in "Brown America," "The crusaders from the North came to a people, flaming with a faith as great as their own."

It is not possible to kindle such faith and fire in a day. Long years of toil brought it. The longing on the part of the slave to control his own life was a moral revolt against slavery. That is where freedom begins—in a deep desire in the soul, to be free—that is where education in the masses begins—in a profound desire to know.

Slavery gave the Negroes faith in God. They kept that faith growing by creating songs of hope. They made their own music to soothe their souls—not a word of hate did they breathe. They saw the hand of God in the night, leading them on into the light. They asked each other in song "Tell Me How Did You Feel. . . . Leaning on the Lord?"

Slavery was a success. The institution was begun with several thousand Negro slaves and ended with over four million free men. It multiplied in various ways. It started with a poor, undeveloped Southland, and ended with plantations rich enough to wage a bloody Civil War over in an effort to continue the institution. It started with slaves and ended with free men. Free men are worth infinitely more to a Democracy than slaves.

Now, as to the by-products. The Negro went into slavery a heathen, he came out a Christian. He went in ignorant, with no inner desire to learn, he came out—hungering and thirsting after knowledge. He went in an unskilled hewer of wood and drawer of water, he came out with many skills and delightful manners.

Mr. Embree gives us a beautiful picture of the Negro, immediately after Slavery, when he says in his "Brown America," "By a fire in the woods at night, a dozen or more people of both sexes and of all ages sat about with their books in their hands, studying their lessons. Out of the House of Bondage. —Sometimes they would fasten their primers between their plough handles, so that they could read as they ploughed." The faith was pathetic—"The enthusiastic learners got up before day and studied in their cabins by light of fire knots." It was ludicrous—"It sometimes happened that those who could read better than they could write became teachers of writing and those who could write better than they could read, teachers of reading." Oh, that the Negro of today would recapture their spirit.

Summed up, the immediate and invaluable by-products of slavery were the love of the early freed men for freedom, education, a little land, and good religion—a passion for these fully possessed them.

Some slave owners helped plant the seed out of their sense of stewardship, but the majority of slaves got it through hard trials and great tribulations. Such trials developed a spiritual ruggedness that produced such men and women as Lott Carey, John Jasper, Sojourner Truth, Richard Allen, Frederick Douglass, Daniel Payne, Harriet Tubman, Robert Williams, Albert T. Jones, W. S. Scarborough and Benjamin T. Montgomery.[35]

Slavery was a success because it gave us men who loved freedom. Yes, the way was devious and difficult, but it was God's plan and now that he has established us in this materially rich country, and each Negro owns himself, it is up to each Negro to do FOR himself,

Mentally and Spiritually—(Wake his Negro up).
Physically—(Make his Negro work).
Socially—(Bring his Negro in—Practice Self-control).

—what the South did to make the physical institution of Slavery a success.

The by-products are gold in the MINE, but the Negro must MINE it. That is God's plan for the Negro in America. There are men and women of good will in the white race who will work with us to reach this Christian goal, but, it is up to the Negro to make his own freedom a success. In order to do it, he must:

1. Wake his Negro up.
2. Make his Negro work.
3. Bring his Negro in.

∞

The Meaning of Cooperation

From Nannie Helen Burroughs, *What Do You Think?* (Washington, DC, n.p., 1950), 124–26.

One of the big words of our day is "cooperation." It is on the lips of all progressive people, and in every workable program. It is a social ideal that enables them to find ways of working together, effectively. It assures achievement, good will, progress and peace on earth. It is made largely of unselfish attitudes, clear vision and common sense—combined to produce definite results in a cause in which two individuals, or groups or organizations are mutually interested or effected.

Cooperation is a planned working relationship of reciprocal benefit to all parties to the compact. Groups that desire the same thing are willing to share in the work incident to getting it because they enjoy, individually and collectively, the benefits that accrue from their united effort. They work as equals. They are co-partners, co-workers, co-sufferers in the undertaking. They share and share alike in labor, sacrifice and results. Each does all he can to help the other. Their common prayer is "help us to help each other, Lord." They share the responsibility in such a way that each does for the other what neither could do, effectively, without the other.

Cooperation enables a group that is distinctly separate organically to submerge its evident difference in order to achieve and glorify nobler ideals for the good of the whole and without which ideals neither group could reach the highest goal.

Cooperation gives us the opportunity of working close enough to people to acquire first hand knowledge of their problems. First hand knowledge makes us more tolerant. In cooperation, we contribute time, mind, influence or means, mutually and jointly to advance a common cause.

Cooperation is never a one-sided service. It is a dual service in which plans or programs are clearly presented and in which each group agrees to help the other and takes pleasure in so doing. Cooperation is a plan by which the left wing group gives six and the right wing group gives a half dozen. The exchange is not similar in kind, but it is similar in spirit and ability. The ideal in cooperation is that each shall do faithfully according to his ability and in the finest kind of spirit.

Without cooperation we can do nothing worth while in any relationship or in any field of service. No individual, no race or nation can live and grow without it. The most essential thing for us to keep on learning, from the cradle to the grave, is how to work with people and like it and like them in spite of marked differences of color, race, character or culture.

This does not mean that we must like peoples' faults and weaknesses, but it does mean that if we are going to get anywhere in this world that we must like them in spite of evident and glaring differences. In Christian cooperation, men of all races enjoy working together for the betterment of their brothers because they believe in the power of the Christian religion as a character building, transforming, equalizing agency.

Learning to work together, happily, helpfully, respectfully and hopefully are the greatest social and spiritual achievements in human relationships. Peoples and races that do it most successfully are the most highly civilized.

Brotherhood and Democracy

From Nannie Helen Burroughs Papers, 1900–1963, Manuscript Division, Library of Congress.

"Greater love hath no man than this." One day, Westminster Abbey was crowded with great men of England, in the midst of whom stood two black men from the jungles of Africa—black men who buried David Livingstone's heart in the heart of Africa, embalmed his body, and carried it on their shoulders a *thousand* miles to the ship, and sat by it night and day until it rested in Westminster Abbey, England's burial place of kings and notables.

David Livingstone was a white man who gave himself a ransom for Africa's millions. His body was worn as thin as parchment, through thirty attacks of African fever, brought on by his relentless search for the headwaters of the Nile River, the hiding place of notorious slave raiders. He died in the densest forest, with no member of his own race near, to cool his fevered brow or close his glazing eyes. From his death bed in that solitude he sent to the world the most challenging message that has ever come out of Africa. "All I can add in my solitude," said he, "is, may heaven's rich blessing come down on everyone who would heal this open sore of the world."

There is another immortal scene. It is at Gettysburg. There stands Abraham Lincoln, the rock in a weary land. He looks out over the hills of Gettysburg, all billowy with the graves of America's noble dead. His face is plowed deep with soul sufferings. His eyes are heavy with sorrow, but his heroic spirit is lifted by power divine, and his lips are anointed with matchless love. He spoke as never man spoke before, nor since, on this Continent.

That was America speaking. That day she rededicated herself to her high purpose—the betterment of *all* the people. Her voice filled the earth with new home.

We have in these two immortal scenes the noblest expression of brotherhood on the one hand, and the most profound meaning of democracy on the other. Regardless of the fact that there is still much land to possess, on all fronts, our country has made marvelous and matchless progress in the fields of inter-racial understanding, cooperation, and good will.

Miracles have been wrought here during the past seventy-five years. The shackles of slavery have been broken; noble teachers and founders of schools for freedmen lived and worked among us; the souls of men have been saved; the scales of ignorance have been removed from the eyes of millions; the love of liberty has become a cherished possession.

In spite of handicaps and barriers of every conceivable kind, the American Negro has made greater progress in religion, in education, in material advancement and in social adjustment, in seventy years, than any group of Negroes anywhere in the world.

In spite of the fact that the Negro suffers from relentless prejudice, as black as a pit from pole to pole, I thank whatever Gods there be for his unsullied and conquerable soul.

The Negro was not left to make his way out of the wilderness alone.

The same spirit that sent Africans to bear the body of David Livingstone to Westminster Abbey sent hundreds of consecrated Americans to labor with him in the name of Jesus of Nazareth and help him break his shackles of ignorance. It moved a noble company of men and women to make sacrificial and princely gifts to Negro education. Pen cannot write nor can tongue tell the far reaching influence and value of their gifts of money and lives.

Only a few years ago men of this race, that was then less than sixty years removed from slavery, fought shoulder to shoulder with men who have been free a thousand years, to make the world safe for democracy.

Today, he is America's safest citizen. Evil forces are at work trying to undermine the very foundation on which the nation is built, but the Negro stands uninfluenced and unmoved. This is his country. He loves it with Seraphic devotion and with everlasting love.

Their noble work will outlast the finest monument in the world. Read the thrilling story of cooperation and good will. A distinguished Hebrew, Julius Rosenwald, gave our rural people four thousand schools and made handsome gifts to Y.M.C.C.s. Various foundations have been laid for our education.

Booker T. Washington's name is immortal, because white men and women, in the North and in the South, in the East and in the West, stood by him, and others endowed him and the institution which he founded. Many of the greatest leaders of the race were educated by individuals and organizations of the white race. Tell the world that the work of the lovers of freedom and justice sat the Negro's soul aflame with hope and established his going.

A great opportunity for race appreciation has come through service in the American home. It is there, in thousands of cases, that each has found the soul of the other. It is there that some of the finest friendships, and most sincere interest in the progress of Negro people have been made. Quiet, unknown, unproclaimed—there are white women—in their homes—in daily contact—who have given to the cause of interracial good will, a thing too valuable for money to buy. They have given the spirit of genuine respect for personality.

In the sacred relationship, members of the two races have learned to care about, and share each other's interests and sorrows and bear each other's burdens.

A democratic atmosphere does something divine to individuals and groups. It releases their souls and makes them dream dreams and aspire, in spite of. As a result the Negro has made original and invaluable contributions to American life.

In the world of music, he has baptized America's spirit in hope and love, and set it on hallowed fire with his spirituals. Through trials and tribulations he sings as he "Wades in the Water." Or he "Steals Away to Jesus," and then "Faces the Rising Sun." As a result, something good is always coming out of Nazareth.

A black man goes into his laboratory in the deep South, and discovers fifty-seven new ways to make common clay, peanuts, and sweet potatoes serve humanity. Unto us a world scientist is born. Men of all races are making a beaten path to George Carver's door, at Tuskegee Institute.

Carter G. Woodson, a Negro, who began life as a laborer, in the coal mines of West Virginia founded the National Association for the Study of Negro Life and History. In the mines, he learned to dig for what he wants. An international institution is the result. Without his organization, Negro contributions to history would be buried deeper and deeper among the forgotten deeds of men who have no facilities for preserving their life story. Individual initiative and American opportunity did it.

Yes now doors of opportunity are opening to the Negro, slowly, *but they are opening*. In our democracy, we are challenged to be well prepared to enter them, and above all to open some door *on our own initiative*. That is the deeper meaning of Democracy. Individuals and groups that are helped must learn and desire to go it for themselves.

The spirit of Christian cooperation is growing. America is becoming more deeply conscious of the meaning of brotherhood. Members of both races are counseling together to find broad and effective ways of cultivating practical and warm hearted cooperation. An organization of white women in the deep south have inaugurated a new program of inter-racial Christian cooperation. It is working and is destined to become leaven in the lump.

A few months ago, one of the most significant events in American church history took place. Distinguished men of the North and the South met in Atlanta, Georgia, with Negro churchmen, to map out a program of inter-racial action. There are spiritual and social forces in America that have put their hand to the plow, and will never turn back.

Lincoln challenged us to build a nation that shall long endure. We can do it. It must be built out of the best in both races—out of justice and good will—out of rugged, honest, intelligence, initiative, industry, and devotion to the fundamental principles of real democracy. We will hit the highway and see humanity glorified when all Americans unite to wipe out ignorance and annihilate race prejudice. These are public enemies number one to our Democracy. They prevent races from working together in the larger common service for the good of the whole nation. A nation that shall endure was Lincoln's hope and it was also the end of which Garrison, Love Joy, Douglass, Stowe, Summer, Beecher, Sojourner Truth, and an innumerable host of clear visioned, courageous men and women gave the last ounce of their devotion; this is the end to which millions have been consecrated, and heaven itself beseeches to let "Thy Kingdom come." This is the end to which Negro women, even the humblest, have made continuous and sacrificial gifts.

Mark this prophesy. Some day some nation is going to build a Christian democracy on this planet. We want America to be that nation. God has already set the stage for it. America can, by noble example, teach the rest of the world how good and how profitable it is to give all citizens full opportunity to develop their latent gifts and make their own distinct contribution to the building of a nation whose God is the Lord. It can be brought to pass by patient, courageous work, undaunted faith in democratic principles and in the power of the Gospel of Jesus Christ at work in the souls of men. The glorification of Brotherhood and Democracy is America's unquestioned opportunity and her supreme sworn duty.

Let no one doubt or despair because of difficulties or any unpromising signs. Some day this nation will be done with hate. Out of the present baffling crisis a third of our population ill fed, ill clothed, and ill housed. Imagination, initiative, industry, and will lead us out and then

"New arts shall bloom
With mightier mould
And loftier music fill the air!"[36]

You who can look with eyes of *faith* beyond the tragedy of a world wrecked by hate and greed, rejoice that God has given you a land from which you can banish ignorance, prejudice, injustice, and hate, by whole hearted cooperation and good will, if you address yourself to this task.

See the powers of evil take their flight
You will see the morn of brotherhood break.

Out of the present race struggle, Christian statesmen and spiritual giants will be born in both races and humble men and women will walk together in heavenly places. They will

"Make firm the bulwark of our country's power
And write a record of human justice
Which all men may read and of which none shall be ashamed."[37]

Beloved America, gird yourself anew, for social, economic, and conquest.

The Only Way to World Peace

From Nannie Helen Burroughs, *What Do You Think?* (Washington, DC: n.p., 1950), 15–19.

A world built on wealth and race for the enjoyment of any one race cannot stand. When Jesus prayed, "Our Father," He included the entire human race. When He said, "Thy kingdom come, thy will be done on earth as it is in heaven," He was asking the Father to put the power within all of His children on this earth that would enable them to use their inner spiritual gifts to transform the world. That prayer of Jesus is a real prayer.

It announces the fact of human brotherhood. God has put everything in us that we need to make this a good world. These innate virtues might not be larger than mustard seed, but like that seed they are capable of yielding abundantly. Here they are. Look at them separately, define them briefly, and analyze them. See what they are good for. These "seeds" are in every mortal. They grow in any individual or race that cultivates them.

Love
The first divine gifts to man is the seed of love. "It is the greatest thing in the world."

Faith
It lights us through the dark to God. It draws the poison from every grief; takes the sting from every loss and quenches the fire of every pain. It is the key that unlocks God's storehouse. It gets us through to God.

Understanding
It opens the eyes and heart. "O, that I might receive my sight"—spiritual and moral.

Sympathy

"Sympathy is two hearts tugging at one load." True sympathy is putting ourselves in another's place. "Next to love sympathy is the divinest passion of the human heart."

Mercy

We pray for mercy for ourselves. "Oh, God have mercy," is our constant cry. That same prayer ought to teach us all to be merciful in dealing with each other.

Humility

Humility is the solid foundation of all virtues. It leads to the highest distinction because it leads to self-improvement.

Long Suffering

Our real blessings often appear to us in the shape of pains, losses and disappointments, but wait on the Lord. "The cross of Christ is the pledge to us that the deepest suffering may be the condition of the highest blessing; the sign not of God's displeasure, but of His widest and most compassionate love." He knows what is best for us and gives it when we need it.

Good Will

He who does not sincerely wish his fellowman well is too base to live. He misses the best of life. Well wishing and kindly feeling doesn't cost anything, but pays handsome dividends to all who give them. Good will blesses the giver and strengthens the receiver.

Justice

"Justice consists in doing no injury to men. It is like the Kingdom of God; it is not without us as a fact; it is within us as a great yearning." All men hunger for justice. All men should deal justly.

Patience

Never think that God's delays are denials. Hold on! Hold fast! Hold out! Patience does not give up. There is no great achievement that is not the result of patient working. God's children are known by their patience and perseverance. Be patient and let God our Father teach His own lesson, in His own way and in His own time.

Sacrifice
"You cannot win without sacrifice." Who lives for humanity, must be content to lose himself. It pays.

Kindness
Kindness has converted more sinners than either zeal, eloquence, or learning. "Kind words produce their own image in man's soul, and a beautiful image it is. They soothe and quiet and comfort the hearer. They shame him out of his sour, morose, unkind feelings. We have not yet begun to use kind words in such abundance as they ought to be used."

Peace
"Peace is the fairest form of happiness." "Five enemies of peace live inside of us: avarice, ungodly ambition, envy, anger and pride. Banish them and peace will come and abide."

Happiness
Human happiness depends mainly upon the improvement of small opportunities—upon giving to the world the best we have.

Hope
Hope is the mother of faith. It keeps us young. It awakens courage. It is like the wing of an angel, soaring up to heaven and bearing our prayers to the throne of God.

Courage
Courage leads to heaven; fear leads to death. "Courage consists not in blindly overlooking danger, but in seeing it and conquering it." "True courage is like a kite, a contrary wind raises it higher." "Without courage there cannot be truth, and without truth there can be no other virtue."

Tolerance

"Has not God borne with you these many years? Then be ye tolerant of others." "Have charity: have patience: have mercy. Never bring a human being, however silly, ignorant, or weak—above all, any little child—to shame and confusion of face. Never by ridicule, even by selfish and silly haste—never, above all, by indulging in the devilish pleasure of sneer—crush what is finest and rouse up what is coarsest in the heart of any fellow-creature."

> "All who share the road with me
> Must share with all upon it,
> So make we all one company,
> Love's golden cord our tether,
> And come what may
> We'll climb the way
> Together, yes, together."[38]

These EIGHTEEN VIRTUES are the blessings, forces and influences for which the world has been fighting for centuries and for which it is fighting now. These are the virtues that all men, everywhere, must cultivate. Millions of people do not know their value. But, that very fact gives every Christian something vital to do. Teach children and grown ups that they are "gold." Whoever has these spiritual in them is rich. Make them shine by using them.

God's plan is to cover the earth with these blessings—expose them to all humanity and expose all humanity to them. Suppose we see how many of these virtues we can make work in our homes, and what effect the practice of them will have on all who live there. Get other members of the household to join you in trying out the eighteen points.

What kind of a world would this be if some people were not living them now? Let us get the spirit—the desire for them and these virtues will grow in us.

> "O God, stir the soil,
> Run the plowshare deep,
> Cut the furrows round and round,

Overturn the hard, dry ground,
Spare no strength nor toil,
Even though I weep.
In the loose, fresh mangled earth
Sow new seed.
Free of withered vine and weed
Bring fair flowers to birth."[39]

Brotherhood and Peace—on earth.

༄

The Path to Real Justice

From Nannie Helen Burroughs, *What Do You Think?* (Washington, DC: n.p., 1950), 105–11.

[Joseph] Addison[40] said, "There is no virtue so truly great and godlike as justice." All men want it, and there will be no peace on this earth and no good will among men until they get it. Wendell Phillips once said, "peace if possible, but justice at any cost!" The leaders of our nation and the leaders of all nations on this planet must decide to find and follow the path of real justice for all men, absolutely unaffected or un-influenced by race or color.

Without justice, no man can give his best to the world because justice stimulates and influences all of those actions which are useful to society. It is the one great interest of man on earth. On the question of justice, there can be no more evasion, no compromise, no "special" arrangement. It is the only way to lasting peace in the world. As long as some races are free and others are half free, the yearning for justice will continue to ferment in the hearts of the half free until new wars shall break out with greater intensity and fury than the one that preceded it. If men must be slaughtered, those whom they leave behind must have it or the slaughter will continue.

"Aye, justice, who evades her?
Her scales reach every heart;

The action and the motive,
She weigheth each apart;
And none who swerve from right or truth
Can 'scape her penalty."[41]

Her laws are immutable because they are the laws of God.

It, therefore, becomes necessary for the nations that would live to find the path and walk in it. This is a challenging fact but it is the truth and the only way by which the nations now contending for world freedom can get from taw in any conference at which they will chart the course for world peace.

Justice for all!
"Ring it aloud from the steeple,
Say it with trumpet and pen;
Freedom and justice for all peoples,
Peace and protection for men—
Sing to the sibilant wire,
That the day of fulfilment is here—
Cry it through thunder and fire;
Nations shall live without fear."[42]

It is a fact that must be taught and accepted by mankind the world over that the path to real justice is lighted by reverence for personality, regardless of race or color. That day has "gone with the wind," when any race can be used as things—as means to an end—as tools and mud sills for other men to step to power and affluence. "JUSTICE FOR ALL" is the battle cry around the world.

We hang our heads and acknowledge that our own nation is woefully lacking in its "inner spirit of reverence for personality." There is a ray of hope! The number of men and women of good will to all, regardless of race, is on the increase in every section, but millions are yet unenlightened.

The gross ignorance, poverty, high death rate, and moral inaptitude of the Negro masses, is due, largely, to the "inner spirit" of our nation in its lack of reverence for personality in black skin. This reverence of personality is the only principle that will ever make this or any other nation, righteous.

Reverence for personality is the only thing of lasting value in the building of a race or a nation. Without it, America will never reach the social goal of a true democracy. The business of giving justice to her own citizens in her own land is more essential to American life, than meddling with governments in other lands.

Those unenlightened ones, who think that reverence for persons should not apply to the Negro, do not know that this is the only spiritual and social principle on which the white race itself can be saved—and lest those who run in fright from the boogaboo—"Social equality we should enlighten them by telling them that the social goal of a true democracy does not arrange for nor prescribe what associates and friends any citizen should have. The attitude of these miseducated or unenlightened citizens has stood in the way of many just and equitable measures for the advancement of the Negro.

The social goals of democracy are universal franchise, personal security, and equal opportunity to all for self-development. No group in a democracy should have the right to abridge or withhold these fundamental rights from any other group under any pretext. Social goals of a democracy have absolutely nothing to do with social affiliation or so-called social equality.

What will it profit America to keep this eternal Negro problem in a position where justice will not be done? The whole scheme in dealing with the problem makes adequate provision for unjust treatment.

Giving the Negro justice does not take a semblance of it from whites. On the other hand, it would relieve them of unnecessary charity burdens and problems of various kinds, and add to the glory of Anglo-Saxon achievements in building a real democracy, and in practicing the religion of Jesus Christ.

"The sacredness of person is not only a fundamental ethical principle, but is a direct expression of Christ's declaration that every man is a child of God." Those who do not believe and accept this fact are playing the hypocrite when they pray "Our Father."

When we teach and preach the value and sacredness of the individual person, all over America and to all classes, we shall begin, by that process, to purify the mind and blood of the nation so that, in the fullness of time, lynching will cease. Reverence for personality is the only cure for lynching.

There is too much good, deep in the heart of America, for her to lose her soul on the race question. It is senseless for America to mark time on this question. A nation that can gear itself for a world war in a day, should be able to gear itself for justice in a half century.

On the highway of American injustice, the Negro suffers, nurses his hurts, waits and watches for the coming of right. Sometimes in anguish and delusion, he cries out—

"Take all the earth, the gold, the land—
But give, O give to me the right to be a man."

And what does it profit a nation to give opportunity to white men and deny it to—Negroes? There is more than enough opportunities to go around.

What kind of opportunity does the Negro ask?

This is all we ask,
The right to learn,
The right to live as free men live
And serve our country as free men ought.

This is the path along which the nation promises in her Bill of Rights and in her Constitution that all her citizens shall travel. Along the path of Justice the nation builds her schools, her shops, her factories—along this path are her hospitals, welfare agencies, and places of recreation and amusement. They are either closed entirely, or opened with limitations.

Justice, in a democracy, provides equal opportunity for all. Human beings cannot develop properly without it. Justice is the bread of the Nation and the Negro is dying for bread. America has

"Sworn to the end of her treasure,
She will conquer the militant sword.
Ring it aloud from the steeple
Tell it from tower and dome,
'Freedom at last for the people
The end of destruction hath come.'
O Country, whose noble confession
Hath given the voiceless a tongue,
Who hath sounded the doom of oppression
As far as thine armies are flung,
To the cripples and weak of the nations
Hast thou uttered the Master's decree,
And thy word, it hath set the foundations
Of that glorious Kingdom to be,
Come swiftly, O wondrous tomorrow
That shall render to Justice a soul,
When the nations shall rise from their sorrow
The sick and the helpless be whole,
Let us cry it aloud from the steeple,
Let us shout where the darkness is hurled."[43]

"Let us give the light to our Negro people
As we carry the torch to the world."[44]

All of the sinning is not on the white side by any means.

The educated Negro is not doing what he should to help the masses. The mass of Negroes need cleaning up, physically, mentally, morally, and spiritually. White Americans cannot do that. That's our job.

The race retards itself when it fails to make the very best of what it has. Dr. Henry Churchill King puts it up to us when he says, "a man should know that he has a calling of his own to fulfill and means to have self-control enough to fulfill it—that he should not fail in those conditions which give the qualities of character or influence, whether his achievements are recognized or not. But if he fulfills the conditions of self-respect, he can hardly fail of winning ultimately the respect of others. The Negro has the hard task, which confronts every growing man and every developing race, to make himself capable, valuable, indispensable: capable of self-support, and of work that needs doing; having a valuable individual and racial contribution to make; then, with his marked individuality, finally demonstrating that the nation cannot spare him, that his unique contribution is indispensable to the perfected national life."

We cannot have a "perfected national life" as long as educated Negroes do little or nothing constructive to help the ones lowest down. Any Negro who tries to escape or wants to be a mere imitation of a white man shuts himself off from being anybody, and does not help democracy to prove that—given the same opportunity—any man in any race can rise to the level of any other man without escaping into another race to get what he needs to develop and utilize his God-given talent.

Negroes should stop apologizing for not being white and rank their own race.

The Hope of the World

From Nannie Helen Burroughs, *What Do You Think?* (Washington, DC: n.p., 1950), 7–10.

PEACE and good will are the hope of the world. THE BIBLE and NOT BOMBS contains the essential elements of peace. What is peace? Basically it is obedience to the law of God. Obey God's law and there can be no WAR. Ignore it and there can be no PEACE. The opposite of peace is NOT WAR. It is attitudes, conditions and practices that lead inevitably TO WAR. WAR ITSELF IS THE RESULT, THE SUM TOTAL of wrong attitudes, conditions and practices, indulged in, tolerated, encouraged, endured, suffered, until they can be borne no longer. War then is the explosion—it is the eruption of a social volcano. Its composition and behavior are similar to that of Vesuvius. The elements of which war is composed remain dormant for a long time, but let nobody fool you.

All of the elements that cause the explosion are there. They are in human beings because the basic powers that are strong enough to eliminate them or over-come them have not been put to work in the hearts of men. The elements out of which the atomic bomb—the mightiest weapon of open war is made—is a secret, but the elements out of which peace, the only means of human welfare, is made, is not a secret.

God tells us in the Book of Books what makes for peace. If you examine the hot lava of a volcano you will see that it is made of fine glass that cuts human beings to pieces—of rocks and mud—and all of these elements are always hot. There are air vents in the volcano, to let the wind fan the molten fire until it becomes as hot as the inferno and then comes the eruption. Wars are made in the same way and out of human elements that are similar in their actions.

They become moral muck. They harden the heart like rock. They burn deeper and deeper into man's spirit. The winds of passion and resentment sweep over them. Then comes the explosion or war. Deep down in the human heart are all the elements of war dormant but dangerous. They are prepared by the centuries for the day of destruction.

Men talk of sudden or undeclared war. Bunk! There is no such thing. It takes a long time to make a war. Men tolerate, condone and encourage and practice envy, malice, greed, hate, discrimination, injustice, and all of the other concoctions of the devil. These are like the heat and fury of Vesuvius pent up in the mind and heart of human beings. The explosion will come just as sure as Vesuvius is going to get into action every time she gets hot enough inside and the wind of discontent rises and sweeps through her.

As long as men are discontented over the way they are treated and no effective forces are put into operation to improve conditions and satisfy their minds and hearts, we are going to have wars and more wars and it is a waste of time to talk about peace.

The atomic bomb is not the answer. It is only a useless threat. It is the Twentieth Century fear breeder. To create an instrument of fear to make the human race behave is to create a colossal Frankenstein. In the end, the atomic bomb will do about as much to make the nations of the earth behave as a snowball would do to cool hell off. Justice is what men want. It is their God-given heritage and bomb or no bomb, God is on the side of men who live and fight for justice.

If men want peace it must be made of the elements of peace and not of the elements or instruments of war. Yes, nations must keep prepared to defend themselves, but fear provoking instruments and injustice are no safeguards against wars. Peace is made out of respect for human personality, education and equality of opportunity for all. Give the races of mankind these, and the atomic bomb will become useless.

The hope of the world lies in making a better brand of human beings and not in making better bombs. Christianity in men's hearts and not bombs in their hideouts is the only force powerful enough to convert the world from war—making proclivities to peace-making pursuits.

America calls itself Christian. Its acts and deeds of injustice as a nation are an abomination in the sight of the Lord. When she decides to spend as much time, concern and money on the peace bomb of justice as she is spending on the atomic bomb of war, the words, "In God We Trust" will become meaningful.

Think of a nation talking about enduring peace when it spends Five Dollars on the education of a white child and Fifty Cents on the education of a Negro child! Think of a nation talking about enduring peace when it sends black men to fight for world freedom and denies these same men a semblance of it when they return to "the land of promise."

Peace is not made of ignorance and prejudice. Peace is made of even-handed justice. The Christian nation's atomic bomb spells destruction of every vestige of civilization. What kind of Christianity is that? Justice alone spells peace on earth. What kind of good-will can a nation make out of an atomic bomb?

Equality of Opportunity Is the Eternal Goal

From *Eleventh Annual Message of Miss Nannie H. Burroughs, President of the Woman's Convention Auxiliary to the National Baptist Convention, U.S.A., Inc., San Francisco, California, September 9, 1959.* (n.p., National Baptist Convention, 1959), 25–27.

God made only one race. He has only one plan for its destiny. The Bible and science declare this fact, unequivocally. Then, the major business of God's Church and of democratic governments is to accept the fact of the brotherhood of man and initiate and promote plans and programs that will insure the development and building of brotherhood and justice for all on this planet.

We cannot deny the oneness of the human race and the oneness of human destiny. Putting the emphasis on the whiteness and the rightness of one race and the inferiority of all men who are not white is not only fictitious but deliberately false. It can bring only endless racial warfare and destruction to the entire world. Men are not going to be mudsills and puppets any longer without exacting an eternal ghastly and costly toll.

The hour has come when the Christian Church and democratic governments must join heart and hand, and clean the world of prejudice and ignorance.

Today, the Nations that call themselves superior got that way by gross exploitation of the races whom they call inferior. Christianity and Democracy were both born to promote brotherhood and justice throughout the world. Neither is living up to its purpose and promise.

Liberty, equality and fraternity are cravings created in the human heart by God himself so that all His children may utilize and enjoy his bounteous provisions.

All members of the human race have the divine gift of native appetite, craving and love. Democracy must stimulate the desire for the full meal. That's what Jesus meant when He said "I am come that they might have life, and that they might have it more abundantly." Snacks will not satisfy man's needs.

We shall not lose out in this race struggle if we decide in our hearts to let nothing stop us in our desire and determination to work until the shackles of injustice are broken.

God wasn't playing when He made man in His own image. Whoever seeks to destroy that image is in danger of hell fire. We are not playing when we declare unto you that we shall not cause God to regret that He took the time and His perfect breath to make us.

Equality of Opportunity to attain unto His high purpose for us is our eternal goal. The weapons of our warfare are—desire, work, faith and unswerving determination to get through to our trust and heritage and possess it.

Write these three words down—IGNORANCE, LETHARGY, INDIFFERENCE and you will spell out the main cause of the present condition of the masses. Practically all of the masses and a majority of the so-called "classes" or educationally and economically advantaged Negroes fall into one or all of these three groups.

The so-called "classes" should be concerned and helpful so as to aid in establishing the upward going of the masses, but they are not.

Let nobody fool you. Race prejudice is not the major cause of the untoward condition of the race. The main trouble is inside the race. If we make up our minds to work on the fundamentals that build human beings—no man—conceived instrument or agency can stay our progress.

Class indifference to mass conditions has contributed largely to the present chaos. Turn this indifference into concern, dedication and dynamic enthusiasm and determined desire for self help and the entire race will be on its way to work and to take its God-ordained place in the galaxy of the progressive races of mankind.

If we do not get from first base, we will at least make A TRY. Even in an effort to reach the Moon, scientists are doing just that.

What seems to be urgently needed by our world is a peace force drawn from people of every country and race and colour, and from every religion and none, who will be the pioneers of a new and undiscovered country. It will not be an army of bigots and fanatics. But it will be a force that has a divine enthusiasm for tolerance and forgiveness. It will glory in the maximum of uncertainty and doubt on many matters of doctrine, definition and name-calling, It will have no loyalty oath to any race or nation or tribe, to any earthly boundaries or arbitrary limitations, because it will be an army more like a religious order with its citizenship in heaven . . . Such an army will not be afraid of breaking laws that are unjust, or of the methods of boycott and non-cooperation where laws and customs prevent people living in peace and friendship with one another and where they wish to, being educated together and worshipping with one another. . . .

The watchwords of this army will be prayer and action. Never one without the other, always together, prayer and action; as from Bethlehem to Gethsemane, its members will never cease from the struggle for right and justice on earth. They will build and work with their brains and their hands for what Lewis Mumford calls "a more co-operative and serviceable civilization."

In this mighty struggle to improve race relations, let us lay aside the weights of doubt, hate and indifference. Let us pray the prayer of the great Franciscan Order—

"Lord make me an instrument of Thy Peace;
Where there is hatred, let me sow love;
Where there is injury, pardon;
Where there is doubt, faith;
Where there is despair, hope;
Where there is darkness, light;
And where there is sadness, joy.
O Divine Master, grant that I may not so much
Seek to be consoled, as to console;
To be understood, as to understand;
To be loved, as to love;
For it is in giving that we receive;
It is in pardoning, that we are pardoned;
And it is in dying that we are born to eternal life."

Therefore, let us selflessly dedicate this Convention to help construct something in America that we can call a Christian civilization. God is for it. Let's join Him.

∽

We Must Fight Back, but with What and How?

From *Pittsburgh Courier*, May 30, 1959, sec. 2.

It is reported that Robert Williams,[45] now the suspended president of the Monroe (N.C.) NAACP branch, told the members of his local organization not long ago, that "We must fight back." Continuing, he said, "I still believe that there can be no progress without friction or some violence. In the fight for freedom, we must be willing to pay the price. There is no cut-rate freedom."

Robert Williams is exactly right. "There is no cut-rate freedom." Whoever makes up his mind to "fight back," must know the strength of his enemy and he must also know with what and how much he himself has to "fight back" with and how he is going to use his weapons of defense.

FREEDOM COSTS far more than physical conflict. Reckless advice, without counting the cost, makes about as much sense as telling the Negroes of the South to commit suicide and thus have the whole ungodly thing over with.

It is reported that the national secretary, Roy Wilkins,[46] suspended Williams, and the national board sanctioned the act of its secretary. This summary act on the part of the secretary and the board can certainly divide the thinking of Negro people throughout the country. Divided, we cannot win. Many may think that this act of Secretary Wilkins and the board is a gesture on the part of the secretary and the board to gain some of the favor that the NAACP has apparently lost in the South because of its consistent militancy.

This is certainly no time to divide the thinking of Negroes on the question of justice. The advice to "fight back" physically might be zeal, but certainly not according to knowledge.

IN A CRISIS such as the kind that we are passing through the South, it is the plain business of the NAACP to spell out in plain United States English the most effective way to "fight back." Advice to "fight back" physically is not only unintelligent but it arms the ignorant whites of the South with a first-hand excuse for using any weapons at their command, in so-called, self-defense. All they want is the least excuse for united action to fight on all fronts and with everything they have, against all Negroes.

One of the most effective ways to fight your enemies is to find out what they want you to do and don't do it. To find out how they expect you to act and do not act that way.

This is not the time for physical combat or to use dastardly words of resentment. Neither is this the time for Negroes to cringe or to take low. Races are not doing that now. This is the time for the NAACP to teach the people what the right weapons are and how to use them effectively.

Mr. Williams' advice sets only a death trap for unwary Negroes. It simply means that with or without the slightest provocation, the cruelly oppressive whites would make pastime of the tortures perpetrated on

Negroes by them. In their ignorance and viciousness, low-down whites would turn some areas into unmitigated Aceldamas.

The only way in a crisis such as the one through which Negroes are passing, in America, is to take the civilized, Christian, God-ordered, stand, which is not low, but is supremely high. Some people think that a soft word means taking low. The Bible teaches exactly the contrary.

"As soft answer turneth away wrath: but grievous words stir up anger."

"The tongue of the wise useth knowledge aright; but the mouth of fools poureth out foolishness." —Proverbs 15:12.

"The word of God is quick, and powerful, and sharper than any two edged sword" (Hebrews 4:12).

"Come boldly . . . and find . . . help in time of need" (Hebrews 4:16). There is nothing cringing about that.

There are many white people in the South who are "fighting back" and to good effect—with the weapons of interest, intelligence, understanding, influence and dedication to the cause of justice, determination and goodwill.

Of course, proper human behavior cannot be learned in a day, but there are people, in America, who know from both sacred and profane history that it is the only sure way UP and OUT. They believe with a faith that will not compromise that wrong was made to LOSE and that right was made to WIN. In this faith, they stand fast or press forward under the leadership of One who has never lost a battle and cares nothing about race or color.

In this crisis, "fight back" with 2nd Corinthians, 10th chapter, fourth and fifth verses, and do it like it's nobody's business, but yours and God's—"for the weapons of our warfare are not carnal, but mighty through God to the pulling down of strongholds" of prejudice and injustice. Intelligence, calm, and a faith that will not shrink are the weapons with which to fight.

THOUGHTS AND WORDS TOWARD THE WHITE WORLD

As much as Nannie Helen Burroughs believed in black self-determination without white interference, she believed that brotherhood and justice could never be achieved independent of interracial cooperation. In "Some Early Trail Blazers in Interracial Service" she recalled a tradition of interracial cooperation that extended all the way back to the antebellum period. The way she saw it, white people were not fundamentally evil, although they were woefully ill informed. They simply lacked enlightenment and truth. To Burroughs, black folks possessed the truth that white Americans could not see. In the same way she outlined a twelve-point thesis for things that black people must do for themselves, she also wrote "Twelve Things Whites Must Stop Doing."

What's interesting is that her belief in interracial cooperation did not necessarily include interracial marriage. In fact, she scoffed at it. Burroughs snorted at Negroes who married whites: "Just something gone, but nothing missing. Let them go. They should have been gone long ago!"[47] She preserved the idea that the black woman would be the white woman's ally in preserving an unmixed race. Nevertheless, blacks and whites could be allies in social matters.

༄

An Appeal to the Christian White Women of the Southland

From *The United Negro: His Problems and His Progress: Containing the Addresses and Proceedings of the Negro Young People's Christian Congress, Held August 6–11, 1902*, ed. Irvine Garland Penn and John Wesley Edward Bowen (Atlanta, GA: D. E. Luther Publishing, 1902), 522–23.

We wish to appeal to you in behalf of the thousands of mothers in this land who have suffered in silence the unchristian humiliation to which they have been subjected in the Southland since the introduction of the separate-coach law. Not so much for these mothers, for their days are numbered; but we do appeal for the young womanhood of the Southland for whom these mothers have lived and labored and trained for useful lives in this strenuous age. We are laboring to develop these young women and transform them into brilliant gems of refinement and culture, but the tide is against us, and though we have struggled on trying to master the situation, still we see breakers ahead.

The separate-coach law in the Southland is not only a reflection upon our advancement, but a stigma upon us, and the better class of whites throughout the country consider it a stigma upon American civilization, and would join heartily in its removal. But the law exists, and we shall not attempt by force to break it—though it has operated seriously against the moral development of the race—a race that has never raised its arms except in defense of the laws of this land and the protection of its liberties.

The honor of black womanhood is at stake, and let those who will, cower before the crisis, but let us here, in this place, put ourselves on record as protectors and defenders of Christian womanhood, white or black.

In traveling through the Southland all Negro passengers are crowded indiscriminately into one coach—as the law ignores the fact that beneath the black skin is a soul as immortal, a pride as exalted, an intellect as keen, a longing as intense and aspirations as noble, as those which peep forth and manifest themselves in the proudest blue-eyed Anglo-Saxon man or woman.

To be ushered from clean homes, with an atmosphere saturated with pure ozone—where we do observe strict sanitary laws—to be huddled together in cars used as smokers in the States where separate-coach laws do not exist, and for colored passengers in the States in which the law does exist, is an insult which we have long endured.

Though we have suffered in silence for years, we cannot longer stand it. We now turn, like Daniel of old, open in our chambers the windows towards Jerusalem and appeal to the white Christian women of the Southland, not for seats in their coaches, not to help us repeal the separate-coach law, but to help us to secure that comfort, that protection, that decency in traveling commensurate with our intelligence, our morals and our conceptions of Christian decency, which principles are as dear to us as to them.

༄

Some Early Trail Blazers in Interracial Service

From Nannie Helen Burroughs, *What Do You Think?* (Washington, DC: n.p., 1950), 54–58.

Do not think that all the Negroes in the South between 1619 and 1860 were slaves. They were not. Free Negroes in the whole South grew from 35,000 in 1790 to 250,787 in 1860. Many of them purchased their freedom, thousands were manumissions—that is they were set free by their owners, others were fugitives; a few came from abroad as free men.

Even during slavery, there were a few schools in towns and cities for slaves and free Negroes in the South. According to Carter G. Woodson, the historian, Julian Troumontaine taught openly in Savannah until 1829 and clandestinely thereafter, until 1844.

The union army in 1864 discovered that a Mrs. Deveaux had been secretly teaching Negroes there for thirty years. A similar school taught by another white woman was discovered in Norfolk in 1854. There was a private Negro school in Newbern about this time, and still another in Fayetteville, North Carolina. John Chavis was teaching whites in that State at this time.

There was not much interference with secret Negro schools in Charleston, Wilmington, Norfolk, and Petersburg prior to the Civil War. Years before emancipation Simeon Beard conducted a Negro school in Charleston. In Baltimore, Louisville, and New Orleans, there was no serious objection to private Negro education. In 1847 W. H. Gibson was teaching in a day and night school in Louisville. In New Orleans the education of the free people of color was regarded as necessary.

In the North, too, especially in the cities, most Negro communities had some of the facilities for education. Abolitionists, Quakers, and other sympathetic groups maintained here and there a few Negro schools. When the idea of education at public expense became incorporated into the laws of Northern states some of them allotted a portion to the education of the Negroes in separate schools.

In 1829, however, Ohio excluded Negroes from the benefits of public education and did not recede from this position until 1849. Indiana did the same in 1837 and re-enforced the prohibition in 1853 by a provision that the names of Negro children should not be taken in the school enumeration and that the property of Negroes should not be taxed for school purposes. Negroes in the District of Columbia first studied privately with white friends, but in 1807 George Bell, Nicholas Franklin and Moses Liverpool built the first Negro schoolhouse in the capital of the Nation.

William Lloyd Garrison was one of America's greatest stalwarts in the cause of freedom. "He came forward with the argument that slavery was contrary to the natural rights of humanity." He stirred the Nation. He was the "John the Baptist" of his day.

A number of men and women stood with him. There stood Wendell Phillips, the brilliant Edmund Quincy, Francis Jackson, one of the first to stand by Garrison when the mob broke up his antislavery meeting in 1835. Maria Weston Chapman, another of this group, contributed much to the support of abolition by raising funds through the Antislavery Bazaar. Charles F. Hovey, the abolition merchant, gave large sums to support the cause.

Lucretia Mott, Eliza Lee Follen, a poet, sang of liberty and freedom. Sydney Howard Gay, the polished writer, boldly advocated instant emancipation. Williams J. Bowditch, a scholarly lawyer, used his talent to promote freedom. With sketches of intelligent Negroes, Lydia Maria Child gave the race a hearing in circles formerly closed. Thomas Garrett kept the same fires burning in proslavery Delaware.

The fact that the first Negro Baptist Church was founded at Silver Bluff, South Carolina, about 1773, is sufficient evidence that Slaves were taking their duty to God seriously. This group was fortunate in having the kind master, George Galphin, who became a patron of this congregation. He permitted David George to be ordained for this special Work after having formerly allowed George Liele to preach there during these early years.

The struggles of George Liele and Andrew Bryan throw additional light on these early efforts. George Liele was born in Virginia about the year 1750, but soon moved with his master, Henry Sharpe, to Burke County, Georgia, a few years before the Revolutionary War.

As his master was a deacon of the Baptist Church of which Matthew Moore was pastor, George, upon hearing this minister preach from time to time when accompanying his owner, became converted and soon thereafter was baptized by this clergyman. Not long thereafter, upon discovering that he had unusual ministerial gifts, this church permitted him to preach upon the plantations along the Savannah River and sometimes to the congregation of the white church to which he belonged. As his master was much more liberal than most of his kind, Liele was permitted to extend his operations down the Savannah River as far as Brampton, Savannah, and Yamacraw, where he preached to the slaves.

His ministerial work became so important that his master finally liberated him that he might serve without interference; but his work was interrupted by the Revolutionary War, during which his master was killed.

Upon the death of his master, moreover, some of the heirs of the estate, not being satisfied with the manumission of George Liele, had him thrown into prison, hoping to re-enslave him; but Colonel Kirkland of the British Army, then in control of Savannah, came to his rescue by securing his release from prison.

When the British evacuated that city, George Liele went with them to Jamaica, indenturing himself to Colonel Kirkland as a servant for the amount of money necessary to pay his transportation. Before leaving Savannah, however, fortune brought it to pass that the vessel in which he embarked was detained for some weeks near Tybee Island, not far from the mouth of the Savannah River. While waiting there, he came to the city of Savannah and baptized Andrew Bryan and his wife Hannah, Kate Hogg, and Hagar Simpson, who became the founders of the first African Baptist Church in Savannah.

The good work went on in Georgia, South Carolina, and Virginia. Strange as it might seem, William Lemon of Virginia was chosen by a white congregation to serve at the Pettsworth or Gloucester church in that State.

In Portsmouth, Virginia, a Negro Baptist preacher attained unusual distinction. There the blacks and whites belonging to the same Baptist church experienced very little difficulty in their acceptance of each other on the basis of religious equality. They were constituted a church by the Virginia Association held in Isle of Wight County in 1798

Pioneering in this same field, in 1792, was the famous "Uncle Jack," a full-blooded African, recognized by the whites as a forceful preacher of the Gospel in the Baptist Church. For some years he preached from plantation to plantation, moving so many to repentance that the white citizens in appreciation of his worth had him licensed to preach and raised a fund with which they purchased his freedom. They bought him a small farm in Virginia, where for more than forty years he continued his ministry as an instrument in the conversion of a large number of white people.

Thus we see that interracial work is not new in America. White Americans in the North and in the South entered the service in State and Church before the Revolutionary War and their ranks have continued to increase. They believed in justice for all. They believed in brotherhood. They worked earnestly, in those early days to make America safe for Democracy and Christianity. Now their tribe is increasing daily.

The Best Way to Resent the White Man's Insults

From Nannie Helen Burroughs, *What Do You Think?* (Washington, DC: n.p., 1950), 67–71.

Every human being is made in the image of God. A human soul spells divinity and eternity. Touch it and you touch God. The majority of white people have little or no respect for personality unless that personality is clothed in white skin. The survival of this civilization depends absolutely upon whether the white race can be cured of its un-Godly white complex. There can be no compromise, or physical arrangement in race relations that will give lasting peace, unless the white race decides to make intensive teaching of reverence for human personality, the fundamental thing in race relations. This is the price of Democracy on this planet.

The Negro does not want to be white and the white man does not want to be black. Each race wants to keep its own color and at the same time have proper respect one for the other and show it in every day relations without any thought of condescension. Neither race can reach this ideal in a day. We have been teaching and acting the other way too long. But we can face the truth together and teach and practice until the new attitude becomes habit. It can be done and men of good will are even now working at it with all their mind, spirit and soul. God is working with them. It is not going to be easy, but it can and will come to pass.

Because of lack of respect for personality, members of the white race insult Negroes every second in every day. It hurts. Let no man tell you that it doesn't. It does something to the Negro's soul. It generates venom. It makes Negroes very uncomfortable. They chafe and burn under it. Men and even animals resent being pricked and kicked. Thoroughbreds kick back. There are any number of basic reasons why Negroes, like all men, should resent intentional studied, stupid, gratuitous insults.

1. It is human.
2. It would "repent" God that he made them if they do not.
3. They would become fixed liabilities to society.
4. It would mean too much of the human race going to waste.
5. It would demoralize the white race. "No man can keep me in the gutter without eventually getting down there himself," said Booker T. Washington.
6. It would make Negroes put all white people in the same category—"mean." That is far from true.
7. It would strengthen the assumption of race superiority on the mere score of color. This is sheer nonsense. God and science are together on the oneness of the human race.
8. Both races would miss heaven.

These eight reasons are sufficient to compel us to bring all of the good sense that each race has to bear on this whole problem of race relations. Since Negroes suffer in mind and soul and spirit over the insults of the white race (insults that seem to give the white race great satisfaction and bolster up their assumption of superiority) Negroes should do two definite things:

1. Ignore the Ignorant Ones Graciously.
"Father forgive them for they know not." Negroes must stop stooping, getting loud and coarse in order to get back at or resent insults offered by ignorant whites, who really do not know any better. Pity them and pass on, unless they register it physically. That's another question.

Always think of the most effective way of taking care of bullies and cowards. The superior thing to do about a studied insult from a supposed intelligent white person is to be perfectly self-possessed and soft-spoken. Think and then speak to the point. Don't fly off. That's what too many of them expect or want. Resent it calmly. Cut like a skilled surgeon—don't hurt—help.

2. Talk It Over with the Open Minded.
There is still another way. An individual cannot do this big job alone. There are small groups of white people who are fair, well-meaning, intelligent, and open-minded. Think out the best way to talk this vital and delicate matter over with them. They can be of tremendous service. They can become leaven in the "white lump." But do not think for once that Negroes are without fault when it comes to this matter of offering insults. Too many of us are boorish. We carry chips on our shoulders. We are looking for insults and we think it is smart to give people as good as they send.

That's the wrong attitude and there is need of much education among Negroes on this point. We must put leaven into the "black lump." Some Negroes can say and do some outlandish things when they get ready to resent insults. It is time that we stop it and acquire another, and more effective technique. The only way under the sun to be a superior person is to do the superior thing. We have opportunities to do it. It is the only way to surprise, disappoint, and disarm, unenlightened white people.

Read the following poem thoughtfully. This little ragged Negro boy has the technique. There are several deep points in his retort. He thought. He was "a nice little match" for that one gallows storekeeper. He left him something different to think about. Here is what happened.

A little urchin, ragged, black,
An old cigar stump found;
And visions of a jolly smoke
Began to hover 'round.

But finding that he had no match,
A big store he espied;
And straightway for it made a dash
To have his want supplied.

"I have no match," the keeper said,
"And even if I do,
I have no match, you understand,
For such a thing as you."

Down in the ragged pantaloons,
The little black hand went;
And forth it came, now holding fast,
A big old copper cent.

"Gimmie a box," the urchin said,
As his face with pride did shine;
"An' nex' time a gen'mum wants a match,
Jes' giv' him one uv mine."

༄

The Dawn of a New Day in Dixie

From Nannie Helen Burroughs, *What Do You Think?* (Washington, DC: n.p., 1950), 25–31.

The Woman's Missionary Union of the Southern Baptist Convention and similar organizations of forward-looking southerners are making progress along the Christian way in race relations right in their own southern communities. I have always contended that when it comes to the race problem in the South, that the southern white woman is the molder, shaper, and changer of attitudes, sentiment and actions of the whites of that entire section.

She holds the key to the solution of the race problem in Dixie. Her word is law and gospel to southern white men. She is the maker of the pattern of southern life. She holds the destiny of more souls in her hands for weal or for woe than does any group of women anywhere in the world. She holds a trust that is no trifle. Whatever the South is, or whatever it will become depends upon her vision, attitude, teachings and desires.

When southern white women go all-out for or against anything, southern white men are all in for it. This is a tremendous responsibility, but southern white women have it. At last the advanced thinkers among them are becoming aware of their stewardship in the realm of race relations.

The indications are that they are going to do a much better job in the field of religion and race relations than has ever been done in America. The best guarantee of the soundness of the new program is that the leaders are not moved by pity or sympathy. The harbingers of the new day are motivated by an overpowering sense of everyday duty, and a new sense of the value and dignity of human personality. The South has loved some Negros (Mammies and other household varieties) for what they were to it economically, and has tolerated the masses for the same reason, but the leaders in this renaissance are teaching love and the right Christian attitude—not mere toleration—but they are emphasizing for the Negro what he is worth to God and the social order as a human personality.

No, the millennium has not come. But God is working on the hearts of Southern Christian women to whom He has committed a great and sacred trust. Basic changes are taking place in their thinking on the race problem. Since we are inclined to put everything—good, bad or indifferent on the War—let me hasten to remind you that these sociological changes are not due to the War, nor to any of its exigencies. They are due entirely to the effectual working of the leaven of intellectual and spiritual enlightenment in the lump. The process is necessarily slow. All worthwhile transformations are. The changes will affect and influence every phase of southern thinking on the race question.

The Christian leaders of the South will have to unteach much that has been taught. They will have to help the people to unlearn many of the biological and sociological untruths that have been taught about the Negro. The ignorant whites will have to be enlightened. They have been taught that just being born white instead of black makes them superior to any and all Negroes, however advanced in learning and living Negroes may be. They have been taught that Negroes have no rights that any white person needs or should respect. It will take a long time to enlighten that large group of unfortunate white people who have been thus mistaught. But it can and will be done!! Enlightenment, understanding, patience, truth and vision will do it.

The hope of the southern renaissance lies in the fact that the outstanding leaders in the white colleges, editors of religious journals and some of the dailies, sociologist and straight-thinking Christian women are not afraid to try their faith, courage, ability and religion on the race problems right in their own communities. They are not talking so much over the air. They are talking face to face with individuals, and small groups throughout the south. They are making progress.

I venture to say that I receive more letters, every week in the year (within the past five years) than any Negro woman in America. These letters and small conferences indicate clearly that Southern white women are not trying to lead Negroes. They are anxious to help Negroes lead themselves. Our files are actually bulging with letters asking for information about a problem to which they have never before given any serious, constructive thinking.

Those who know conditions might be inclined to doubt the power of these women to change the thinking, attitudes and age old prejudices of Southern communities, but those who doubt do not know what is actually taking place in the hearts of Southern Christian women.

Let me share with you a few excerpts from letters that have come very recently. I have never had the privilege of meeting some of these women, personally. But they seem to desire to share with me the work of preparing Negro Christian women to meet the challenge of the new day. Here are just a few excerpts from letters:

"I have been interested for a long time in promoting the work among the many colored women and children in the Negro churches in this community. I am hindered from many actual contacts by racial prejudices among the people. However, I would be willing to foster the work of missionary societies in the churches if we could get the work organized. If you know of a Field Worker among your people who could come here and help begin the work it would be a great help." (South Carolina.)

"We have on our island three Negro Baptist Churches—all have a house of worship and are self-supporting. They put us to shame as we have no church house and only part-time preaching. Our church is only six years old, though, and the others have been established many years. Our women are coming to a realization of our obligation to our less fortunately situated sisters. Some of the women have not had educational advantages. Most of them own a home and are in fairly good circumstances, but cannot read. We want to help them." (Georgia.)

"You are doing a great work. May the Lord use you on and on many years to come. I am the wife of a retired preacher." (Louisiana.)

"Our Inter-racial Institute was a meeting of good fellowship. These days of testing are a challenge to our faith and God must get glory out of it in bringing his children to a closer walk with Him. I am greatly interested in your people, but I am at sea as to what to do. I want some firsthand information from one who is a leader of her people. What are some of the practical things that can be done? Please send me any suggestions that you think can be worked out locally or used in the State. My latest project is a Circulating Library. I would like to have suggestions as to the best way to make it of greatest service. We will have sets of books that will be loaned to the Churches." (Oklahoma.)

"I have been trying to help the Negro women here. Some of us have been giving them our literature and magazines, but I felt that they were not just what was needed. I will gladly pass on any help you send me." (Georgia.)

"I cannot sit still and see these agents of the devil teaching hate. If you have anything you think these people need to help them fight some of the evil influences, I shall be glad to get it or send you the names of active workers who need such help. I am helping the school to put on a patriotic program and am giving two prizes." (North Carolina.)

"I am very interested in the Negroes here and am anxious to help them, but we must start from the beginning as they have no organization. Please send me some suggestions at once." (Alabama.)

But, certainly, one of the most interesting letters that we have ever received came to us recently from a *white preacher*, who lives in a little town in the State of Kentucky. I am happy to share this entire letter with you.

"I am much interested in the colored Baptist ministers. I am anxious to translate that interest into practical value to them. In cooperation with some of our brethren in the South, we have established a free lending Library for colored Baptist ministers in the State of Georgia. So far, so good. I am happy but not satisfied. I am anxious that the best books be in reach of every colored Baptist preacher in all the land. Is this worth-while? Needed? Will you help? If we can get some responsible person in each State to assume the care of books, I am satisfied that within a few years, or probably months, that thousands of good books can be gathered and placed at the free disposal of your brethren. This would enrich their ministry greatly. For twenty-five years, I conducted such a Library among my brethren. It is a blessing to many men who have no other means to get books. I just wish you knew how willing, ready and anxious I am to help in this great work. It would be a great service for your Woman's Missionary Union. Please let me hear from you, at once."

I shall have more to say about signs that herald the dawn of a New Day in Dixie.

WHAT ARE MEN FIGHTING FOR?

What are men fighting for, you ask?
The answer is not far to find.
They're fighting for peace on earth
And, then, good-will to all mankind.

They're fighting to conquer the forces arrayed,
Against their freedom and justice and place,
Their place on earth, wherever they be,
On land, in air, on ocean or sea.

They're fighting that all men shall earn their bread
To lift their hearts, hold high their heads,
To enjoy the earth and be fully free,
As God intended mankind to be.

They're fighting for peace for every race,
Regardless of creed or color or place,
This is the justice that all men crave;
For which they'd rather die, than for despots slave.

No race on earth will live again.
Beneath another's rod,
Or take the chaf that's offered it.
In place of their gifts from God.

Not land divided as the spoil,
Or words writ in gold,
Nor armies circled 'round the earth
Can bring peace to this troubled globe.

For justice as solid as pure gold,
And freedom for all who breathe,
Are the only blessings that mankind hungers for,
And will fight 'til the price is paid.

Twelve Things Whites Must Stop Doing

From Nannie Helen Burroughs Papers, 1900–1963, Manuscript Division, Library of Congress.

STOP penalizing Negroes for not being white. Color is not character. It is only a badge of distinction.

STOP making social excursions into the Negro race, depositing white offspring and then crying out against social equality.

STOP fighting integration in public education in the daytime, and practicing social equality anytime they want to.

STOP teaching basic untruths about race.

STOP trying to disprove the biblical and scientific fact that "God hath made of one blood all races of men to dwell on the face of the earth."

The New Testament re-affirms this fact when Jesus declared, "One is your Master, even Christ; and all ye are brethren." All scientists are agreed that biologically, sociologically, physiologically, ethnologically, all races are the same. Why this difference of color? This superficial difference was made by time, climate, soil, food, and environment. Men scattered and lived in different parts of the earth, and the five factors listed above accomplished incidental, pigmentary, difference on races.

STOP misinterpreting Genesis 9:19–27. The Bible does not say that God cursed Ham. It says that "Noah cursed his son, Ham." God did not even appear on the scene while Noah was drunk. Noah did the same kind of "running off at the mouth" that drunks usually do. Noah's cursing and assigning his son to everlasting servitude was about as effective as would be the cursing and assignment to servitude, of any son by any father, today. God has never cursed any race. Man must STOP cursing and destroying any race under the pretext that he is only helping God carry out His plan and purpose. On this point God speaks in Galatians 6:7 without equivocation—"Be not deceived . . . whatsoever a man soweth, that shall he reap." Races and nations always reap, in various ways, the ungodly things that they sow.

STOP making unjust discriminatory laws, molding social sentiment against respect for human personality, building up customs, continuing outmoded attitudes in an effort to prove that the Negro is inferior. In any race, only those are inferior who do inferior things.

STOP putting all kinds of barriers in the way of the progress of the Negro race, and then declaring that America's high purpose is to build "one nation indivisible, with LIBERTY and JUSTICE for ALL."

STOP making laws to protect the legal and civil rights of *all* citizens and when the rights of the Negro are involved, allow white citizens to put themselves *above* the law and not only deny Negroes their legal rights but persecute and lynch them. Such acts express vicious race prejudice. Out of such acts and attitudes America can never build a Christian democracy.

STOP using Negroes as political mud sills and stepping stones, to get whites in power, politically, and then deny Negroes full citizenship rights and equal opportunities, through education and employment, to secure their own rightful place in the labor world and enjoy full citizenship rights, responsibilities, rewards and privileges.

STOP teaching race prejudice to children in order to perpetuate contempt for people who are not white and thus make segregation a permanent institution in a democracy.

STOP calling this land "Christian" and the government thereof a democracy. The fact is brotherhood and fellowship are not the practice in many American churches. In the majority of them, Negroes are only welcome or tolerated on specially arranged occasions, and this arrangement is not for long nor frequent. Most white Christian churches and organizations export their religion through missionaries. They do keep a spurious brand for home consumption. Americanism and the attitudes of most whites are intended to "keep the Negro in his place"—give him an inferior complex and do injury to his mind, spirit and soul, and thus make him a second class citizen.

The only hope and the redeeming factor in race relations in America is that there is and always has been an appreciable number of whites—and thank God, the number is increasing, in the North and in the South, who have been just, kind and generous. Many white people are embarrassed, hurt and often articulate in expressing themselves and are active against injustice. But compared with the total population that is active and articulate against justice to the Negro, this fair minded number is small.

America could practice the teachings of Jesus Christ in human relations and brotherhood; justice and goodwill could be applied in education, labor, civil rights and religion without making the white race any blacker or the black race any whiter.

It is not at all necessary to further MIX UP and MESS UP the two races in order to clean up the results of the kind of ungodly social mixing and grave injustice that have been going on for over three hundred years.

America should decide, once and for all, to give the Negro his full citizenship rights. Those whites, who make social excursions into the Negro race, should stop it and "shinny on their own side" forever.

Booker T. Washington, the wisest man of his generation would put it this way, "the races can be one as the hand, and as separate as the fingers thereon."

Write this one fact on the fly leaf of your Bible, —this private mixing and then a public protest against mixing, is a stench in the nostrils of a just God.

With a political and social justice, as the eternal basis, two races working together, could cooperate in building the greatest Christian Democracy the world has ever seen.

PART THREE

THE FIGURE OF NANNIE HELEN BURROUGHS IN POPULAR THOUGHT

BURROUGHS IN POPULAR THOUGHT

During her long career, Burroughs was upheld nationally as a monument to Negro womanhood. Her Victorian sensibilities and deep sense of humility often meant that she was not particularly introspective about her past. Always conscious to avoid frivolity, she only offered personal anecdotes that supported her overall message of uplifting the race. She was always clear about the future. As a witness to her appeal, one journalist remarked that Burroughs was not "measured . . . as a Negro woman, but as a woman" (Hammond, "Saving an Idea"). The writings contained in this section reveal how journalists approached Burroughs and how she, in turn, articulated herself to the world.

∾

Saving an Idea

Lily Hardy Hammond

From Lilly H. Hammond, *In the Vanguard of a Race* (New York: Council of Women for Home Missions and Missionary Movement of the United States and Canada, 1922), 47–62.

Some people seem born to get those things done which nobody else would even attempt. Some driving force within sends them out on a new, untried, hard way, on what seems to all their friends to be a wild-goose chase. To them, however, it is a veritable quest of the Holy Grail. They go from one difficulty to another, with no better sense, the onlookers think, than to tackle the impossible; and then, all at once, when the wild project is thought to be dead and as good as buried, the thing, in some amazing way, is done—a success beyond dispute. Then people begin to praise it and the doer of it, and forget that they said it couldn't be done. That is what happened to Nannie Burroughs and her big idea. She says the Lord worked it out, and that it couldn't possibly have been done without prayer and faith.

Nannie was born in Orange, Virginia. Her mother's people and her father's belonged to that small and fortunate class of ex-slaves whose energy and ability enabled them to start towards prosperity almost as soon as the war which freed them was over. When she was still a very little girl, one of her grandfathers owned a good farm, and the other made a comfortable living as a skilled carpenter. Her mother, left with her little girl to provide for, could have been supported by either of these men, but she was unwilling to be dependent on relatives; and besides, she wanted her child to have a better education than the country town could afford. When Nannie was five years old, her mother went to Washington. Here she worked and kept her child in school until Nannie graduated with honor from high school.

The young girl took a thorough business course, and special work in domestic science. She wanted to teach the latter branches, and as she had led her class in all her work, she was given to understand that if she would take this special preparation, she would be made assistant teacher of domestic science in the high school. The position was given, however, to some one else, who, it was rumored, had "pull" with the authorities.

"I can't tell you how it broke me up," she said, "I had my life all planned out—to settle down in Washington with my mother, do that easy, pleasant work, draw a good salary, and be comfortable the rest of my life, with no responsibilities to weigh me down. I never would have done the thing I have done; I would not even have thought of it.

"But somehow, an idea was struck out of the suffering of that disappointment—that I would some day have a school here in Washington that politics had nothing to do with, and that would give all sorts of girls a fair chance and help them overcome whatever handicaps they might have. It came to me like a flash of light, and I knew I was to do that thing when the time came. But I couldn't do it yet, so I just put the idea away in the back of my head and left it there."

She went to Philadelphia and worked in an office for a year. Then she went to Louisville, Kentucky, where, at the headquarters of the National Baptist Convention of the Colored Church, she became bookkeeper and editorial secretary. Like her mother, she had been a devoted church member from childhood, and she put her energy, her training, and her great gifts into the service of her church.

But even the heavy official work for both the men's and the women's conventions could not consume the energy of this human dynamo.

Because she had had such good opportunities at school and knew so much about right ways of living, Miss Burroughs felt a responsibility toward helping those who had had no chance to learn. She was teaching in Sunday-school and was being asked to talk at all kinds of church meetings. "But what's the sense of talk," she said, "if you don't do something? You talk, and people get stirred up and think they'd like to do something, and that makes them feel good, and they go off happy and satisfied, feeling as though they're some account in the world because they've felt like doing something—and they haven't done one thing to help one soul alive. If you're going to be a Christian, you've got to do something weekdays as well as talk and feel about it Sundays."

So she organized a Woman's Industrial Club. They rented a house and served cheap, wholesome lunches for colored working-folk. In the evenings she taught domestic science there. She started a class in millinery and a class in what she called, "every-day things needed in the home." This included sanitation, hygiene, suitable dress, care of children, cooking, sewing, and laundry work. The women of the Industrial Club, her helpers and backers, each paid ten cents a week toward the work, and she managed the rest of it herself. She carried on this work during the nine years she lived in Louisville.

One day one of the leading white women of the city came into her office and asked if she was running the cooking-school at the colored women's club. When Miss Burroughs said yes, the woman asked how she got the money for it.

"Why, we club women pay ten cents a week, and we make pies and cakes and sell them."

"Well," said the white woman, "don't give your lessons for nothing any longer. People value more highly that which they pay for. If they can afford only a penny, let them pay that. I will pay you regularly for every pupil you have, so that you can get whatever you need for the school."

After this, the club grew until Miss Burroughs was forced to put others in charge of the classes, merely supervising the work herself.

In 1900 she went to the annual meeting of the Colored Baptist Convention and gave a talk which seems to have electrified the assembly. As one result, she was made secretary of the Woman's Auxiliary, a small and feeble missionary organization of this great Church which had raised the year before just $15 for the general mission work of the denomination. She has been its secretary ever since. In her first year as secretary, the women raised over $1,000. In 1920 they raised over $50,000, and in the twenty years of her leadership they have put $366,000 into the missionary treasury of their Church.

But while Miss Burroughs worked with enthusiasm and energy for her denomination, she wanted to enlist her churchwomen in something, which would draw together and help all the women of her race.

That idea of a school for girls who needed help had been tucked away for some time in the back of her head; now she took it out and considered it.

There were schools for colored girls, of course; but they were, for the most part, founded and all were largely supported by white people. While Miss Burroughs knew how invaluable this help to her race had been, and is, yet she felt that the Negroes were far enough along now to begin to do more for themselves.

The year after she became secretary of the Woman's Auxiliary, she tried to get her Baptist women together as a starting point for this broader work.

"We will work harder than ever for the foreign fields of our Church," she said; "but let us start a national school for girls here at home—not a Baptist school, but one that all Negro women, of every creed, can come together on. We don't know what we can do until we all get together."

But the women would not listen. They would have none of Miss Burroughs' school. They were Baptists, working for the great Baptist Church. Again she put her idea away in the back of her head for safe-keeping and returned to her work in Louisville and to the building up of her Baptist organization in the one direction it was as yet willing to take—that of Baptist good works.

Five years later the Auxiliary was raising $13,000 a year. The women had just put up a brick building for some of their mission work in Africa. Miss Burroughs told them that they needed to help girls here in America as well as in Africa, and that if they had the school she proposed, they could bring girls here from Africa and prepare them to go back as missionaries. They liked that idea and proposed to rent a little cottage somewhere and put some African girls in it to be trained as Baptist missionaries.

"That's not my idea," said the secretary. "It must be national, not Baptist—something all colored women can do for all colored girls."

They appointed a committee. "You know," she said, with a flash of the laughter that is always ready to bubble up, "when we women just must dodge an issue, we put it over on a committee. But when the committee met in Louisville, in January, 1907, they endorsed the plan I suggested." When Miss Burroughs had her vacation that summer, she went to Washington to look for a site. With a horse and buggy she drove all over that part of the District, and found a hill site.

"Somehow I felt the school had to be set on a hill. It was all red gullies up here and a sight to see, with a dilapidated eight-room house atop of it all; but there were six acres of land and this beautiful view. It was for sale for $6,500, $500 to be paid in ten days and $500 more twenty days later; the remainder could wait at interest. I took it."

"Had the women given you the money?"

"Why, no, not a cent."

"Had you saved all that yourself?"

Again that look of flashing laughter.

"Why, no; I hadn't saved any money. I'd had too many things to do with my money. I had saved an idea."

"I see. But what about the $500?"

"I went to Louisville and raised it. From my own people—yes. You see"—soberly—"I'd prayed about this thing for a long time. I felt God wanted me to go ahead, and I knew if I did what I could and trusted Him, He would see it through. And He did."

She stayed on in Louisville for two years until the whole $6,500 was raised and the place paid for. Then she went to Washington and opened her school in October, 1909, with eight pupils. The property is vested in a self-perpetuating board of trust, the majority of the members being women. If the board is ever dissolved, it goes to the Baptist Convention and the Women's Auxiliary jointly, to be used for educational purposes.

Both races bewailed Miss Burroughs' leaving Louisville. She was offered a site for her school as a gift if she would stay, but she felt that as a national institution, it should be in the nation's capital. The Louisville *Courier-Journal*, one of the most distinguished papers of the South, paid her a remarkable tribute: "Probably no woman's organization in Louisville or, for that matter, elsewhere is doing as much practical, far-reaching good" as the organization founded by "this remarkable young colored woman, Miss Nannie Burroughs."

Of course the school grew. And its young principal, still secretary of the Women's Auxiliary and having to raise money for her teachers' salaries, must provide means for enlargement. She decided to turn an old stable back of the house into classrooms and a dormitory.

But for once it looked as though she must fail. The women who had wanted the school to be a Baptist training-school did not call it the National Training School, as Miss Burroughs did. Most of them just called it, "Nannie Burroughs' school" and washed their hands of it. But one Baptist woman stood by her. When things looked most hopeless, Mrs. Maggie L. Walker, the woman banker of Richmond, gave her $500 on condition that she would not tell any one who gave it to her. That started the fund, and soon all the money needed was in hand.

"I had to keep my promise, of course," said Miss Burroughs, "and not say a word. But you see what I did."

My eyes followed hers to a substantial, well-painted building which bore above its white columns the legend, "Maggie L. Walker Hall"—a monument to a woman's faith in a woman and in her idea of service.

The briers and weeds were gone by this time; the girls were cultivating a three-acre garden and canning the surplus yield; they had filled the gullies themselves, students and teachers; they had set out trees; and soft green slopes covered the once-bare hill. Concrete walks came next, and then Pioneer Hall, built new from the ground up, three stories and a basement. A white man lent the money for this building, but colored people paid for it. During the war two additional acres were purchased, with a dwelling which was remodeled for sleeping-rooms, industries, and a clubroom. The Northern Baptist white women then offered $3,500 for a model cottage to be used in the domestic science work. Negroes added $500 for the building and furnished the cottage tastefully. The senior class in domestic science runs the Home on a practical and profitable basis. Conventions meeting in Washington and all sorts of local organizations, clubs, and groups come out for luncheons and dinners. The girls serve them, and the money goes to the school.

One day a Washington bank called up Miss Burroughs and told her they had $1,000 for her.

"For me?" she gasped. "Where'd you get it? Are you sure it's for me?"

"It's for Nannie H. Burroughs of the National Training School. Come down here and we'll tell you what we know about it."

She lost no time. The money, she learned, came from the estate of a white Californian who had left a certain sum for work begun and developed by Negroes who showed initiative and vision. A colored man had told the executors about Miss Burroughs' school, and after due investigation they had sent her $1,000 for her work.

"I couldn't put a big gift like that into something already started," she said. "There's always a place for money—our water-works cost us $7,000 up on this hill, and we've put in steam heat and electric lights. But this money had to give us something we never would have had without it. I got $3,000 more from my own people and we built the community house down there at the foot of the hill, across the road. Then we put four thousand books into it, upstairs. The public schools and our school and the whole community use those books."

They showed use when we went to look at them—use, not abuse. They are undoubtedly appreciated. They are in a big room used for community gatherings and entertainments. Downstairs is a store. Formerly there was not a place within a mile where a spool of thread could be bought. Here the neighbors can get notions, staple groceries and canned goods, and almost anything that a housekeeper is likely to need in a hurry. The girls of the domestic science department have a cake and pie department that is very popular.

The community house quickens the mental and spiritual life of the whole neighborhood, ties the school and the community together, gives the girls training both in business and in service to the community, and yields the school an annual cash income of nine per cent on the investment. Doesn't a thousand dollars have to be energized with vision, business ability, and human sympathy before it can bring in returns like that?

With the war came a severe testing of the quality of the work the school was doing for the souls of the students. The bitter cold of the war-winter put the school pump quite out of commission—this was before the $7,000 water-works went in. All winter long—and how long that winter lasted—teachers and girls carried in buckets every drop of water used on the place from the neighborhood springs and wells up that steep, icy hill to the tank in the third story of Pioneer Hall: water for cooking, bathing, laundry, dish-washing, cleaning for a hundred and fifty people. "And we all kept clean, and we all kept sweet," said Miss Burroughs, who did her full share of water-carrying.

They carried coal, too, —all of them, Miss Burroughs included—for the coal companies, hard pressed for labor, refused to carry coal up the difficult hill. They would dump it at the bottom, at the entrance to the grounds, or they would not deliver it at all.

"I just explained it to the girls," said the principal. "I showed them it was really a part of our service to our country, —and a mighty small part compared to what our boys were doing without a word of complaint, — and they caught the spirit and the coal-scuttles too. We all did. We brought every piece of coal the school used that winter all the way up this hill. Not a man on the place, you understand. We carried coal and water, tended to our pigs and chickens, cooked, cleaned, and did our school work in a cheerful, happy spirit. You know," she went on thoughtfully, "I think the 'hard' years were the best ones we had. We built more character. Souls grow under pressure."

So do ideas—the kind Miss Burroughs saved in the back of her head so long. That special idea took a fresh start once the water-works were in, and assumed the shape of a laundry. The girls had done their personal laundry with the primitive equipment of wooden tubs, but the school had been paying $500 a year for laundering its household linen, and its principal has that rarest of business gifts which can turn liabilities into assets. Since sheets must be laundered, they should bring money in by the process instead of taking it out. If they had a big, modern laundry, the girls who desired to do so could learn the work as a trade, and by taking in outside work, those who needed to earn their school expenses could do so, at least in part, and the school could earn a profit on its investment—all instead of paying out $500 a year to somebody else for washing sheets. Miss Burroughs worked it all out after due investigation and so convinced her board of trustees that they told her to go ahead. If she could raise $10,000, the remainder could remain on mortgage for a while. One of her trustees told her if she would get $9,000 by a certain date, he would give her a thousand himself. So she did an amazing thing.

She went to white contractors, told them she hadn't a cent as yet, and asked them to begin on the building at once; and they did. When the building was almost finished —a fine, big, modern plant, —she was asked, "Have you got the money?"

"I haven't tried yet," she answered. "I've just been preparing for my campaign. I'll get it, because God will give it to me. I look to Him, and He never fails me. It's His work. I began it for Him, I take it to Him day by day. When we need anything, I look to Him for it, then I think and pray and work over my part of it the very best I can, and what we need is given."

A $15,000 building almost finished on pure faith—faith of white contractors in a Negro woman, faith of the woman in God! The school has been run like that throughout its twelve years of life. In the first eleven years $232,000 in cash has gone into it. Of this, the Women's Auxiliary has given $4,300, the white Baptist women, $3,500, a white Californian, $1,000, and a few thousand dollars have come from the students in board. All the remainder has been raised by the principal from people of her own race, and secured while she has been raising the income of the Baptist Women's Auxiliary from $15 a year to $50,000.

Yet the test of a school is not the money put into it, but the character that comes out of it. By this standard the National Training School is an asset to the nation. No one can see the girls without being impressed with their efficiency and their spirit of service. It is hard to estimate the loss to both races from lack of room at the school for those who apply for admission.

"But I believe," says the woman who has built all this out of the idea she saved so carefully, "that some day God will move some white person to give the school something big—endowment and equipment to do the best work it is capable of. I've felt all along that if we colored people could start it and prove that it is worth while and would do our very best for it, that before I am clean worn out and can't do any more, He would put it into the heart of some one of His rich white children to do what we can't—endow it and make it a permanent help to my people and my country after I'm dead and gone. I pray for that, and I'm trusting for it, too. But I'm not asking anybody but God for it. It must come from Him."

Miss Burroughs is at present working to unite the women of her race for mutual service. She is organizing them as workers—including artists, teachers, business and professional women, domestics, and home women in one big group, without regard to class distinctions. She wants them to stand together as women with common ideals of work, of standards of living, of service, and of self-respect. She wants the most favored women of her race to stand beside the poorest and, in doing so, to give the latter a new respect for themselves and their work, new hope, and new ambition, that, through a better service, they may win a better reward.

Miss Burroughs' influence over her people can hardly be estimated. She has dynamic power. Measured, not as a Negro woman, but as a woman, she has extraordinary ability; and her living faith in God and in all His children, of whatever race, her spirit of service and sacrifice have energized her gifts as only faith and love can do.

Evanston Hears Miss Burroughs: Educator, Club Worker Discusses What to Do with Life

Mary E. Depugh

From *National Notes*, May 1926.

Miss Nannie H. Burroughs President of the National Training School for Girls, Washington, D.C., and one of the most forceful women speakers of the Race, addressed a large gathering at the Second Baptist Church, Evanston, Sunday on the subject, "What to Do with a Life."

In a speech punctuated with the sharp witticisms and telling anecdotes characteristic of her platform utterances, Miss Burroughs scored her hearers for failing to get the most out of their lives, for neglecting to live up to the fullness of the opportunities daily presented to them. Her address was an earnest plea for a clearer vision and a stronger determination to make "the business of living more profitable."

Miss Burroughs has been for several years a contributor to the leading Race papers of the country. She has been corresponding secretary of the Women's auxiliary of the National Baptist Convention and chairman of the business department of the National Association of Women's Clubs. She is a member of the board of directors of the National Association for the Advancement of Colored People, and has been listed among the speakers at several of the annual spring conferences of the association.

"Live your life physically to the best of your ability," urged Miss Burroughs. "Respect your bodies, and let your habits of posture, of diet and of daily living be those that will build the strongest and most efficient physical foundations for an active life. Too many of us slouch along city streets, stump down in office chairs and in general deport ourselves as if the mere business of living was more of a burden than we could bear. Let us brace up and be more erect and alert men and women.

"Live your life intellectually to the fullest. Think in terms of real responsibilities. Too many of us fritted away our time and our talents and in the end have nothing to show for a life half spent. Women fail to keep mentally abreast of their husbands, and husbands fall short of the consideration they owe their wives. Read more and aim for more light and less heat.

"Live your life spiritually on the highest possible plane. Serve your fellow men freely and generously. Glorify life by taking what you find in it, and making that better."

∾

Pointing the Way to Better Womanhood: That's Nannie Helen Burroughs's Job and She Does It

Floyd J. Calvin

From *Pittsburgh Courier*, June 8, 1929, 6.

Nannie Helen Burroughs is looking to the future. High on a hill, about three miles northeast of the National Capitol, stands a monument to her unflagging energy and determination. This is also a monument to Negro womanhood, for in the achievement of Nannie Burroughs, Negro womanhood has achieved.

The National Training School for women and girls at Lincoln Heights, Washington, is the creation of Miss Burroughs. Twenty years ago she saw the need of a school for the training of young colored women along certain lines of Christian service and home improvement and she went out to Lincoln Heights and began work. At the time she started "Lincoln-ville" there were only four other buildings in the neighborhood, and where she started was on a rugged clay hill that nobody else had ever dreamed of beautifying. But Miss Burroughs has seen "Lincoln-ville" transformed and built up to not only a thickly populated, but a valuable part of the city of Washington. And she has seen her own school grow from nothing to a plant with eight acres and eight buildings, worth $225,000. There is a total of 102 students. The business staff is composed of one manager of the laundry, two matrons, two secretaries, a book-keeper and a store keeper. The last building erected was the new Trades Building, which, when completed, will cost $54,000. The buildings on the campus are administration (Trades Hall, fireproof), two stories completed; Chapel, Maggie L. Walker Hall, laundry, Alpha Hall, library (community center); Pioneer Hall and Burdett Hall.

With this much done, however, Miss Burroughs has just begun to fight. One might think that she would be ready to rest for a while, but right now she is planning the supreme struggle of her career. She will soon launch a campaign for $225,000 to finance her program for the next three years. This money will be used for the following:

1. Dormitory (to accommodate 150 girls).
2. Dining room (seat 300).
3. Chapel, with pipe organ (to seat 1,000).
4. A fund of $10,000 for improvement of campus and grounds.

One might say—"An ambitious program for a woman." But it is an ambitious program for anybody. Yet Miss Burroughs is going into it with that calmness of purpose and determined zeal that has characterized all of her efforts in behalf of the institution. She believes in the program herself, and suffice to say, if she believes in it, it will go over.

What is going on at the school at present that would warrant this program of expansion? It might be said, first of all, that the mere fact of Miss Burroughs' leadership of the institution would be enough to commend the expansion of the work to the general public. Two white people who know both her and her work, and whose word can safely be taken at face value, say of her; "Nannie Burroughs as a public servant is worth as much to her race and our community as the splendid school which she has founded for Negro girls. She should receive larger support for the school so that she can give more of her time to public speaking and serving all the people in those wider fields of human welfare for which she is pre-eminently fitted." The second says: "I am thinking that we should call together a group of people and see what can be done to give more help to your work and thereby save you for the largest possible public service to the American people."

But to be more specific: "The aim of the National Training School is to give a training of head, hand and heart and develop a definite and active social interest in the spiritual and moral forces that make for human welfare. To accomplish this high purpose the school has an atmosphere that is Christian; a spirit that is aggressive, unostentatious but happy; surroundings that are clean; personal ideals that are simple; academic and trade courses that are high standards. A school with an open door to all sects."

Students enter at the Junior High school grade and may complete a regular four years of high school and a two-year normal course. They are taught, in addition to their literary work, social service, domestic science and art, dressmaking, tailoring and millinery, industrial art and practical housekeeping, including actual home making, which is practiced in the dormitory. A commercial course in shorthand, typewriting and book-keeping is offered. This writer was permitted to inspect the dormitory accompanied by Miss Burroughs and in the absence of the students, and every room in the building was neat and orderly, and had been graded for the day (the rooms are graded everyday and a mark given which is a part of the regular report card of each student). An average of 150 graduates have been turned out by the institution for the past 15 years, and for the first four years of the existence of the school the average was 10 graduates.

The department of Negro History is of especial pride at the National Training School. A special room is set aside for the study of this subject, and every student must take the course in Negro History. Recitation everyday for two months is held in the subject, then an examination is held, both written and oral. The students then write orations on Negro achievements, and by a process of elimination the two best orators from each class are selected. From these winners an oratorical contest is held annually, at which three awards in gold are made. The contests have created wide interest and a healthy familiarity with Negro history and with current events among Negroes.

Developing the National Training school has been no easy task. To hear Miss Burroughs relate some of her experience is to live through all the human emotions incident to carrying to success an uncertain enterprise. The day this writer visited the school was calm and peaceful enough. A lazy Washington spring time sun gave no hint of the fierce struggles that had been faced unflinchingly on the National Training hill. Miss Burroughs was calm herself, almost indifferent to the story she was telling in such a casual manner. But she did have the air of one who was master of the situation, although she would only exert herself when it was necessary. The story of how water was finally brought to the school from the city system was but one of the many instances where faith had to lead the way. Miss Burroughs paid high tribute to the (white) Washington business men. They stood by her, even when they couldn't see themselves where and how she would come out. They believed in her.

And now comes the great new task of making the National Training school higher and better. The foundation for a splendid school has been laid and Miss Burroughs is going out and as both white and colored people to help enlarge the plant and secure the future of the institution. She will go out and ask them, man to man and woman to woman, to help more firmly establish the only Christian institution for Negro girls north of Richmond, Va. She will ask you and you, and she wants you and you to help.

A Message from a Mahogany Blond

Era Bell Thompson

From *Negro Digest*, July 1950, 33.

You never had it so good, says the Grand Old Lady of Lincoln Heights, pioneer religious leader.

"We have to get used to being colored," said Miss Nannie H. Burroughs. "We must like it and glorify it. That is the first step to race appreciation."

Miss Burroughs has been colored for a good many years. She was liking it and glorifying it back in 1909 when she founded her Training School for Women and Girls high on a Washington, D.C., hill, and all through her 40 years of service in the woman's division of the National Baptist Convention which she now heads. Miss Burroughs, the self-dubbed Mahogany Blond, has been preaching the gospel of race pride all of her full and energetic days. She is proud to be black.

"Not all the Jim Crow cars that can be made from now until Shiloh comes," she once told an interracial audience, "not all the discrimination and prejudice, not all the handicaps and barriers white people can put in the way will teach this Mahogany Blond that she is innately inferior to the proudest blue-eyed Anglo Saxon that walks the earth!"

The portly woman in the neat grey dress folded her dark hands on the work-piled desk. Intelligent brown eyes looked out of the window of the book-lined study down into the valley of houses below Lincoln Heights, but her mind was focused beyond the horizon, envisioning a new and better day for the race with which she is so impatient, of which she is so proud.

"Never have times for the Negro been so good. There is *nothing* in the world he cannot do. If they stop him in Mississippi, then he can start over in Maine. But keep that beefsteak appetite," she warned, "for it is better to be ready for opportunities than to prepare oneself after they come."

"The Negro has great undeveloped mental and spiritual resources which America needs, yet he stands back on his color. Despite the unparalleled strides he has made as a race and phenomenal success as an individual, he still lacks faith in his own ability."

Miss Burroughs chuckled. "You know, just last summer a friend and I were walking along a street where the homes were particularly neat and attractive. 'Why can't colored people live in beautiful neighborhoods like this,' said my friend. 'It's a shame the way we have to live in second-hand houses and in the worst part of town.' I was agreeing with her heartily when we saw a nice-looking colored girl sitting on the lawn of one of the prettiest homes. For a minute we just stared. 'Surely she doesn't *live* there,' exclaimed my friend, 'not in *that* house—in *this* neighborhood!' 'No,' I said, 'It can't be true.' Yet, the girl's poise and appearance fit the setting so well she seemed to belong. We crossed the street so that we might get a better view. The girl was unmistakably colored. Finally I could stand it no longer. I had to know if Negroes lived in that house. Going up to the door, I rang first, then realized that I'd look pretty foolish unless I could think of something intelligent to say. A neat colored woman came to the door.

"'Does Mrs. Jones live here?' I asked using the first name that came into my mind. 'I'm Mrs. Jones,' said the lady. When I recovered a measure of my composure, I told her the truth, that her home was so nice and the surroundings so pretty, we just couldn't believe it belonged to colored. Mrs. Jones smiled. She was used to questions like that, she said. White people stopped to ask her the same thing.

"We have a complex about things like that. If it is nice we think it is not for us; if it is well done, we didn't do it. In school we are taught the white man's theory: his philosophy, his attitude and his faith, and we accept them. What schools need to teach is the oneness of the human race. Until all the schools, north, south, east and west teach without apologies and explaining away the Negro, until they spell it out in books that all men are equal, they cannot teach sound Americanism, democracy or Christianity."

Her lower jaw settled into a grim line. The brown eyes flashed. Nannie Burroughs was angry. "The Negro lacks imagination, initiative, creativeness—and the motivating force behind all three—industry! He lives too much in the present, accepting the ready-made patterns of white people because that is the easy way. He didn't invent television because he knew that if he waited long enough white people would invent it for him. When he destroys his set he will buy another one.

"I was showing one of my school girls how to make a bed the other day," said Miss Burroughs, the heavy folds of her face relaxing into her usual pleasant smile. "I folded the sheet at the corner and tucked it in. The girl just stood there. I went to the other corner of the bed and repeated the process and waited. The girl did not move. 'Why don't you try your hand?' I asked, exasperated. 'You're *doing* it,' she replied."

Miss Burroughs shook her head slowly. "The civilization and environment of the white man's world has done something to the Negro—has done *too much* for him. He is content to live only in the present. He isn't even satisfied because he hasn't thought about his position long enough to come to a conclusion.

"Unless the Negro, as a race," Miss Burroughs said slowly, "measures up and contributes to the development of standards of today, he will become a thing apart. He already has a bad reputation to overcome. White America has told the world that he is lazy, unreliable, immoral and smells—that is why he must be segregated. Knowing this, Negroes must do everything under the sun (without announcing it) to disprove these charges."

Few can deny there is much truth in what Miss Burroughs says about the short comings of Negroes, but the way she says it often rankles her colored brethren. Capitol citizens still remember her pithy summary of the alley dwellers a few years ago. "The problem," thundered Nannie Burroughs, "is not getting the Negro out of the alley, but to get the alley out of the Negro!"

And again, when she said of the average Negro, "He gets up on the installment plan—never gets dressed fully until night, and by then he is completely disorganized. That is because," explains the lady on the hill, "he really has nothing to get up to."

A secretary brought in the morning mail and was given a list of songs to type and items to look up for *The Worker*, an attractive quarterly magazine (circulation 47,000) which Miss Nannie Burroughs has been publishing for the past 16 years. She also edits some eight or 10 smaller booklets for church and club circles.

"The American Negro is walking over a gold mine," Miss Burroughs lamented, frowning. "He undervalues his greatest gifts. White people make a living off the Negro's humor, put it on stage and radio, and reap a fortune. Like his laughter, the Negro's humor in its native state is loud, vulgar and so unrefined that he doesn't know its value.

"Music is the most valuable, most sacred thing the Negro has, yet he and he alone is destroying it. In trying to produce a new type of music, to commercialize spirituals and gospels, the beautiful God-given music of our fathers is lost. The Negro church is more guilty than any other group for turning heart-made music into home-made boogie woogie with its accompanying physical contortions and sensual body movements. They believe like the words of that once-popular song, 'It don't mean a thing if it ain't got that swing.'

"Church literature like church music, has also suffered but in a different way. The church is 50 years behind the times in its literature. A fortune awaits the person who is willing to furnish plays and programs for special days and events," said Miss Burroughs, whose one act comedy, *The Slabtown District Convention* written over 20 years ago, is still in big demand (in 13th edition) all over the country.

Woman's Day, a fixture in the services of all Negro churches, was originated by Miss Burroughs "years and years ago." It was the grandmother of all the other special days observed by churches and church organizations. "I could kick myself around the Potomac for starting this 'day' fad," said its author with a twinkle in her eye. "Now, there are more days than the calendar allows!"

Miss Burroughs searched among the papers on her desk. "There are many fields overlooked by the present generation that are ripe and waiting. Interior decorating is made to order for Negroes. We buy all the run-down houses white people discard. With their long windows and high ceilings, their narrow doorways and old fashioned fixtures, none but the trained could make them attractive.

"Like Booker T. Washington said, Negroes must learn a trade, acquire a skill at which they can earn a decent living." She found the note she was looking for. "But first there are 12 important things he must do for himself before he can demand full acceptance and equal opportunity from the majority group."

She began to read from the paper. "One. Put first things first. The Negro puts too much of his earnings on his back, in his stomach, and into having what he calls a 'good time.' The late Dr. Kelly Miller used to say, 'The Negro buys what he wants and begs for what he needs.'

"Two. The Negro must stop expecting God and white folks to do for him what he can do for himself. God intends that he shall do exactly what Jesus told the man (in John 5:8) to do—carry his own load.

"Three. The Negro must take better care of his possessions: support his wife and children, make his home surroundings more attractive. He must learn how to run a community up—not down.

"Four. He must learn to dress more appropriately. Knowing what to wear, how to wear it, when to wear it and where to wear it are earmarks of common sense and good breeding, and an index to character.

"Five. He must make his religion an everyday practice and not just a Sunday-go-to-meeting performance.

"Six. Negro leaders must resolve to wipe out mass ignorance. Teach! The masses must become obsessed with desire and determination to meet the basic requirements of decent living and good citizenship. More must learn to read and write. Ignorance—satisfied ignorance—is a millstone about the neck of the race. It is democracy's greatest burden.

"Seven. The Negro must stop apologizing for not being white. He must qualify for the position that he wants. Purpose, initiative, ingenuity, skill and industry are the keys that open doors for all men. The Negro must make himself a workman who is too skilled not to be wanted, and too dependable not to be on the job.

"Eight. He must overcome his bad job habits, such as absenteeism, funerals to attend, or a 'little business' to look after. Also overcome bad conduct habits on the job, such as petty quarreling with other help, incessant loud talking about nothing, loafing, carelessness due to lack of job pride, insolence, gum chewing and too often, liquor-drinking.

"Nine. He must improve his conduct in public places. Taken on the whole, he is the loudest, most ill-mannered race group in the world. He is *rights* mad, but *duty* dumb.

"Ten. The Negro must learn to operate business, not Negro business. He must remove his typical trademarks, learn sound business principles, measure up to accepted business standards and meet all competition graciously and by equal or superior service.

"Eleven. The Negro must develop good leadership. A race transforms itself through its own leaders. It rises on its own wings, or is held down by its own weight. True leaders never set themselves apart. They are with the masses in their struggle. They simply got to the front *first*. Their only business at the front is to inspire the masses by hard work and noble example and to challenge them to come on.

"Twelve. The Negro must stop forgetting his friends. He has had and still has friends in the North and in the South who not only pray, speak, write, influence others, but make unbelievable, unpublished gifts for the advancement of the race. The noblest thing that the Negro can do is to so live and labor that these gifts shall not have been made in vain. He must make his heart warm with gratitude, his lips sweet with praise and his heart and mind resolute with purpose to stand on his feet and go forward in mass, knowing that the captain of his salvation 'is no respecter of persons.'

"In every nation, he that feareth Him, and worketh righteousness, is accepted with Him. The Negro must deliver himself. That's the deep meaning of democracy."

Miss Burroughs laid the paper down. "Get used to being colored," she repeated. "Have faith in yourselves and in your race. Be proud that you are black. Negroes who buy Cadillacs to bolster their ego are whistling in the dark. They are confused and don't want to be left out of things.

"Those who marry whites?" Miss Nannie Burroughs snorted and arose from her chair. "Just something gone, but nothing missing. Let them go." She started for the door. "They should have been gone long ago!"

APPENDIX

Chronology of the Life and Times of Nannie Helen Burroughs

1879	Born 2 May in Orange, Virginia, to Jennie Poindexter and John Burroughs.
February 1883	Moves to Washington, DC, with mother.
1896	Graduates from M Street High School, Washington, DC.
ca. 1897	Serves as associate editor of the *Christian Banner*, Philadelphia.
1897	Moves to Philadelphia and takes job with the Baptist church.
1898	Serves as bookkeeper and stenographer for the Foreign Mission Board of the National Baptist Convention.
January 1900	Delivers speech, "How the Sisters Are Hindered from Helping," at the annual meeting of the National Baptist Convention.
1900	Founds Woman's Industrial Club in Louisville, Kentucky.
1901	Elected corresponding secretary of the Women's Convention, Auxiliary to the National Baptist Convention.
1902	Takes up studies at business college.
1905	Delivers keynote address at the first congress of the Baptist World Alliance in Hyde Park Corner, London, England.
1907	Receives honorary master's degree from Eckstein-Norton University in Kentucky.
1908	Initiates National Woman's Day and inaugurates annual celebration in local churches. Writes *The Slabtown District Convention*, a satirical play.
1909	Opens National Training School for Women and Girls (renamed National Trade and Professional School for Women and Girls).
ca. 1920s	Serves as recurring columnist for the *Pittsburgh Courier*.
1921	Founds National Association of Wage Earners.

1923	Helps organize International Council of Women of the Darker Races.
1930	Denied membership to the American Automobile Association (AAA).
1934	Gives commencement address at Tuskegee University.
1934–61	Serves as editor in chief of *The Worker* magazine.
1948–61	Serves as president of the Women's Convention, Auxiliary to the National Baptist Convention.
1950–60	Serves on the executive committee of the Baptist World Alliance.
1961	Dies 20 May in Washington, DC.

NOTES

Introduction

1. This description of Burroughs is by the *Pittsburgh Courier*. See Nannie Helen Burroughs, "Negro Women Must Make Future Brighter, or Continue an Economic, Social Slave," in part 2 of this volume.

2. Burroughs to Woodson, December 28, 1931, quoted in Traki Taylor, "God School on the Hill: Nannie Helen Burroughs and the National Training School for Women and Girls, 1909–1961" (PhD diss., University of Illinois at Urbana–Champaign, 1998), 43.

3. See Earl L. Harrison, *The Dream and the Dreamer: An Abbreviated Story of the Life of Dr. Nannie Helen Burroughs and the Nannie Helen Burroughs School at Washington* (Washington, DC: N. H. Burroughs Literature Foundation, 1956); and Opal V. Easter, *Nannie Helen Burroughs* (New York: Garland, 1995).

4. See Evelyn Brooks Higginbotham, "Religion, Politics, and Gender: The Leadership of Nannie Helen Burroughs," in *This Far by Faith: Readings in African American Women's Religious Biography*, ed. Judith Weisenfed and Richard Newman (New York: Routledge, 1996), 140–57; and Higginbotham, *Righteous Discontent: The Women's Movement in the Black Baptist Church, 1880–1920* (Cambridge, MA: Harvard University Press, 1994).

5. Bettye Collier-Thomas, *Jesus, Jobs, and Justice: African American Women and Religion* (New York: Borzoi Books, 2010).

6. See Sharon Harley, "Nannie Helen Burroughs: 'The Black Goddess of Liberty,' *Journal of Negro History* 81, no. 1 (Spring 1996): 62–71; and Audrey McCluskey, "We Specialize in the Wholly Impossible: Black Women School Founders and Their Mission," *Signs: Journal of Women in Culture and Society* 22, no. 2 (Winter 1997): 403–26.

7. Susan Lindley, "Neglected Voices and Praxis in the Social Gospel," *Journal of Religious Ethics* 18, no. 1 (Spring 1990): 75–102.

8. See Karen Johnson, "Uplifting Women and the Race: A Black Feminist Theoretical Critique of the Lives, Works, and Educational Philosophies of Anna

Julia Cooper and Nannie Helen Burroughs" (PhD diss., University of California, 1997), later published as *Uplifting the Women and the Race: The Lives, Educational Philosophies, and Social Activism of Anna Julia Cooper and Nannie Helen Burroughs* (New York: Routledge, 2000). Citations in the current volume are to the dissertation. See also Traki Taylor, "God School on the Hill: Nannie Helen Burroughs and the National Training School for Girls, 1909-1961" (PhD diss., University of Illinois at Urbana-Champaign, 1998); Lolita C. Boykin, "Integrating Natural Coping and Survival Strategies of African American Women into Social Work Practice: Lessons Learned from the Works of Nannie Helen Burroughs" (PhD diss., Louisiana State University and Agricultural and Mechanical College, 2003); Ann Michele Mason, "Nannie H. Burroughs' Rhetorical Leadership during the Inter-War Period" (PhD diss., University of Maryland, College Park, 2008); and Shantina Shannell Jackson, "To Struggle and Battle and Overcome: The Educational Thought of Nannie Helen Burroughs, 1865-1961 (PhD diss., University of California, Berkeley, 2015).

9. "College and School News," *Crisis* (July 1944): 212.

10. Taylor, "God School on the Hill," 8-9.

11. Some sources list her birth year as 1878, but most literature on her life defers to 1879.

12. See Eric Foner, *Reconstruction: America's Unfinished Revolution, 1863-1877* (New York: Harper and Row, 1988); and Douglas Egerton, *The Wars of Reconstruction: The Brief, Violent History of America's Most Progressive Era* (New York: Bloomsbury, 2015).

13. Rayford Logan, *Betrayal of the Negro: From Rutherford B. Hayes to Woodrow Wilson* (Cambridge, MA: Da Capo Press, 1997).

14. Ibid., 3.

15. Audrey Thomas McCluskey, *A Forgotten Sisterhood: Pioneering Black Women Educators and Activists in the Jim Crow South* (Lanham, MD: Rowman and Littlefield, 2014), 3.

16. Johnson, "Uplifting Women and the Race," 89-90.

17. Henry McNeal Turner, "The Barbarous Decision of the Supreme Court," quoted in Cornel West and Eddie S. Glaude, eds., *African American Religious Thought: An Anthology* (Louisville, KY: Westminster John Knox Press, 2003), 755.

18. Quoted in Michele Mitchell, *Righteous Propagation: African Americans and the Politics of Racial Destiny after Reconstruction* (Chapel Hill: University of North Carolina Press, 2004), 5.

19. McCluskey, *A Forgotten Sisterhood*, 3.

20. See Lily Hardy Hammond, "Saving an Idea," in part 3 of this volume.

21. Both Booker T. Washington and Anna Julia Cooper were born into slavery and were the children of white slave owners. W. E. B. Du Bois was not born into slavery, and he came from a long line of black activists. Du Bois claimed to be the great-grandson of Elizabeth Freeman (colloquially known as Mum Bett) who helped destroy slavery in Massachusetts. His maternal great-grandfather was a Revolutionary War veteran. See Douglas R. Egerton, *The Wars of Reconstruction: The Brief, Violent History of America's Most Progressive Era* (New York: Bloomsbury, 2015). Mary Church Terrell's aristocratic pedigree and wealthy family is well documented. See Terrell, *A Colored Woman in a White World* (Amherst, NY: Humanity Books, 2005); and Willard B. Gatewood, *Aristocrats of Color: The Black Elite, 1880–1920* (Fayetteville: University of Arkansas Press, 2000).

22. See Nannie Helen Burroughs, "Not Color but Character," in part 2 of this volume.

23. Harrison, *The Dream and the Dreamer*, 8.

24. For more on the history of Richmond Theological Seminary and Virginia Union University, see Charles H. Corey, *A History of the Richmond Theological Seminary* (Richmond, VA: J. W. Randolph, 1895); and Adolph H. Grundman, "Northern Baptists and the Founding of Virginia Union University: The Perils of Paternalism," *Journal of Negro History* 63, no. 1 (January 1978): 26–41.

25. Higginbotham, *Righteous Discontent*, 217–18.

26. Taylor reports that Burroughs's father died, while Jackson states that he deserted the family. Higginbotham's works on Burroughs corroborates the idea that her father died. See Taylor, "God's School on the Hill," 8–9; Jackson, "To Struggle and Battle and Overcome," 17; and Evelyn Brooks Higginbotham, "Nannie Helen Burroughs," in *Black Women in America*, ed. Darlene Clark Hine, vol. 1 (London: Oxford University Press, 2005), 174.

27. Quoted in Taylor, "God's School on the Hill," 8.

28. See Nannie Helen Burroughs, "From a Women's Point of View," in part 2 of this volume.

29. Ibid.

30. Mary Church Terrell, "History of the High School for Negroes in Washington," *Journal of Negro History* 2, no. 3 (July 1917): 232–66; Henry S. Robinson, "The M Street High School, 1891–1916," *Records of Columbia Historical Society* 51 (1984): 119–43; and Johnson, "Uplifting Women and the Race," 93–99.

31. For more on Anna Julia Cooper see Charles Lemert and Esme Bhan, eds., *The Voice of Anna Julia Cooper: Including* A Voice from the South *and*

Other Important Essays, Papers, and Lectures (Lanham, MD: Rowman and Littlefield, 1998); Vivian M. May, "Anna Julia Cooper: Black Feminist Scholar, Educator, and Activist," in *North Carolina Women: Their Lives and Times*, ed. Michele Gillespie, and Sally G. McMillen (Athens: University of Georgia Press, 2015), 192–212; and Margaret Nash, "Patient Persistence: The Political and Educational Values of Anna Julia Cooper and Mary Church Terrell," *Educational Studies* 35 (April 2004), 122–36. For more on Mary Church Terrell, see Terrell, *A Colored Woman in a White World*.

32. Robinson, "The M Street High School, 1891–1916," 119–43.
33. Johnson, "Uplifting Women and the Race," 100.
34. Gatewood, *Aristocrats of Color*, 59–60.
35. Quoted in Gatewood, *Aristocrats of Color*, 165.
36. Quoted in Harrison, *The Dream and the Dreamer*, 10.
37. Taylor, "God's School on the Hill," 14–15.
38. Higginbotham, "Nannie Helen Burroughs," 174–76.
39. Jackson, "To Struggle and Battle and Overcome," 33.
40. See the Nannie Helen Burroughs entry in Gerald L. Smith, Karen McDaniel, and John A. Hardin, eds., *The Kentucky African American Encyclopedia* (Lexington: University Press of Kentucky, 2015), 79.
41. Quoted in Harrison, *The Dream and the Dreamer*, 12.
42. Harrison, *The Dream and the Dreamer*, 79.
43. Higginbotham, "Religion, Politics, and Gender," 148; see also Harley, "Nannie Helen Burroughs."
44. See Higginbotham, *Righteous Discontent*; Taylor, "God's School on the Hill"; and Bettye Collier-Thomas, *Jesus, Jobs, and Justice*.
45. Harrison, *The Dream and the Dreamer*, 8.
46. See Barbara Welter, "The Cult of True Womanhood, 1820–1860," *American Quarterly* 18, no. 2 (Summer 1966): 152.
47. Susan M. Cruea, "Changing Ideals of Womanhood during the Nineteenth-Century Woman Movement," *General Studies Writing Faculty Publications* 1 (2005), https://scholarworks.bgsu.edu/gsw_pub/1.
48. Linda Perkins, "The Impact of the 'Cult of True Womanhood' on the Education of Black Women," *Journal of Social Issues* 39, no. 3 (1983): 18.
49. Lemert and Bhan, *The Voice of Anna Julia Cooper*, 78.
50. Kelly Miller, "The Risk of Woman Suffrage," *The Crisis* (November 1915): 37–38.
51. Anna Julie Cooper, "The Higher Education of Woman (1890–1891), in Lemert and Bhan, *The Voice of Anna Julia Cooper*, 27.
52. Chanta Haywood, "Prophesying Daughters: Nineteenth-Century Black Religious Women, the Bible, and Black Literary History," in *African

Americans and the Bible: Sacred Texts and Social Textures, ed. Vincent L. Wimbush (Eugene, OR: Wipf and Stock), 356.

53. Quoted in Harrison, *The Dream and the Dreamer*, 37.
54. Harrison, *The Dream and the Dreamer*, 44.
55. Ibid.
56. See Nannie Helen Burroughs, "Woman's Day," in part 1 of this volume.
57. Feminism has been the dominant conceptual framework through which Burroughs's life and work has been traditionally interpreted. Notable scholars have ventured beyond this tendency to conscript all black women's activism into a feminist genealogy. I tend to agree with those who interpret black women according to Africana womanist discourses. In this way, I follow the thought of Valethia Watkins Beatty, Clenora Hudson Weems, and Tommy J. Curry.
58. Harrison, *The Dream and the Dreamer*, 79.
59. Quoted in Lily Hardy Hammond, "Saving an Idea," in part 3 of this volume.
60. Harrison, *The Dream and the Dreamer*, 38.
61. Taylor, "God's School on the Hill."
62. Quoted in Harrison, *The Dream and the Dreamer*, 37.
63. Quoted in ibid., 38.
64. Rom. 8:28.
65. Quoted in Harrison, *The Dream and the Dreamer*, 34.
66. Susan Lindley, "Neglected Voices and Praxis in the Social Gospel," 91–93.
67. Ibid., 93.
68. Higginbotham, "Religion, Politics and Gender," 12.
69. See Nannie Helen Burroughs, "Race Attitude," in part 2 of this volume.
70. See Nannie Helen Burroughs, "What the Bible Is and What It Does For the Human Race," in part 1 of this volume.
71. See Nannie Helen Burroughs, "With All Thy Getting," in part 2 of this volume.
72. W. E. B. Du Bois, "The Conservation of Races," in *W. E. B. DuBois: A Reader*, ed. David Levering Lewis (New York: Henry Holt and Company, 1995), 20–27.
73. Anna Julia Cooper, "Has America a Race Problem? If So, How Can It Be Solved?" in Lemert and Bhan, *The Voice of Anna Julia Cooper*, 121–33.
74. Chike Jeffers, "Anna Julia Cooper and the Black Gift Thesis," *History of Philosophy Quarterly* 33 (January 2016): 79–97.
75. See Burroughs, "With All Thy Getting," in part 2 of this volume.
76. See Burroughs, "Slavery Was a Success," in part 2 of this volume.

77. Ibid.

78. Ibid.

79. See Nannie Helen Burroughs, "This Is the War of the Five Rs: Race, Room, Raw Materials, Rights, Religion," in part 2 of this volume.

80. See Burroughs, "From a Woman's Point of View," in part 2 of this volume.

81. See Nannie Helen Burroughs, "The Only Way to Victory," in part 2 of this volume.

82. Nannie Helen Burroughs, letter to the editor, Nannie Helen Burroughs Papers, Manuscript Division, Library of Congress, quoted in Taylor, "God's School on the Hill," 47.

83. Quoted in Harrison, *The Dream and the Dreamer*, 26.

84. See Nannie Helen Burroughs, "Industrial Education—Will It Solve the Negro Problem?" in part 2 of this volume.

85. See Burroughs, "Up from the Depths," in part 2 of this volume.

86. See Nannie Helen Burroughs, "Educated Parasites and Satisfied Mendicants," in part 2 of this volume.

87. See Nannie Helen Burroughs, "Get Ready—Winter Is Coming, Says Educator, Leaders Idle," in part 2 of this volume.

88. See Burroughs, "Educated Parasites and Satisfied Mendicants," in part 2 of this volume.

89. See Nannie Helen Burroughs, "Twelve Things Whites Must Stop Doing," in part 2 of this volume.

90. See Burroughs, "Up from the Depths" in part 2 of this volume.

91. See Burroughs, "Writer Asks How Dems Election Will Affect Negro?" in part 2 of this volume.

92. See Burroughs, "From a Woman's Point of View," in part 2 of this volume.

93. Ibid.

94. Ibid.

95. Quoted in Higginbotham, "Religion, Politics and Gender," 147.

96. Credit must be given to Africana philosophers Dr. Tommy Curry and Dr. James Haile III for their pioneering work in cultural-logics.

97. James B. Haile III, "The Cultural-Logic Turn of Black Philosophy," *Radical Philosophy Review* 18 no. 1 (2015): 126–50.

98. See Burroughs, "From a Woman's Point of View," in part 2 of this volume.

99. Ibid.

100. See Burroughs, "With All Thy Getting," in part 2 of this volume.

101. Ibid.

102. See "Proceedings of the Spring Conference of the Association for the Study of Negro Life and History Held in Philadelphia, April 3 and April 4, 1924," *Journal of Negro History* 9 (July 1924): 375–80; and Pero Gaglo Dagbovie, "Black Women, Carter G. Woodson, and the Association for the Study of Negro Life and History, 1915–1950," *Journal of African American History* 88, no. 1 (Winter 2003): 21–41.

103. "Proceedings of the Spring Conference," 3.

104. "Proceedings of the Annual Meeting of the Association for the Study of Negro Life and History, Inc., Held in Pittsburgh, October 24, 25, and 26, 1927," *Journal of Negro History* (January 1928): 1–6.

105. Laurie F. Maffly-Kipp and Kathryn Lofton, eds., *Women's Work: An Anthology of African-American Women's Historical Writings from Antebellum America to the Harlem Renaissance* (London: Oxford University Press, 2010), 204.

106. Christine Woyshner and Chara Bohan, eds., *Histories of Social Studies and Race: 1865–2000* (New York: Palgrave MacMillan, 2012), 88.

107. Sarah Bair, "Educating Black Girls in the Early 20th Century: The Pioneering Work of Nannie Helen Burroughs," *Theory and Research in Education* 36 (Winter 2008): 19–20.

108. Alana D. Murray, "Countering the Master Narrative: The Development of the Alternative Black Curriculum in Social Studies, 1890–1940" (PhD diss., University of Maryland, College Park, 2012), 2.

109. Ibid., 81.

110. Bair, "Educating Black Girls," 19; Francesca Morgan, *Women and Patriotism in Jim Crow America* (Chapel Hill, University of North Carolina Press, 2005), 123.

111. See Cheikh Anta Diop, *The African Origin of Civilization: Myth or Reality* (Chicago: Chicago Review Press, 1989); Molefi Asante, *The Afrocentric Idea* (Philadelphia, PA: Temple University Press, 1998); John Henrik Clarke, *African People in World History* (Baltimore, MD: Black Classic Press, 1993); Maulana Karenga, *Maat: The Moral Ideal in Ancient Egypt* (New York: Routledge, 2004); Ivan Van Sertima, *They Came before Columbus: The African Presence in Ancient America* (New York: Random House, 1976); Jacob Carruthers, *Divine Speech: A Historiographical Reflection of African Deep Thought from the Time of the Pharaohs to the Present* (London: Karnak House Publishers, 1995).

112. Lewis Gordon, *Existentia Africana: Understanding Africana Existential Thought* (New York: Routledge, 2000).

113. Bair, "Educating Black Girls," 19.

114. Ibid., 12.

115. King to Burroughs, March 8, 1958, in *The Papers of Martin Luther King Jr.*, vol. 4, *Symbol of the Movement January 1957–December 1958*, edited by Carson et al. (Berkeley: University of California Press, 2000), 378.

116. See Nannie Helen Burroughs, "Twelve Things the Negro Must Do for Himself," and Burroughs, "Twelve Things Whites Must Stop Doing," both in part 2 of this volume.

117. Phil. 2:12 (King James Version).

118. See Nannie Helen Burroughs, "Unload the Leeches and Parasitic 'Toms' and Take the Promised Land," in part 2 of this volume.

Part One. Things of the Spirit

1. John Lord, "Cleopatra: The Woman of Paganism" in *Beacon Lights of History*, vol. 3, *Ancient Achievements* (New York: Fords, Howard, and Hulbert, 1883), 311–48; Arthur T. Pierson, "Removal of Barriers" in *The Crisis of Missions, Or, The Voice Out of the Cloud* (London: James Nisbet and Co., 1886), 29–36.

2. Frances E. W. Harper, "Women's Political Future," *World's Congress of Representative Women*, ed. May Wright Sewall (Chicago: Rand, McNally and Co., 1894), 434. Burroughs was still a student at M Street High School when Frances E. W. Harper delivered this speech.

3. In this paragraph and the one preceding it, Burroughs quotes directly from John Lord's "Cleopatra: The Woman of Paganism," 311–48. John Lord (1810–94) was a nineteenth-century historian and lecturer. His fifteen-volume set *Beacon Lights of History* covered six thousand years of European and American history, exploring the past from old pagan civilizations to modern leaders and culture on both sides of the Atlantic.

4. Here Burroughs quotes Pierson's "Removal of Barriers."

5. See David M. Goldenberg, *The Curse of Ham: Race and Slavery in Early Judaism, Christianity and Islam* (Princeton, NJ: Princeton University Press, 2003).

6. Burroughs is referring to Hosea 4:17.

Part Two. The Way Up and Out

1. Earl L. Harrison, *The Dream and the Dreamer: An Abbreviated Story of the Life of Dr. Nannie Helen Burroughs and the Nannie Helen Burroughs School*

at Washington (Washington, DC: N. H. Burroughs Literature Foundation, 1956), 8.

2. For more on Burroughs's relationship with the National Baptist Convention, see Bettye Collier-Thomas, *Jesus, Jobs, and Justice: African American Women and Religion* (New York: Alfred A. Knopf, 2010).

3. An Italian, Spanish, or Portuguese speaking person.

4. Gen. 3:19.

5. Horace Greeley (1811–72) was an American statesman and journalist.

6. Called the "black enchantress" and "the Senator's Lady," Hannah Elias was an early twentieth-century black woman who passed as Cuban in New York City. She had a twenty-year affair with a white millionaire named John R. Platt whom she convinced was the father of her child. Over the duration of their relationship Platt gave Elias $685,000. Around 1905, Platt sued Elias for extortion. Her black lover killed a white multimillionaire, Andrew Green, in a case of mistaken identity. For more, see J. A. Rogers, *Sex and Race: A History of White, Negro, and Indian Miscegenation in the Two Americas,* vol. 2, *The New World* (New York: Helga M. Rogers, 1942); "Hannah Elias—The Senator's Lady," *Baltimore Afro-American*, November 4, 1952, 3; and "Hannah Elias Talks Freely," *San Francisco Call*, January 19, 1905.

7. The name of the supreme god worshipped in ancient Canaan and Phoenicia. Commonly associated with the ancient Canaanites who considered Baal to be a fertility deity. Baal worship was rooted in sensuality and involved prostitution. The worship of Baal also required human sacrifice. Burroughs draws this reference from Old Testament biblical literature. For more, see Norman Geisler and Joseph M. Holden, *The Popular Handbook of Archaeology and the Bible* (Eugene, OR: Harvest House Publishers, 2012).

8. The "encroachments" Burroughs refers to is the sexual abuse black women suffered en masse during the period of enslavement and the subsequent Civil War.

9. Italics added.

10. For more on ethnology and scientific racism, see Tommy J. Curry, "Ethnological Theories of Race/Sex in Nineteenth-Century Black Thought: Implications for the Race/Gender Debate of the Twenty-First Century," in *The Oxford Handbook of Philosophy and Race,* ed. Naomi Zack (London: Oxford University Press, 2017), 565–75; George M. Frederickson, *The Black Image in the White Mind: The Debate on Afro-American Character and Destiny, 1817–1914* (Middletown, CT: Wesleyan University Press, 1971); Reginald Horsman, *Race and Manifest Destiny: The Origins of American Racial Anglo-Saxonism* (Cambridge, MA: Harvard University Press, 1981).

11. For more on nineteenth-century black ethnology, see Mia Bay, *The White Image in the Black Mind: African American Ideas about White People, 1830-1925* (London: Oxford University Press, 2000).

12. Burroughs refers to the following: Benjamin Banneker (1731-1806), mathematician and astronomer; Frederick Douglass (1818-95), abolitionist and author; "our Bruce": possibly a reference to politician Blanche K. Bruce (1841-98), an alternative suggestion, although not as likely would be a reference to John Edward Bruce, the black nationalist thinker and writer; John Mercer Langston, 1829-97, abolitionist and attorney; Edward Wilmot Blyden (1832-1912), diplomat, writer, and politician; William Sanders Scarborough (1852-1926), classical scholar and first African American member of the Modern Language Association; T. Thomas Fortune (1856-1928, journalist and editor, founder of the weekly newspapers *People's Advocate*, and the *New York Age*; Roscoe Conkling Bruce (1879-1950), the son of Senator Blanche K. Bruce and black educator who stressed industrial and business skills; Booker T. Washington (1856-1915), author, educator, Tuskegee Institute founder.

13. Eleanor Rowland Wembridge (1882-44) was a pioneer in the field of psychology. A nationally known author on juvenile delinquency, she served as a girls' referee for the Cuyahoga County Juvenile Court.

14. Burroughs quotes John Addington Symonds, "Hymn of Peace." Symonds (1807-71) was an English poet, literary critic, and cultural historian. For the full poem, see Symonds, "Hymn of Peace," *Christian Register*, October 6, 1904, 12.

15. Italics added for this text written by Roy L. Hill, editor *Rhetoric of Racial Hope*, in which Burroughs's essay appeared.

16. Wendell Phillips (1811-84), William Lloyd Garrison (1805-79), Charles Sumner (1811-74), Harriet Beecher Stowe (1811-96), and Henry Ward Beecher (1813-87) were early nineteenth-century white abolitionists.

17. This quote was used as the title of a recent documentary film, *Tell Them We Are Rising: The Story of Black Colleges and Universities*, directed by Stanley Nelson and Marco Williams.

18. Here Burroughs references the National Association for the Advancement of Colored People.

19. Burroughs is referring to General Jan Smuts, the South African and British Commonwealth statesman, soldier, and prime minister from 1919 to 1939.

20. Burroughs is referring to Robert Russa Moton (1867-1940), the African American educator and author, informally known as Major Moton. Moton succeeded Booker T. Washington as the second principal of Tuskegee Institute

after Washington's death. He rebuked Jan Smuts during a speech the latter delivered in New York. As David J. Paul writes:

> General Jan Smuts, the leader of the white population in South Africa and the chief architect of her apartheid policy of complete segregation, was the keynote speaker. He gave the American audience a brief amount of background information of the native people and praised them for their patience in the resolution of race conflict, saying that it was like "the patience of the ass." Members of the audience were so shocked by this unflattering comparison that they gasped in astonishment, but Smuts did not notice and kept on speaking. He would have ended the evening on that note were it not for Dr. Moton, who had silently waited behind Smuts during the speech but now took the podium and began to speak. He diplomatically praised Smuts for his sympathetic treatment of black South Africans but admitted that something was troubling him. Moton explained to Smuts that his comparison between Africans and the ass "shot a pang through the hearts of my people and many others who are kindly disposed towards us. I wish you would explain to these people what you meant when you compared the Negro with the ass." Smuts, visibly shaken, quickly apologized to Moton and explained that he had not meant to be insulting. Local papers that were published the next day carried the headline "MOTON REBUKES GENERAL SMUTS."

David J. Paul, "This Great and Sacred Trust: Robert R. Moton's Legacy at Tuskegee Institute, 1916–1930," *Honors Projects* 33 (1996): 32, https://digitalcommons.iwu.edu/history_honproj/33/. For more on Moton, see Robert Russa Moton, *Finding a Way Out: An Autobiography* (Garden City, NY: 1920), https://docsouth.unc.edu/fpn/moton/moton.html.

21. Benjamin R. Tillman (1847–1918) was a democratic politician and governor of South Carolina from 1890 to 1894 and a U.S. senator from 1895 to 1918. Coleman L. Blease (1868–1942) was a democratic politician and governor of South Carolina from 1911 to 1915. Both Tillman and Coleman were virulent racists who adamantly opposed black equality.

22. Kelly Miller (1863–1939) was one of the most prolific African American intellectuals of the late nineteenth and early twentieth centuries.

23. Suzanne O'Dea Schenken, *From Suffrage to the Senate: An Encyclopedia of American Women in Politics*, vol. 1 (Santa Barbara, CA: ABC-CLIO, 1999), 483–84.

24. In this article Burroughs responds to an editorial written by E. W. Carrington. For Carrington's essay, see E. W. Carrington, "An Earnest Inquiry," *Voice of the Negro* 1 (October 1904): 452.

25. Jer. 31:29.

26. James "Sunny Jim" Rolph, Jr. (1869–1934) was the governor of California from 1931 to 1934.

27. A reference to Rom. 7:24.

28. Prov. 14:34.

29. Alfred Lord Tennyson, "From Locksley Hall."

30. The Harlem race riot of 1935 is often considered the first modern American race riot. On March 19, Lino Rivera, a sixteen-year-old Puerto Rican, was caught stealing a penknife from a local store. The riot happened when rumors spread that police had killed Rivera. The truth was that Rivera had not been killed but released through the backdoor of the store.

31. The communist movement in America first took flight in the 1920s. Widespread fear of Bolshevism and anarchism provoked the first Red Scare in the years immediately following World War I. Leftist sympathizers became known as "Red." The first Red Scare revolved around a perceived threat from the American labor movement, anarchist revolutions, and political radicalism. FBI Director J. Edgar Hoover equated any kind of protest or uprising with communist subversion. For more on the Red Scare and the Communist Party in America, see Erica J. Ryan, *Red War on the Family: Sex, Gender, and Americanism in the First Red Scare* (Philadelphia, PA: Temple University Press, 2016); and Paul Kengor, "Red Herring: The Great Depression and the American Community Party," a white paper for the Center for Vision and Values at Grove City College (unpublished), http://www.visionandvalues.org/docs/Kengor_Great_Depression_and_American_Communist_Party.pdf.

32. World War II.

33. Aceldama, or Akeldama, means "field of blood" in Aramaic. It is the name given by Jews to a field south of Jerusalem purchased by Judas with the money that he received for the betrayal of Christ.

34. Edwin Rogers Embree (1883–1950) was one of the most influential philanthropists of the twentieth century.

35. Burroughs provides a roll call of notable formerly enslaved African Americans who emerged from slavery equipped with incredible spiritual strength, grit, and intellect. Some of the lesser known names she mentions include: Lott Carey (1780–1828), a formerly enslaved Baptist minister who was a missionary leader in the founding of the colony of Liberia; John Jasper (1812–1901), a formerly enslaved Baptist minister who was heralded as "unmatched" in his crusade for Christianity and the gospel; Richard Allen (1760–1831), founder of the first national black church in the United States, the African Methodist Episcopal Church (AME Church); Daniel Payne (1811–93), often considered the premier bishop of the AME Church who stressed education and

preparation of ministers; William Sanders Scarborough (1852–1926), considered the first African American classical scholar; and Benjamin T. Montgomery (1819–77), formerly enslaved inventor and landowner in Mississippi.

36. Excerpt from John Addington Symonds's "Hymn of Peace." Burroughs slightly misquotes the poem. It should read: "New arts shall bloom, of loftier mould, / And mightier music thrill the skies . . . ." See Symonds, "Hymn of Peace," *Christian Register*, October 6, 1904, 12.

37. Susan Coolidge, "True Service." Coolidge was the pen name of the nineteenth-century American author Sarah Chauncey Woolsey (1835–1905). For the full poem, see Coolidge, "True Service," *Christian Work and Evangelist*, June 30, 1906, 874.

38. John Oxenham, "Roadmates." Oxenham was the pen name of William Arthur Dunkerley (1852–1941), who was an English journalist, novelist, and poet.

39. The poem is titled "Stir the Soil." The author credit reads: "Anonymous: A Prayer from Singapore."

40. Joseph Addison (1672–1719) was an English essayist, poet, playwright, and politician.

41. Poem by Sarah Josepha Hale (1788–1879), an American journalist, author and poet.

42. Burroughs quotes Angela Morgan's "Torch of the World." Morgan dedicated this poem to President Woodrow Wilson, who "has given a new ideal to the nations." See Angela Morgan, *Forward, March!* (New York: John Lane Company, 1918), 99–102.

43. Morgan, "Torch of the World." The first line "Justice for all!" is Burroughs's insertion.

44. Burroughs changes the verbiage in Morgan's "Torch of the World" to make it racially specific to black people. Burroughs inserts "Let us give light to our *Negro* people, / As we carry the torch to the world" (italics mine). The final stanza of Morgan's poem actually reads: "Lo, look to the light of the people, / America, Torch of the world." See Morgan, *Forward, March!*, 102.

45. Robert F. Williams was a civil rights activist from Monroe, North Carolina. He was a proponent of self-defense/armed resistance.

46. Roy Wilkins was national secretary of the NAACP during the early 1950s.

47. Nannie Helen Burroughs, quoted in Era Bell Thompson, "A Message from a Mahogany Blond." See Thompson's essay in part 3 of this volume.

FURTHER READING

Aiello, Thomas. *Battle for the Souls of Black Folks: W. E. B. Du Bois, Booker T. Washington, and the Debate That Shaped the Course of Civil Rights.* Santa Barbara, CA: Praeger, 2016.

Anderson, James D. *Education of Blacks in the South, 1860–1935.* Chapel Hill: University of North Carolina Press, 1988.

Anderson, Noel. *Education as Freedom: African American Educational Thought and Activism.* Lanham, MD: Lexington Books, 2010.

Collier-Thomas, Bettye. *Jesus, Jobs, and Justice: African American Women and Religion.* New York: Alfred A. Knopf, 2010.

Dorrien, Gary. *The New Abolition: W. E. B. Du Bois and the Black Social Gospel.* New Haven, CT: Yale University, 2018.

———. *Social Ethics in the Making: Interpreting an American Tradition.* Malden, MA: Wiley-Blackwell, 2010.

Easter, Opal V. *Nannie Helen Burroughs.* New York: Garland, 1995.

Egerton, Douglas. *The Wars of Reconstruction: The Brief, Violent History of America's Most Progressive Era.* New York: Bloomsbury, 2015.

George, Ann M., Elizabeth Weiser, and Janet Zepernick, eds. *Women and Rhetoric between the Wars.* Carbondale, IL: Southern Illinois University Press, 2013.

Harley, Sharon. "Nannie Helen Burroughs: 'The Black Goddess of Liberty.'" *Journal of Negro History* 81, no. 1 (Winter–Autumn, 1996): 62–71.

Harley, Sharon, and Rosalyn Terbourg-Penn, eds. *The Afro-American Woman: Struggles and Images.* Port Washington, NY: National University Publications, 1978.

Harrison, Earl L. *The Dream and the Dreamer: An Abbreviated Story of the Life of Dr. Nannie Helen Burroughs and the Nannie Helen Burroughs School at Washington.* Washington, DC: N. H. Burroughs Literature Foundation, 1956.

Higginbotham, Evelyn Brooks. *Righteous Discontent: The Woman's Movement in the Black Baptist Church.* Cambridge, MA: Harvard University Press, 1994.

Johnson, Karen. *Uplifting the Women and the Race: The Lives, Educational Philosophies, and Social Activism of Anna Julia Cooper and Nannie Helen Burroughs*. New York: Routledge, 2000.

Luker, Ralph E. *The Social Gospel in Black and White: American Racial Reform*. Chapel Hill: University of North Carolina Press, 1998.

McCluskey, Audrey Thomas. *A Forgotten Sisterhood: Pioneering Black Women Educators and Activists in the Jim Crow South*. Lanham, MD: Rowman and Littlefield, 2014.

Mitchell, Michele. *Righteous Propagation: African Americans and the Politics of Racial Destiny after Reconstruction*. Chapil Hill: University of North Carolina Press, 2004.

Morgan, Francesca. *Women and Patriotism in Jim Crow America*. Chapel Hill: University of North Carolina Press, 2005.

Ross, Rosetta E. *Witnessing and Testifying: Black Women, Religion, and Civil Rights*. Minneapolis, MN: Fortress Press, 2003.

Savage, Barbara. *Your Spirits Walk Beside Us: The Politics of Black Religion*. Cambridge, MA: Belknap Press, 2008.

Watkins, William. *The White Architects of Black Education: Ideology and Power in America, 1865–1954*. New York: Teachers College Press, 2001.

Weisenfed, Judith, and Richard Newman. *This Far by Faith: Readings in African American Women's Religious Biography*. New York: Routledge, 1996.

Woyshner, Christine, and Chara Bohan, eds. *Histories of Social Studies and Race: 1865–2000*. New York: Palgrave MacMillan, 2012.

INDEX

abolitionists, 158, 205n16
absolutism, 125
Adams, Henry, xx
Adams, Samuel, 118
Addison, Joseph, 143, 208n40
Advancement Association, 78
Africa
   civilization in, xl
   mission work in, 177–78
Allen, Richard, 130, 131, 207n35
ambition, 46, 100–103
American Baptist Home Mission Society, xxi
Americanism, 127, 171, 189
Aristocrats of Color (Gatewood), xxiii
art of living, 57
Asante, Molefi K., xlii
Aspasia, 9
Association for the Study of African American Life and History (ASALH), xxv
Association for the Study of Negro Life and History (ASNLH), xxv, xl, xli, xlii
Association of Southern White Women Against Mob Violence, 105
atomic bomb, 149–50
axiology, xxxiii

Baal deity, 34, 204n7
Bair, Sarah, xvii, xliii
ballots as weapon, 116–18
Banneker, Benjamin, 48, 205n12
Baptists, colors used to identify, 11–13

Baptist theology, 2
barbarism, 53
Bay, Mia, xvi
Beacon Lights of History, vol. 3, *Ancient Achievements* (Lord), 2
Beard, Simeon, 158
Beecher, Henry Ward, 71, 205n16
behavior
   of races, 56
   reform of individual, 75
Bell, George, 159
Bethune, Mary McLeod, xvi, xxv
betrayal, 12
Betrayal of the Negro (Logan), xix
Bibbs, Joseph D., 68
Bible, the, xxx–xxxi, 2–3
   belief in, 49
   education on principles of, 7
   influence of, on human race, 6
   interpretation of, 20
   race referenced in, 150
   speech referenced in, 155
   as stepping stone to greatness, 71
Bill of Rights, 95, 146
birth of Burroughs, xviii–xix, 175, 197n11
Black Arts movement, xxvi
Black Panthers, xxvi
Black Power, xxvi
Black Women's Intellectual Traditions (Conway), xvi
Blease, Coleman L., 86, 206n21
blue-vein society, xx
Blyden, Edward Wilmot, 205n12

Boston tea party, 118
Bowditch, Williams J., 159
Boykin, Lolita C., xvii
Brown, Charlotte Hawkins, xxv
Brown, Hallie Quinn, 24
Bruce, John Edward, xxiii–xxiv
Bruce, Roscoe Conkling, xx, xxxv, 48, 205n12
Bryan, Andrew, 160
Bunker Hill, 60
Burroughs, Jennie Poindexter, xxi
Burroughs, John, xxi
Burroughs, Nannie Helen. *See specific topics*
business unions, 76

Caesar, 8
callous class, 64
Campaign of Education, 98–99
"Can all you can" movement, 83
Candace, Queen of Meroe, xlii
Cardozo, Francis L., xxiii
Carey, Lott, 131, 207n35
Carrington, E. W., 95–97, 206n24
Carruthers, Jacob, xlii
caste system, 103
Central Intelligence Agency (CIA), xlii
Chapman, Maria Weston, 159
character, 33, 103
  development of, 88, 133
  dress as marker of, 89, 192
  formation of, 47
  nobility of, 87
  power of, 115
  race not related to, 169
  transformation of, 66
  as triumphant, 66
  uptightness of, 35
chastity, 24
Chavis, John, 158
Chesterfieldian act, 59
Child, Lydia Maria, 159

child conservation, 37
children
  fair chance for, 37
  intellectual growth of, xlii
  as neglected, 21
  teaching, 57–58, 87, 142
chivalry, 45, 57–58, 61
Christian Banner, xxiv
Christian Church, 17–18
  attitudes of, 126
  beginning of, 19–20
  burdens of, 36
  in debt, 21
  support for, 35
Christianity, xxviii, 150
  application of, 17
  authentic, 44
  democracy and, 151
  empowerment through, xxxiv
  exporting, 16–17
  influence of, 15
  as infrastructure, xxvii, xxxviii
  money for campaign for, 26
  power of, 133
  teaching, 189
Christianization, 17
chronology of life, 194–95
CIA (Central Intelligence Agency), xlii
circumcision, 6
citizenship, xix, 171
civilization, xxvii, xxxii
  in Africa, xl
  gifts of the spirit needed by, 53
  handicaps of, as stepping stones, 114–15
  making, 112–13
  as material, 52
  as matter of standards, 63, 89
  survival of, 161
civil rights movement, xxvi, xliv
  activism for, 95
  organizations for, 75

Civil War, American, xix, 70, 130
Clarke, John Henrik, xlii
cleanliness, 31
  of body, 61–63
  as habit, 90
  importance of, 89
  increasing, 69
Cleopatra, 8
Collier-Thomas, Bettye, xvii, xxvii
colorphobia, 32
colors
  use of, for reference of Baptists, 11–13
  value of, 33
commencement address, Tuskegee Institute (1934), 108–15
communist movement, 207n31
communists, 70, 120
community, xxxvii
  Baptist Church in, 12
  improvement in, 66
  programs for, 21
  race problems in, 166
community-building enterprises, 24
concubinage, 79
condemnation, 4
conduct
  improving of, 68, 90
  transformation of, 66
Congress, U.S., 60
Constitution, U.S., xx, 57, 95, 107
Conway, Carol B., xvi
Cooper, Anna Julia, xvi, xx, xxii, xxxii, xxxv, 198n21
cooperation, interracial, 132–33, 135–37, 152, 156, 168
cotton industry, 128
courage, 14, 18, 45, 57–58, 141
  cultivating, 61
  hope and, 109, 114
  utilizing of, 82

crimes
  concealing of, 96–97
  responsibility for, 103
Crisis of Missions, Or, the Voice of the Cloud (Pierson), 2
Cruea, Susan M., xxvii
Crummell, Alexander, xix, xxvi
cults, 15, 20, 21
cultural assimilation, xl
cultural development, 62
cultural identity, xxxviii
cultural integrity, xlvi
cultural-logic, xxxvii–xliii, 201n96
cultural values, xxxviii
culture
  dress as marker of, 89
  virtue, refinement, and, 33
Curry, Tommy, xxxix, 201n96

Daniel, Sadie, xv
debt, Christian Church in, 21
Declaration of Independence, 95, 107, 110, 119
defamations, 64
degradation of women, 28
dehumanization, xix
Delany, Martin Robinson, xix–xx, xliv
deliverance, 56–57
deliverers, 86
democracy, xx, 193
  brotherhood and, 134–38
  as built on rights, 121–22
  capability of, 22
  Christianity and, 151
  deeper meaning of, 137
  duty of, 102
  education, justice, and, 123–24
  equality in, 64
  laws to prevent, 127
  meaning of, xlv
  as opportunity, 138
  power of, 124

democracy (*cont.*)
  price of, 161
  social goals of, 145
  survival of, 70
  teaching, 189
  wealth and, 125
demoralization, 50
  examples of, 78–79
  self-destruction and, 67
dependability, 90
destiny, 102, 151
devil, 15–16
devotion, 137
  to Christian Church, 175
  to Jesus Christ, 17
  of leaders, 67
  symbol of, 9
dignity, xxxviii, 25, 43
Diop, Cheikh Anta, xlii
diseases, 32
displacement, 44, 69
divine plan, 88, 113
domestic science, 27
domestic work, professionalization of, 25
dominant racial theory, xxxii
double standards, 102
Douglass, Frederick, xx, 48, 71–72, 131, 205n12
down-to-earth plan, 16, 22
Du Bois, W. E. B., xvi, xx, xxxii, xxxv, xlii, 14, 198n21

Easter, Opal V., xvi
economic recovery, 37
economics, cooperative, xxxvii
education, xviii, xxiii, 88
  attaining, 46
  continuous program of, 62
  fund for, 72
  gifts to aid, 135
  industrial, xxxv, 44–49
  justice, democracy, and, 123–24
  kinds of, 48
  money for, 84
  of principles of Bible, 7
  private, 158
  programs for, 81
  public, 158–59
  race work, self-determination, and, 93
  right to, 72
  as universal, 10
  used to stop mob violence, 105
  for women, 28
  See also schools
educational evangelist, xv, xlv
Elias, Hannah, 32, 204n6
emancipation, xix, 40, 117
Embree, Edwin Rogers, 130–31, 207n34
Emerson, Ralph Waldo, 114
emigrationism, xix
emotionality, xxvii
emotions, 65, 187
employment
  equality for, 126
  for women, 30–31
encroachments, 34–35, 204n8
enlightenment, xxx, 2
  new, 7
  patience, understanding, and, 165
equality, xix–xx, 34, 170
  in democracy, 64
  desire for, 97
  for employment, 126
  human, xxxi
  in opportunities, 97, 117–18, 150–53
  religious, 161
  of sexes, 8
  social rights confused with, 99–100
  steps to achieving, 192–93
evangelist, xxvi, xxviii, xxix, xlv
evil, xxxiii, 4, 21–22
exploitation, xix, xxi, xxxiv, 64

faith, xxix, 5, 18, 130, 138
  challenge to, 167
  as critical, 174
  hope and, 61
  lacking in, 189
  love and, 183
  in sacred documents, 93
  as virtue, 139
feminism, xxix, 200n57
fidelity, 29
Fifteenth Amendment, 104, 106–7
Flanders Field, 60
folk wisdom, xxii, xxxix
Follen, Eliza Lee, 159
Foote, Julia, xxviii
forgiveness, 152
Fortune, T. Thomas, 205n12
Franklin, Nicholas, 159
fraternal organizations, 85
freedom, xxxix–xl
  as absolute, 110
  desire for, 130–31
  fight for, 39
  lack of, 78
  from oppression, 126
  price of, 60, 153–54
  of religion, 122
  as successful, 132
Freeman, Elizabeth, 198n21
friendship, 9–10, 92, 193
Fuller, T. O., 70
funding for National Training School for Women and Girls, 177–86

Galphin, George, 159
Garnett, Henry Highland, xx, xliv
Garrett, Thomas, 159
Garrison, William Lloyd, 71, 159, 205n16
Garvey, Marcus, xliv, 94
Gatewood, Willard, xxiii
Gaudet, Frances, xxviii

Gay, Sydney Howard, 159
George, David, 130
Gettysburg Speech, 109, 134
Gibson, W. H., 158
Gilded Age, xxxiv
"Glorify the Best I Have" crusade, 20–21
God, xxxiv
  belief in, 16
  helping with race problem, 67
  human beings made in image of, 161
  laws of, 4, 144
  as love, 122
  support from, 182
  trust in, 65
  value given by, xxxix
good will, 140
Gordon, Lewis, xlii
grace, 14, 18, 43, 55
Great Depression, 75, 111
greed, 149
Greeley, Horace, 31, 82, 204n5
Green, Andrew, 204n6
greenhouse business, 84
group welfare, 85

habits
  cleanliness as, 90
  controlling, 130
  overcoming bad, 192
Haile, James, xxxix, 201n96
Hale, Edward Everett, 101
Hale, Sarah Josepha, 208n41
happiness, 100, 141
  capacity for, 55
  promoting, 40
  pursuit of, 56, 103, 120
Harlem Riot, 118–20, 207n30
Harley, Sharon, xvii
Harper, Frances E. W., 2–3, 203n2
Harriet Beecher Stowe Literary Society, xxiii
Harris, Leonard, xvi

Harrison, Earl L., xvi, xxi, xxviii
hate, 149
   as poison, 79, 106
   spreading of, 121
Hayes, Rutherford, xx
Haywood, Chanta, xxviii
health, 40, 54, 62
Health Week, 62
Hell, 15, 21
Henry, Patrick, 110
Higginbotham, Evelyn Brooks, xvi–xvii, xxvii, 198n26
History of the Negro Church, The (Woodson), 14
Hogg, Kate, 160
holy grail, 24–25
homemaking, 40–42, 51
home ownership, 88, 127
honesty, 24, 31
honor
   integrity and, 60
   virtue and, 31
Hoover, Herbert, xv, 94
Hoover, J. Edgar, 207n31
hope, xxxiv, 18, 136, 141, 148–50
   courage and, 109, 114
   faith and, 61
Houston, Drusilla Dunjee, xli
Hovey, Charles F., 159
humiliation, 64
humility, 14, 18, 55, 140, 174

ICWDR. *See* International Council of Women of the Darker Races; National Association of Wage Earners, the International Council of Women of the Darker Races
ignorance, 31, 144
   attitudes growing from, 66
   consequences of, 51
   ignoring, 163
   laziness and, 41
   lethargy, indifference, and, 151–52
   satisfied, 89
   surrounding social rights, 100
   wiping out, 89, 192
imagination, initiative, and industry, 138, 189–90
immorality, 2
impossible class, 64
income, sufficiency of, 50
independence, 52
indifference, ignorance, and lethargy, 151–52
individualism, 87, 101
industrial efficiency, 80
industry, 31, 45, 57–58
   cultivating, 61
   imagination, initiative, and, 138, 189–90
   self-respect and, 28
   utilizing of, 82
initiative, imagination, and industry, 138, 189–90
integrity, 60
intellectual development, xviii
intelligence, 45, 57–58, 61, 73
International Council of Women of the Darker Races (ICWDR), xlii–xliii
International Order of Human Brotherhood, 101

Jackson, Francis, 159
Jackson, Shantina, xvii
Jasper, John, 131
jealousy, 11
Jeffers, Chike, xxxii
Jesus, Jobs, and Justice (Collier-Thomas), xvii
Jesus Christ, xv, xviii, xxviii, xlv
   brotherhood promoted by, 171
   as captain of soul, 61
   coming of, into the world, 124
   declarations by, 145, 170

devotion to, 17
knowledge of, 16
transformation from, 13
wisdom from, 54
Jim Crow cars, 126, 188
Johnson, Karen, xvii
John the Baptist, xxviii, 29
Jones, Albert T., 131
Judeo-Christian philosophy, xlv
justice, 97, 140
  desire for, 74
  dying for, 86–87
  economic, 69
  education, democracy, and, 123–24
  influence of, 143
  in laws, 170
  opportunities provided through, 146
  peace made of, 150
  race problem as problem of, 72
  See also social justice
justification, 4
  for sacrifices, 92
  for segregation, 90

Karenga, Maulana, xlii
kindness, 141
King, Henry Churchill, 147
King, Martin Luther, Jr., xxvi, xliv, 114
Ku Klux Klan (KKK), xix

labor, 27, 111
  dignity of, xxxvi, 25
  free, 128
  manual, 45
  nobility of, 29
  women's suffrage, lynching, and, 97–98
laboring class, 47–48, 62, 80
laziness, 22, 25, 58
  ignorance and, 41
  reputation for, 64

leaders, xxxvii
  Christian, 166
  devotion of, 67
  duty of, 69
  as parasitic, 86
  of racial groups, 85
  responsibility of, 83
  teaching by, 19
leadership, xxvii, xlv
  churches needing, 19
  developing strong, 193
  as noble, 91
  style of, 75
  of Washington, Booker T., 80–81
Lee, Jarena, xxvi, xxviii
legacy, xvi
leisure, 111
Lemert, Charles, xvi, xxvii–xxviii
Lemon, William, 160
lethargy, ignorance, indifference, and, 151–52
Lewis, David Levering, xvi
liberty, 7, 60, 74, 87
Library of Congress, xliii
Liele, George, 130, 159–60
lifestyle, xliii
Light of Truth, The (Bay), xvi
Lincoln, Abraham, 70, 109, 134, 137
Lindley, Susan, xvii, xxx
literacy campaign, 89
Liverpool, Moses, 159
Livingstone, David, 134–35
Locke, Alain, xvi, xl
Logan, Rayford, xix
Lord, John, 2, 203n3
Lord's supper, 5
love, 139, 165, 183
loyalty, 47, 102
lynching, 59, 119, 128
  crusade against, 78, 94
  cure for, 146
  laws against, 96

lynching (*cont.*)
  participation in, 104–5
  reasons for encouraging, 106–7
  women's suffrage, labor, and, 97–98

magnetism, 10
malignment, 64
mammy, 25, 42–43
manners, 58, 63
marriage, 8–9, 32, 156
Mary McLeod Bethune (Smith), xvi
Mason, Ann Michele, xvii
material goods
  competition for, 53
  as taken away, 112
McCluskey, Audrey, xvi, xvii
mercy, 116, 140
Military Intelligence Division (MID), xlii
Miller, Kelly, xxvii, 88, 192, 206n22
miracles, 135
missiology, 2
missionaries, xlv, 17, 20
missionary programs, 21, 177–78
mob violence, 96
  education used to stop, 105
  endorsement of, 106
Montgomery, Benjamin T., 131
Moore, Matthew, 160
moral code, 35
morality, 73
moral stamina, 36
Moton, Robert Russa, 205n20
Mott, Lucretia, 159
Mumford, Lewis, 152
Murray, Alana, xvii, xlii
music, 38, 136, 191

narcissism, xliv
National Association for the Advancement of Colored People (NAACP), xxv, 153–54, 184, 205n18

National Association of Colored Women (NACW), xxv, 98
National Association of Exterior Decorators, 50–51
National Association of Wage Earners, the International Council of Women of the Darker Races (ICWDR), xxv
National Association of Women's Clubs, 184
National Baptist Convention (NBC), xxv, 24
National Baptist Convention of the Colored Church, 175
National Colored Colonization Council, xx
National League of Republican Colored Women, xxv, 94
National Training School for Women and Girls, xv, xvii, xxv, 37–38, 177–87
National Union of Negro Undertakers, 84
Negro Church, The (Du Bois), 14
neighborhoods, decorating of, 51

obedience, 56
open-mindedness, 163
opportunities
  democracy as, 138
  equality in, 97, 117–18, 150–53
  justice providing, 146
  living up to fullness of, 183
  responsibility promoted through, 176
  seeking of, 92
optimism, xxix, xxxviii
  demonstration of, 94
  from slavery, 57

Pagan days, 8
paganism, 2, 8

Parrish, Mary Virginia Cook, xxiv
patience, 140–41, 165
patriotism, xl, 45, 57–58
   cultivating, 61
   foundation for, 75
   as genuine, 85
   identifying with, 94
   role of, 60
Payne, Daniel, 131
peace, 139–43, 148–50
Pericles, 9
Perkins, Linda, xxvii
persecution, 64
perseverance, xxix
personality, 126
   respect for, 66, 136, 150, 162
   reverence for, 144–45
   as sacred, 94
Peters, Jessie, 130
philanthropists, 47, 52, 81
Phillips, Wendell, 71, 143, 159, 205n16
philosophy
   on life, xxx
   of race, 15
   understanding, xxxviii
Philosophy of Alain Locke, The (Harris), xvi
Pierson, Arthur T., 2
Platt, John R., 32, 204n6
poetry, xviii, 115–16
Poindexter, Maria, xxii, xxxix–xl
political activism, xvii, xxx, 93
political assimilationism, xix
political corruption, xxxiv
political parties, 97–98
politics, xviii
   group, xxxvii
   race-first, xliv, 44
popularization
   of fundamental ideals, 61
   of race, 54
poverty, 28, 44, 53, 144

power
   of character, 115
   of Christianity, 133
   of democracy, 124
   of ideals, 42
   mental, 46, 111
   new, 7
   for self-help, 80
   of virtue, 53–54
   of women, 166
Preparatory High School for Colored Youth, xxii
press, equality in publications by, 103
professionalization, xxxvi
   of domestic work, 25
   race and, 47
Progressive Era, 14
propaganda, Communistic, 118
prosperity, xx
prostitutes, 34
purity, 34

Quakers, 158
Queen of Sheba, xlii
Quincy, Edmund, 159

race, xv, 120–23
   advancement of, 20
   apologizing for, 148
   building of, 41
   business based on, 76–77
   cultural identity and, xxxviii
   domination of, 6–7
   dwelling of, 49
   failures blamed on, 90
   fundamentals of superior, 58
   imitation of, 54
   marriage based on, 32
   not related to character, 169
   popularization of, 54
   professionalization and, 47
   qualification based on, 34

as referenced in Bible, 150
responsibility of, xxxii
as superficial, 170
transformation of, 91, 193
uplifters of, 39
Washington, Booker T., on, 52, 172
See also colors
race appreciation, 136, 188
race attitude, 107–8
race conservationism, 44–45
race prejudice, 64–65, 70, 152
    cultivating, 16–17
    expressions of, 170–71
    as fading, 90
    as relentless, 65
    suffering from, 135
race problem, 27, 44–49
    in communities, 166
    God helping with, 67
    as problem of justice, 72
    progress shown through, 73
    solution to, 48
race progress, 14, 22, 53
race relations, 6, 17, 165, 171
race work, 75–76, 93
racial evangelist, xxvi
racketeering, 18
radicalism, 102
raw materials, 120–23
Reconstruction period, xviii–xix, xx, 68
redemption, xxxi, 4
reforming individual behavior, 75
regeneration, 5
religion, 24, 120–23
    as everyday practice, 89, 192
    freedom of, 122
    as necessity, 61
    sociology of, xxxvii
religious thought, xxvii
religious typology, 15
repentance, 5, 14

Republican National Committee's Speaker's Bureau, 94
resentment, 120, 149
resurrection, 5
Revolutionary War, 118, 160
Righteous Discontent (Higginbotham), xvi–xvii
righteousness, xxxi, 54, 193
    principles of, 4
    pursuit of, 94
Rolph, James, 106–7
room, 120–23
Rosenwald, Julius, 135
Ruffin, Josephine St. Pierre, 24

Sabbath, 5
sacrifices, 141
    gifts as, 137
    justification for, 92
    spirit of service and, 183
salvation, 47, 87
    of sinners, 4
    transformation, identity, and, 3
    of womanhood, 27
satisfied class, 64
Scarborough, William Sanders, 48, 131, 205n12, 207–8n35
schools
    contributions to, 110
    establishing, 10, 91
    need for, 177
    public, 37
    See also National Training School for Women and Girls
scorn, 30, 31
segregation, 64, 103
    fighting against, 51
    justification for, 90
    reasoning behind, 190
self-aggrandizement, xxxvii
self-defense, 95
self-destruction, 58, 67

self-determination, xxxvi, xl, 24
    belief in, 156
    race work, education, and, 93
self-improvement, 31
self-respect, xxxix, 52, 147
    as common ideal, 183
    industry and, 28
sensitivity, xviii
sensitization, degrees of, 65
sensitized class, 64
Sertima, Ivan Van, xlii
sex, 10
sexual freedom, 58
shame, 12
Sharpe, Henry, 160
Simpson, Hagar, 160
Slabtown District Convention, The, 191
slave owners, 129–30
slavery, xix, xxi, xxii, 42, 126
    attitudes toward, 56
    by-products of, 131
    emergence from, 207n35
    Maria Poindexter's attitude toward, xxxix–xl
    optimism from, 57
    as success, xxxii, 128–32
    as tragedy, 56
    Washington, Booker T., born into, 198n21
Smith, Elaine, xvi
Smuts, Jan, 79, 205nn19–20
social achievement, 42
social deterioration, 59
social integration, 89
social justice, xliv, 43, 113
social order, 68–69, 108, 110–12
social paralysis, 83
social-political thought, xxxiv–xxxvii
social problems, 59
social recognition for women, 29–30
social reform, 14

social rights, 121–22
    confused with social equality, 99–100
    ignorance surrounding, 100
    recognition of, 101–2
    See also voting rights
Socrates, 9
spirituality, 45, 184
    cultivating of, 61
    depths of, 19
    growth of, 64
spiritualization, xxxii, 17
stewardship, 11, 131
Stewart, Maria, xxvi, xxviii
Stowe, Harriet Beecher, 71, 137, 205n16
subordination, xix
suffering, xxxiii, 12, 140
    of homes, 51
    from insults, 162–63
    of mothers, 49–50
    from racial prejudice, 135
    as silent, 157
suicide, 9
Sumner, Charles, 71, 205n16
superficiality, 33
Symonds, John Addington, 205n14
sympathy, 7, 140, 165

Taylor, Traki, xvii, xxvii, 198n26
teaching, 18
    children, 57–58, 87, 142
    Christianity, 189
    democracy, 189
    of gospel, 26
    health, 62
    by leaders, 19
    long range program of, 41
    love, 165
    truth, 66
tenderness, 42
Terrell, Mary Church, xvi, xx, xxii
theological anthropology, xxx–xxxi

Tillman, Benjamin R., 86, 206n21
tolerance, 118, 142, 152
Toward an Intellectual History of Black Women (Bay), xvi
trades, 47
  learning of useful, 69–70, 191–92
  requirements for professional, 81
traditions
  intellectual, xvi
  preserving, xli
tragedy
  happiness amidst, 55
  slavery as, 56
transformation
  blue print for, 67
  of character, 66
  of conduct, 66
  from Jesus Christ, 13
  of race, 91, 193
  salvation, identity, and, 3
Troumontaine, Julian, 158
Truth, Sojourner, xxvi, 131, 137
Tubman, Harriet, xxvi, 131
Turner, Henry McNeal, xix–xx, xxvi

unenlightened class, 64
United Negro Improvement Association, 94
upbringing, 175
uplifters, 20, 66–67
  importance of, 68
  of race, 39
uplifting
  of masses, 81
  for reform, 75
urbanization, xxxiv, 44

value, xxix
  of ballot, 36
  of color, 33
  correct sense of, 87
  as given by God, xxxix
  as sacred, 17
  war for, 123
vanity, 2, 11
virtue
  honor and, 31
  power of, 53–54
  refinement, culture, and, 33
Voice of Anna Julia Cooper, The (Lemert), xvi
Volstead Act, 105
voting rights, xix, 104

Walker, Maggie L., 179
"war of the five Rs," 120
Washington, Booker T., xvi, xx, xxxv, 48, 191–92
  admiration for, 136
  as born into slavery, 198n21
  leadership of, 80–81
  on race, 52, 172
Washington, George, 60
Washington, Josephine Turpin, 24
Washington, Margaret Murray, xxv
wealth, democracy and, 125
W. E. B. Du Bois: A Reader (Lewis), xvi
Wells-Barnett, Ida B., xvi, 14
Wembridge, Eleanor R., 55, 57, 205n13
Wheatley, Phillis, 48
When Truth Gets a Hearing, xli–xlii
Wilkins, Roy, 154, 208n46
Williams, Fannie Barrier, 14, 24
Williams, Robert F., xxvi, 95, 131, 153–54, 208n45
womanhood, black, xxvii, xliv, 24, 38
  examples of, 167
  honor of, 157
  monument to, 174, 184–85
  salvation of, 27
Woman's Auxiliary, 177–79, 182
Woman's Day, 8–10, 61, 191
Woman's Industrial Club, xxiv, 176
Woman's Missionary Society, 25–26

Woman's Missionary Union of the Southern Baptist Convention, 164–65, 168
Woman Suffrage Association, 98
women
  burdens carried by, 37, 88
  development of, 157
  as economic and social slave, 39
  as liability, 40
  love of, 87
  organization and unification of, 183
  power of, 42–43, 166
  protection for, 96
  resources for, 8
  respect for, 34
  rights for, 125
  social recognition for, 29–30
  strength of, 35–36
Women Builders (Daniel), xv
Women's Convention (1904), Austin, Texas, xxx, 24
women's history, xxxvii
women's suffrage, xlv, 25, 93, 97–98
Wonderful Ethiopians of the Ancient Cushite Civilization (Houston), xli
Woodson, Carter G., xv, xxv, xlii, 14, 88, 136–37, 158
Worker, The (magazine), 190–91
World's Congress of Representative Women (1893), 2–3
World War I, 93, 207n31
World War II, 93
Woyshner, Christine, xvii

xenophobia, xxxv

yeast, 124
Young People's Society, 11, 12, 13

NANNIE HELEN BURROUGHS, born in 1879 in Orange, Virginia, was an African American educator and activist. In 1909, she founded the National Training School for Women and Girls in Washington, DC. She continued to work there until her death in 1961.

KELISHA B. GRAVES is an honors and undergraduate research programs advisor and adjunct instructor at Fayetteville State University. She is completing a Doctor of Education in Educational Leadership.

Printed in the USA
CPSIA information can be obtained
at www.ICGtesting.com
CBHW020805271124
18062CB00004B/191